FODOR'S BED & BREAKFASTS AND COUNTRY INNS

The Upper Great Lakes' Best Bed & Breakfasts

3rd Edition

Delightful Places to Stay and Great Things to Do When You Get There

Fodor's Travel Publications, Inc.
New York • Toronto • London • Sydney • Auckland
http://www.fodors.com/

Third Edition

ISBN 0–679–03293–2

The Upper Great Lakes' Best Bed & Breakfasts

Editor: Robert I. C. Fisher
Editorial Contributors: Robert Blake, Janet Foley
Creative Director: Fabrizio La Rocca
Cartographer: David Lindroth
Illustrators: Alida Beck, Karl Tanner
Cover Design: Guido Caroti
Cover Photograph: Zane B. Williams

Special Sales

PRINTED IN THE UNITED STATES OF AMERICA

10 9 8 7 6 5 4 3 2 1

Contributors

Tom Davis updated the section on Door County, Wisconsin, where he makes his home. The author of two books, he also serves as senior editor for *Wisconsin Trails* and for *Sporting Classics*. His freelance writing and photography has appeared in *Cross-Country Skier, Country Inns/Bed & Breakfasts, Milwaukee Magazine, Gray's Sporting Journal*, and *New England Review/Bread Loaf Quarterly*.

Deborah Hawkins is a freelance writer whose articles appear regularly in various regional newspapers and magazines; she is also the co-founder of *Traverse, The Magazine*. She lives in Traverse City and wrote the Little Traverse Bay Region, Grand Traverse Region, and Mackinac Island sections of the Michigan chapter.

Konnie LeMay was born and raised in Duluth, Minnesota, and recently got the chance to return to her home port as assistant editor of the *Daily Telegram* in Superior, Wisconsin (Duluth's "twin" port). Updater of the Mississippi River Valley and Bluff Country and the Duluth and North Shore sections of the Minnesota chapter, Konnie has also worked for newspapers in France and South and North Dakota.

Brenda Steinbring, a third-generation Minnesotan, lives in uptown Minneapolis. She updated the Twin Cities Area, the Northwest and the Cuyana Iron Range, and the Southwestern Prairie sections of the Minnesota chapter.

Tina Lassen wrote and updated the Upper Peninsula section of the Michigan chapter. A freelance writer based in Madison, Wisconsin, Tina writes about travel, outdoor sports, and recreation for *Northwest Airlines World-Traveler, Midwest Living, Midwest Express Airlines Magazine, Outside, Country Inns*, and other national magazines. She and her yellow lab, Brunswick, spend whatever free time they can hiking in the Upper Peninsula.

Kristin Visser is a travel writer based in Madison, Wisconsin. Her articles have appeared in regional and national publications. She is the author of four travel books: *Wisconsin with Kids, Frank Lloyd Wright and the Prairie School in Wisconsin*, the *Acorn Guide to Door County*, and *Wisconsin Trivia*. She updated every section of the Wisconsin chapter but Door County.

Khristi Zimmeth is a freelance writer based in Grosse Pointe Park, Michigan, and a former editor of *Travel & Leisure*. She is also author of two guidebooks—*The Family Adventure Guide to Ohio* and *Quick Escapes from Detroit/Ann Arbor*—and a senior editor at *Michigan Living*, where she covers the state's bed-and-breakfast beat. She updated the Southeastern and Southwestern sections of the Michigan chapter.

Contents

Foreword

While every care has been taken to ensure the accuracy of the information in this guide, the passage of time will always bring change, and, consequently, the publisher cannot accept responsibility for errors that may occur.

All prices and listings are based on information supplied to us at press time. Details may change, however, and the prudent traveler will avoid inconvenience by calling ahead.

Fodor's wants to hear about your travel experiences, both pleasant and unpleasant. When an inn or B&B fails to live up to its billing, let us know and we will investigate the complaint and revise our entries where the facts warrant it.

Send your letters to: Editor, The Upper Great Lakes' Best Bed & Breakfasts, Fodor's Travel Publications, 201 East 50th Street, New York, NY 10022.

Introduction

You'll find bed-and-breakfasts in big houses with turrets and little houses with decks, in mansions by the water and cabins in the forest, not to mention structures of many sizes and shapes in between. B&Bs are run by people who were once lawyers and writers, homemakers and artists, nurses and architects, singers and businesspeople. Some B&Bs are just a room or two in a hospitable local's home; others are more like small inns. So there's an element of serendipity to every B&B stay.

But while that's part of the pleasure of the experience, it's also an excellent reason to plan your travels with a good B&B guide. The one you hold in your hands serves the purpose neatly.

To create it, we've handpicked a team of professional writers who are also confirmed B&B lovers: people who adore the many manifestations of the Victorian era; who go wild over wicker and brass beds, four-posters and fireplaces; and who know a well-run operation when they see it and are only too eager to communicate their knowledge to you. We've instructed them to inspect the premises and check out every corner of the premier inns and B&Bs in the areas they cover, and to report critically on only the best in every price range.

They've returned from their travels with comprehensive reports on the very best B&Bs—establishments that promise a unique experience, a distinctive sense of time and place. All are destinations in themselves, not just spots to rest your head at night, but an integral part of a weekend escape. You'll learn what's good, what's bad, and what could be better; what our writers liked and what you might not like.

At the same time, Fodor's reviewers tell you what's up in the area and what you should and shouldn't miss—everything from historic sites and parks to antiques shops, boutiques, and the area's niftiest restaurants and nightspots. We also include names and addresses of B&B reservation services, just in case you're inspired to seek out additional properties on your own. Reviews are organized by state, and, within each state, by region.

In the italicized service information that ends every review, a second address in parentheses is a mailing address. A double room is for two people, regardless of the size or type of its beds. Unless otherwise noted, rooms don't have phones or TVs. Note that even the most stunning homes, farmhouses and mansions alike, may not provide a private bathroom for each individual. Rates are for two, excluding tax, in the high season and include breakfast unless otherwise noted; ask about special packages and midweek or off-season discounts. What we call a restaurant serves meals other than breakfast and is usually open to the general public.

The following credit-card abbreviations are used throughout this guide: AE, American Express; D, Discover; DC, Diners Club; MC, MasterCard; V, Visa.

Where applicable, we note seasonal and other restrictions. Although we abhor discrimination, we have conveyed information about innkeepers' restrictive practices so that you will be aware of the prevailing attitudes. Such discriminatory practices are most often applied to parents who are traveling with small children and who may not, in any case, feel comfortable having their offspring toddle amid breakable bric-a-brac and near precipitous stairways.

When traveling the B&B way, always call ahead; and if you have mobility problems or are traveling with children, if you

*prefer a private bath or a certain type of bed, or if you have
specific dietary needs or any other concerns, discuss them with
the innkeeper. At the same time, if you're traveling to an inn
because of a specific feature, make sure that it will be
available when you get there and not closed for renovation.
The same goes if you're making a detour to take advantage of
specific sights or attractions.*

*It's a sad commentary on other B&B guides today that we feel
obliged to tell you that our writers did, in fact, visit every
property in person, and that it is they, not the innkeepers, who
wrote the reviews. No one paid a fee or promised to sell or
promote the book in order to be included in it. (In fact, one of
the most challenging parts of the work of a Fodor's writer is to
persuade innkeepers and B&B owners that he or she wants
nothing more than a tour of the premises and the answers to a
few questions!) Fodor's has no stake in anything but the truth.
If a room is dark, with peeling wallpaper, we don't call it
quaint or atmospheric—we call it run-down, and then steer
you to a more appealing section of the property.*

*So trust us, the way you'd trust a knowledgeable, well-traveled
friend. Let us hear from you about your travels, whether you
found that the B&Bs you visited surpassed their descriptions
or the other way around. And have a wonderful trip!*

*Karen Cure
Editorial Director*

Special Features at a Glance

Name of Property	Accessible to Guests with Disabilities	Antiques	On the Water	Best Value	Car Not Necessary	Historic Building	Romantic Hideaway	Luxurious	
MICHIGAN									
Aspen House		✓				✓	✓	✓	
Bay View at Mackinac		✓	✓		✓		✓	✓	
Bear River Valley									
Belvedere Inn					✓	✓			
The Benson House	✓						✓		
Big Bay Point Lighthouse			✓			✓	✓		
Blanche House Inn		✓	✓			✓	✓		
Bogan Lane Inn					✓	✓			
Bowers Harbor Bed & Breakfast			✓						
The Bridge Street Inn		✓				✓			
Brookside Inn							✓	✓	
Celibeth House		✓				✓			
Centennial Inn				✓		✓			
Chateau Chantal	✓						✓	✓	
Cherry Knoll Farm									
Chicago Pike Inn	✓	✓				✓	✓	✓	
Chicago Street Inn		✓		✓			✓		
Cloghaun Bed & Breakfast		✓			✓	✓			
Corktown Inn B&B		✓				✓	✓	✓	
Crane House	✓	✓				✓	✓		
Dundee Guest House		✓		✓					
Fairchild House		✓					✓	✓	
The Gingerbread House	✓			✓		✓			
Greencrest Manor		✓				✓	✓	✓	
Haan's 1830 Inn		✓		✓	✓	✓			

Pets Allowed	No Smoking Indoors	Good Place for Families	Boating Nearby	Beach Nearby	Cross-Country Ski Trails	Golf Within 5 Miles	Fitness Facilities	Good Biking Terrain	Skiing	Horseback Riding	Tennis	Swimming on Premises	Fishing Nearby	Hiking Nearby
	✓			✓	✓	✓		✓	✓				✓	✓
	✓		✓	✓				✓		✓				✓
	✓			✓	✓	✓		✓	✓					✓
	✓	✓		✓		✓		✓	✓					
	✓		✓	✓		✓		✓	✓					✓
	✓		✓	✓	✓			✓			✓		✓	✓
	✓	✓	✓			✓					✓		✓	✓
	✓	✓	✓	✓	✓			✓		✓				✓
	✓		✓	✓				✓	✓				✓	✓
	✓		✓	✓		✓		✓	✓					✓
	✓			✓				✓	✓				✓	✓
	✓		✓	✓	✓			✓					✓	✓
	✓			✓	✓			✓	✓				✓	✓
	✓			✓	✓			✓	✓					
	✓			✓				✓	✓				✓	✓
		✓		✓		✓								
			✓	✓		✓		✓					✓	
	✓	✓	✓	✓				✓		✓				✓
			✓											
			✓	✓	✓			✓					✓	✓
	✓							✓						✓
			✓	✓	✓	✓		✓			✓	✓	✓	✓
	✓	✓	✓	✓		✓		✓	✓					✓
	✓				✓	✓		✓					✓	
	✓	✓	✓	✓				✓		✓				✓

Special Features at a Glance

Name of Property	Accessible to Guests with Disabilities	Antiques	On the Water	Best Value	Car Not Necessary	Historic Building	Romantic Hideaway	Luxurious	
The House on the Hill		✓					✓	✓	
The Inn at Union Pier	✓	✓	✓	✓			✓		
The Inn on Mackinac	✓			✓	✓				
Kimberly Country Estate		✓					✓	✓	
Kingsley House		✓	✓				✓		
Laurium Manor Inn		✓		✓		✓	✓	✓	
Leelanau Country Inn									
Linden Lea			✓	✓			✓		
Maplewood Hotel	✓		✓		✓	✓	✓		
McCarthy's Bear Creek Inn		✓	✓			✓			
Mendon Country Inn	✓	✓				✓	✓		
Metivier Inn	✓					✓	✓	✓	
Montague Inn	✓	✓				✓			
Murray Hotel	✓					✓			
National House Inn	✓	✓				✓	✓		
Neahtawanta Inn			✓			✓			
1900 Market Street Inn					✓				
North Shore Inn	✓		✓				✓		
Old Mill Pond Inn				✓			✓		
Omena Shores		✓				✓	✓	✓	
Open Windows B&B									
Parsonage 1908		✓				✓	✓		
Pebble House	✓	✓	✓				✓		
Pinewood Lodge	✓	✓	✓	✓			✓		
Raymond House Inn						✓			
Sand Hills Lighthouse Inn		✓	✓			✓	✓		

Pets Allowed	No Smoking Indoors	Good Place for Families	Boating Nearby	Beach Nearby	Cross-Country Ski Trails	Golf Within 5 Miles	Fitness Facilities	Good Biking Terrain	Skiing	Horseback Riding	Tennis	Swimming on Premises	Fishing Nearby	Hiking Nearby
	✓			✓	✓	✓		✓	✓					✓
		✓	✓	✓	✓			✓					✓	✓
	✓	✓	✓	✓				✓		✓				✓
	✓			✓	✓	✓		✓	✓			✓		✓
	✓		✓	✓				✓	✓	✓			✓	✓
	✓	✓		✓	✓	✓		✓			✓		✓	✓
	✓			✓	✓	✓		✓	✓				✓	✓
	✓	✓	✓	✓		✓		✓	✓			✓	✓	✓
	✓	✓	✓	✓	✓	✓		✓		✓		✓	✓	✓
		✓			✓	✓		✓					✓	✓
	✓	✓	✓			✓		✓					✓	✓
	✓		✓	✓				✓		✓				✓
			✓				✓					✓	✓	✓
	✓		✓	✓				✓		✓				✓
		✓			✓	✓		✓			✓		✓	✓
	✓	✓	✓	✓				✓	✓				✓	✓
	✓		✓	✓				✓		✓				✓
	✓		✓	✓	✓			✓	✓			✓	✓	✓
	✓		✓	✓				✓					✓	✓
	✓	✓	✓	✓	✓	✓	✓						✓	✓
	✓		✓	✓		✓		✓					✓	✓
	✓		✓	✓	✓	✓		✓			✓		✓	✓
	✓		✓	✓	✓	✓		✓			✓		✓	✓
	✓	✓	✓		✓			✓				✓	✓	✓
	✓		✓	✓				✓					✓	✓
	✓		✓	✓	✓			✓					✓	✓

Special Features at a Glance

Name of Property	Accessible to Guests with Disabilities	Antiques	On the Water	Best Value	Car Not Necessary	Historic Building	Romantic Hideaway	Luxurious	
Snowbird Inn		✓					✓		
South Cliff Inn		✓	✓				✓	✓	
The Stacy Mansion	✓	✓				✓	✓	✓	
Stafford's Bay View Inn						✓			
Stuart Avenue Inn		✓				✓	✓	✓	
Thunder Bay Inn		✓				✓	✓		
Torch Lake Bed & Breakfast									
Twin Oaks Inn		✓				✓	✓		
Veranda at Harbor Springs							✓		
The Victoriana 1898		✓			✓	✓	✓		
Victorian Inn		✓				✓	✓	✓	
Victorian Villa Inn		✓				✓	✓	✓	
Walloon Lake Inn			✓						
Water Street Inn	✓	✓	✓				✓		
Wickwood Country Inn	✓	✓					✓	✓	
William Clements Inn	✓	✓		✓		✓		✓	
Yelton Manor		✓	✓			✓	✓	✓	
MINNESOTA									
The Anderson House		✓		✓		✓			
The Ann Bean House		✓			✓	✓	✓	✓	
The Archer House	✓		✓		✓	✓			
Asa Parker House		✓				✓	✓	✓	
Bearskin Lodge			✓				✓		
Bluff Creek Inn		✓				✓	✓	✓	
Bridgewaters Bed and Breakfast		✓	✓	✓			✓	✓	

Pets Allowed	No Smoking Indoors	Good Place for Families	Boating Nearby	Beach Nearby	Cross-Country Ski Trails	Golf Within 5 Miles	Fitness Facilities	Good Biking Terrain	Skiing	Horseback Riding	Tennis	Swimming on Premises	Fishing Nearby	Hiking Nearby
	✓			✓		✓		✓	✓				✓	✓
			✓	✓	✓	✓		✓			✓		✓	✓
✓						✓		✓					✓	
		✓	✓	✓		✓		✓	✓					✓
	✓	✓				✓		✓						
			✓	✓	✓			✓	✓				✓	✓
	✓		✓	✓		✓		✓	✓					✓
		✓	✓	✓	✓	✓		✓					✓	✓
	✓		✓	✓		✓								
	✓			✓		✓		✓	✓		✓			
			✓	✓	✓	✓	✓				✓		✓	✓
	✓	✓	✓	✓		✓		✓	✓					✓
	✓		✓	✓	✓	✓		✓	✓				✓	✓
			✓	✓	✓	✓		✓		✓	✓		✓	✓
			✓	✓		✓		✓					✓	
			✓	✓	✓	✓		✓					✓	✓
✓	✓	✓	✓	✓	✓	✓		✓	✓		✓		✓	✓
	✓		✓	✓	✓	✓		✓			✓		✓	✓
		✓	✓	✓	✓	✓		✓			✓		✓	✓
	✓		✓	✓	✓	✓		✓			✓		✓	✓
		✓	✓	✓	✓	✓		✓				✓	✓	✓
	✓				✓	✓		✓		✓	✓			✓
	✓		✓	✓	✓	✓		✓	✓		✓		✓	✓

Special Features at a Glance

Name of Property	Accessible to Guests with Disabilities	Antiques	On the Water	Best Value	Car Not Necessary	Historic Building	Romantic Hideaway	Luxurious	
The Candle Light Inn		✓			✓	✓	✓	✓	
Carriage House Bed & Breakfast		✓		✓	✓	✓			
Carrington House		✓	✓						
Carrolton Country Inn				✓		✓			
Chatsworth B&B		✓			✓	✓			
Covington Inn			✓				✓		
Elephant Walk		✓					✓	✓	
The Ellery House		✓		✓	✓	✓	✓		
Elm Street Inn		✓							
Elmwood House				✓		✓			
Evelo's Bed & Breakfast		✓		✓	✓		✓	✓	
Fering's Guest House									
Finnish Heritage House		✓		✓		✓			
Fitger's Inn	✓		✓	✓	✓	✓			
The Garden Gate Bed and Breakfast				✓	✓				
Hallett House		✓					✓		
Harvest Restaurant & Inn		✓		✓	✓				
Heartland Trail Inn									
Historic Scanlan House		✓		✓		✓	✓		
Hospital Bay B&B		✓	✓	✓		✓			
Hungry Point Inn		✓		✓		✓	✓		
The Inn at Palisade Bed & Breakfast			✓	✓			✓		
JailHouse Inn		✓		✓		✓	✓	✓	
James A. Mulvey Residence Inn		✓		✓	✓	✓	✓		
Laurel St. Inn		✓				✓	✓		
Le Blanc House		✓		✓	✓	✓	✓		

Pets Allowed	No Smoking Indoors	Good Place for Families	Boating Nearby	Beach Nearby	Cross-Country Ski Trails	Golf Within 5 Miles	Fitness Facilities	Good Biking Terrain	Skiing	Horseback Riding	Tennis	Swimming on Premises	Fishing Nearby	Hiking Nearby
	✓		✓		✓	✓		✓	✓				✓	✓
	✓		✓	✓	✓	✓		✓		✓	✓		✓	✓
✓	✓		✓	✓	✓	✓		✓		✓	✓	✓	✓	✓
	✓	✓	✓			✓	✓		✓		✓	✓		✓	✓
	✓					✓	✓	✓			✓			
	✓		✓					✓			✓		✓	✓
	✓		✓	✓	✓	✓		✓			✓		✓	✓
	✓	✓	✓	✓	✓	✓			✓		✓		✓	✓
	✓						✓	✓				✓	✓	✓
	✓	✓	✓	✓	✓	✓		✓			✓		✓	✓
	✓		✓	✓	✓			✓			✓		✓	✓
	✓		✓			✓							✓	✓
	✓	✓	✓			✓	✓		✓				✓	✓
		✓	✓	✓	✓	✓		✓	✓		✓		✓	✓
✓	✓	✓				✓		✓			✓			✓
	✓		✓	✓	✓	✓		✓					✓	✓
	✓		✓	✓	✓	✓		✓			✓		✓	✓
	✓		✓	✓	✓	✓		✓		✓			✓	✓
	✓				✓	✓		✓		✓	✓		✓	✓
	✓		✓			✓		✓			✓		✓	✓
	✓	✓			✓	✓		✓	✓	✓			✓	✓
	✓	✓	✓	✓	✓			✓					✓	✓
	✓					✓	✓		✓	✓	✓			✓	✓
	✓		✓	✓				✓			✓		✓	✓
	✓	✓			✓	✓		✓			✓		✓	✓
	✓		✓					✓			✓		✓	✓

Special Features at a Glance

Name of Property	Accessible to Guests with Disabilities	Antiques	On the Water	Best Value	Car Not Necessary	Historic Building	Romantic Hideaway	Luxurious
Lindgren's Bed & Breakfast			✓					
Log House on Spirit Lake and Homestead		✓	✓				✓	
Lumber Baron Hotel			✓			✓	✓	
The Mansion Bed & Breakfast Inn		✓		✓		✓	✓	
Martin Oaks		✓		✓		✓		
Mathew S. Burrows 1890 Inn		✓			✓	✓	✓	✓
Mrs. B's Historic Lanesboro Inn			✓	✓		✓		
Naniboujou Lodge	✓		✓	✓		✓	✓	
Nicollet Island Inn	✓		✓	✓	✓	✓	✓	
Nims' Bakketop Hus			✓					
1900 Dupont		✓		✓	✓	✓	✓	✓
Oakhurst Inn								
Olcott House		✓				✓		✓
Park Row Bed and Breakfast		✓		✓			✓	
Park Street Inn		✓				✓	✓	
Peters' Sunset Beach		✓	✓			✓		
Pincushion Mountain Bed & Breakfast				✓			✓	
Prairie House on Round Lake			✓	✓				
Prairie View Estate		✓		✓				
Pratt-Taber Inn		✓		✓	✓	✓	✓	✓
Quill & Quilt	✓	✓		✓		✓	✓	
Red Gables Inn		✓		✓	✓	✓		
The Rivertown Inn		✓				✓	✓	
The Rose Bed and Breakfast				✓			✓	✓
St. James Hotel	✓		✓		✓	✓		
Schumacher's New Prague Hotel						✓	✓	✓

Pets Allowed	No Smoking Indoors	Good Place for Families	Boating Nearby	Beach Nearby	Cross-Country Ski Trails	Golf Within 5 Miles	Fitness Facilities	Good Biking Terrain	Skiing	Horseback Riding	Tennis	Swimming on Premises	Fishing Nearby	Hiking Nearby
			✓	✓	✓	✓		✓	✓	✓	✓		✓	✓
	✓		✓	✓	✓	✓		✓		✓	✓	✓	✓	✓
			✓			✓		✓			✓		✓	✓
			✓	✓	✓	✓		✓	✓		✓		✓	✓
	✓		✓	✓	✓	✓		✓			✓		✓	✓
	✓		✓	✓	✓	✓			✓		✓		✓	✓
		✓	✓		✓	✓		✓		✓	✓		✓	✓
			✓	✓	✓	✓		✓					✓	✓
		✓	✓		✓			✓			✓		✓	✓
✓	✓		✓	✓	✓			✓		✓		✓	✓	✓
	✓		✓	✓				✓			✓		✓	✓
	✓		✓	✓	✓	✓		✓			✓		✓	
	✓	✓	✓	✓	✓	✓			✓				✓	✓
	✓		✓	✓	✓	✓		✓			✓		✓	✓
	✓		✓	✓	✓				✓				✓	✓
			✓	✓		✓		✓			✓	✓	✓	✓
	✓		✓		✓	✓		✓					✓	✓
	✓		✓							✓	✓	✓	✓	✓
✓	✓		✓		✓	✓						✓	✓	✓
✓		✓	✓		✓	✓		✓	✓		✓		✓	✓
	✓		✓	✓	✓	✓		✓			✓		✓	✓
	✓		✓	✓	✓	✓		✓	✓	✓	✓		✓	✓
	✓		✓	✓	✓	✓		✓			✓		✓	
	✓				✓	✓		✓			✓			
		✓	✓		✓	✓		✓	✓		✓		✓	✓
					✓	✓		✓			✓			✓

Special Features at a Glance

Name of Property	Accessible to Guests with Disabilities	Antiques	On the Water	Best Value	Car Not Necessary	Historic Building	Romantic Hideaway	Luxurious
Sod House on the Prairie		✓						
Spicer Castle		✓	✓			✓	✓	✓
The Stone Hearth Inn Bed & Breakfast		✓	✓	✓		✓	✓	
Stonehouse Bed and Breakfast								
The Superior Overlook B&B			✓	✓		✓	✓	
Thorwood Historic Inns	✓	✓				✓	✓	✓
The Victorian Bed & Breakfast		✓	✓	✓	✓	✓	✓	
Walden Woods		✓	✓	✓			✓	
Whistle Stop Inn		✓		✓			✓	
The William Sauntry Mansion		✓			✓	✓	✓	✓
WISCONSIN								
Allyn Mansion Inn		✓				✓	✓	✓
Arbor House	✓	✓				✓	✓	
Arbor Inn		✓		✓				
The Barbican Guest House		✓				✓	✓	✓
Bettinger House		✓		✓		✓		
Breese Waye		✓		✓		✓		
Cameo Rose	✓	✓					✓	
Candlewick Inn		✓				✓	✓	
Canterbury Inn	✓				✓		✓	✓
Cedar Trails Guesthouse		✓		✓				
College Avenue B&B		✓		✓	✓	✓		
Collins House		✓	✓			✓	✓	
The Creamery			✓			✓		
Crystal River Inn		✓	✓	✓		✓	✓	

Pets Allowed	No Smoking Indoors	Good Place for Families	Boating Nearby	Beach Nearby	Cross-Country Ski Trails	Golf Within 5 Miles	Fitness Facilities	Good Biking Terrain	Skiing	Horseback Riding	Tennis	Swimming on Premises	Fishing Nearby	Hiking Nearby
	✓	✓								✓				✓
			✓	✓	✓	✓	✓	✓		✓		✓	✓	✓
	✓		✓	✓	✓			✓					✓	✓
		✓	✓	✓	✓	✓		✓		✓			✓	✓
	✓	✓	✓	✓	✓	✓		✓			✓		✓	✓
	✓		✓	✓	✓	✓		✓	✓		✓		✓	✓
	✓		✓	✓	✓	✓		✓	✓		✓		✓	✓
	✓	✓	✓	✓	✓	✓		✓	✓	✓	✓		✓	✓
	✓		✓	✓							✓		✓	
	✓		✓	✓	✓	✓		✓			✓		✓	✓
	✓		✓	✓	✓	✓		✓	✓	✓	✓		✓	✓
	✓	✓		✓	✓	✓		✓			✓			
	✓		✓	✓	✓	✓		✓					✓	✓
			✓	✓	✓	✓		✓		✓	✓		✓	✓
			✓	✓	✓	✓		✓	✓				✓	✓
	✓		✓	✓	✓	✓		✓	✓				✓	✓
	✓				✓	✓		✓						✓
	✓		✓	✓	✓	✓		✓	✓				✓	✓
	✓				✓	✓		✓						
	✓	✓	✓		✓	✓		✓	✓			✓	✓	✓
	✓		✓	✓		✓		✓					✓	
		✓	✓	✓	✓	✓		✓	✓			✓	✓	✓
		✓	✓		✓	✓		✓	✓				✓	✓
	✓		✓	✓	✓	✓		✓					✓	✓

Special Features at a Glance

Name of Property	Accessible to Guests with Disabilities	Antiques	On the Water	Best Value	Car Not Necessary	Historic Building	Romantic Hideaway	Luxurious	
Dreams of Yesteryear		✓			✓	✓	✓		
The Duke House		✓		✓		✓			
Eagle Centre House		✓					✓		
The Eagle Harbor Inn	✓	✓						✓	
Eckhart House		✓				✓			
Elizabethan Inn	✓	✓	✓		✓	✓	✓		
The Ephraim Inn	✓	✓	✓			✓	✓		
Fargo Mansion Inn		✓				✓	✓	✓	
The Franklin Victorian		✓				✓			
The French Country Inn of Ephraim		✓		✓		✓			
The Gallery House			✓	✓		✓			
The Geiger House		✓		✓		✓			
Grapevine Inn		✓		✓			✓		
The Gray Goose Bed and Breakfast		✓		✓		✓			
Great River Bed & Breakfast		✓				✓	✓		
The Griffin Inn	✓	✓		✓		✓	✓		
The Harbor House Inn	✓	✓		✓		✓			
The Harrisburg Inn		✓		✓					
Hill Street		✓		✓					
Historic Bennett House		✓				✓	✓	✓	
The Hitching Post		✓				✓			
The Inn at Cedar Crossing		✓				✓	✓		
The Inn at Old Twelve Hundred		✓				✓	✓	✓	
The Inn at Wildcat Mountain		✓				✓			
The Inn on Maple		✓		✓		✓	✓		
Jamieson House		✓				✓	✓	✓	

Pets Allowed	No Smoking Indoors	Good Place for Families	Boating Nearby	Beach Nearby	Cross-Country Ski Trails	Golf Within 5 Miles	Fitness Facilities	Good Biking Terrain	Skiing	Horseback Riding	Tennis	Swimming on Premises	Fishing Nearby	Hiking Nearby
	✓		✓	✓	✓	✓		✓	✓		✓		✓	✓
	✓		✓		✓	✓		✓	✓				✓	✓
	✓				✓	✓		✓		✓				✓
	✓	✓	✓	✓	✓	✓	✓	✓		✓	✓	✓	✓	✓
	✓				✓	✓		✓						✓
	✓		✓	✓	✓	✓		✓	✓	✓	✓	✓	✓	✓
	✓		✓	✓	✓	✓		✓		✓	✓		✓	✓
	✓	✓	✓	✓	✓	✓		✓	✓				✓	✓
✓	✓	✓	✓	✓	✓	✓		✓	✓				✓	✓
	✓		✓	✓	✓	✓		✓		✓	✓		✓	✓
	✓		✓	✓	✓	✓		✓	✓		✓		✓	✓
	✓		✓	✓	✓	✓		✓	✓				✓	✓
	✓		✓	✓	✓	✓		✓					✓	✓
			✓	✓	✓	✓		✓		✓	✓		✓	✓
	✓	✓		✓		✓		✓						
	✓		✓	✓	✓	✓		✓		✓	✓		✓	✓
	✓		✓	✓	✓	✓		✓		✓	✓		✓	✓
✓		✓	✓	✓	✓	✓		✓	✓				✓	✓
	✓		✓	✓	✓	✓		✓	✓	✓	✓		✓	✓
	✓		✓	✓	✓	✓		✓	✓		✓		✓	✓
	✓	✓		✓	✓	✓		✓	✓		✓			
	✓		✓	✓	✓	✓		✓		✓	✓		✓	✓
	✓		✓	✓		✓							✓	
✓	✓	✓	✓	✓	✓	✓		✓	✓	✓			✓	✓
	✓		✓	✓		✓		✓		✓			✓	✓
	✓		✓			✓	✓		✓	✓				✓	✓

Special Features at a Glance

Name of Property	Accessible to Guests with Disabilities	Antiques	On the Water	Best Value	Car Not Necessary	Historic Building	Romantic Hideaway	Luxurious	
The Jefferson-Day House		✓				✓	✓		
The Jones House		✓		✓		✓	✓	✓	
Just-N-Trails	✓						✓		
The Knollwood House		✓		✓		✓			
Lakeside Manor			✓	✓			✓		
Lawrence House		✓			✓		✓	✓	
Lazy Cloud Lodge	✓						✓		
The Manor House	✓	✓	✓			✓	✓	✓	
The Mansards on-the-Lake		✓	✓						
Mansion Hill Inn		✓			✓	✓	✓	✓	
Martindale House		✓				✓	✓	✓	
Mascione's Hidden Valley Villas	✓						✓		
Nash House				✓		✓			
Oak Hill Manor		✓		✓		✓			
Oakwood Lodge		✓	✓	✓		✓			
Otter Creek Inn		✓					✓		
Parkview		✓		✓		✓			
The Parson's Inn		✓		✓		✓			
Past and Present Inn	✓	✓					✓		
The Pederson Victorian Bed & Breakfast		✓		✓		✓			
The Phipps Inn		✓				✓	✓	✓	
Pine Creek Lodge	✓						✓	✓	
Pinehaven			✓	✓					
Pleasant Lake Inn			✓	✓			✓		
Rosenberry Inn	✓	✓		✓		✓	✓		
Roses		✓		✓					

Pets Allowed	No Smoking Indoors	Good Place for Families	Boating Nearby	Beach Nearby	Cross-Country Ski Trails	Golf Within 5 Miles	Fitness Facilities	Good Biking Terrain	Skiing	Horseback Riding	Tennis	Swimming on Premises	Fishing Nearby	Hiking Nearby
	✓		✓	✓	✓	✓		✓	✓		✓		✓	✓
	✓		✓	✓	✓	✓		✓	✓		✓		✓	✓
	✓	✓	✓	✓	✓	✓		✓	✓	✓			✓	✓
	✓	✓	✓	✓	✓	✓	✓	✓	✓			✓	✓	✓
	✓		✓	✓	✓	✓		✓	✓	✓	✓	✓	✓	✓
	✓		✓	✓	✓	✓		✓	✓		✓		✓	✓
	✓		✓	✓	✓	✓		✓	✓	✓			✓	✓
			✓	✓	✓	✓		✓	✓		✓		✓	✓
	✓		✓	✓	✓	✓		✓	✓		✓		✓	✓
	✓		✓	✓	✓	✓	✓	✓	✓		✓		✓	✓
	✓	✓	✓	✓	✓	✓		✓	✓		✓		✓	✓
			✓	✓	✓	✓		✓	✓	✓		✓	✓	✓
	✓	✓	✓		✓	✓		✓	✓				✓	✓
	✓	✓	✓		✓	✓		✓	✓				✓	✓
	✓	✓	✓	✓	✓	✓		✓			✓	✓	✓	✓
	✓					✓		✓					✓	
		✓	✓	✓	✓	✓		✓	✓				✓	✓
✓	✓	✓	✓	✓	✓	✓		✓	✓				✓	✓
	✓	✓	✓	✓	✓	✓		✓	✓				✓	✓
	✓				✓	✓		✓	✓	✓				✓
	✓		✓	✓	✓	✓		✓	✓		✓		✓	✓
	✓				✓	✓		✓						✓
	✓	✓	✓	✓	✓	✓		✓	✓				✓	✓
	✓	✓	✓	✓	✓	✓		✓	✓			✓	✓	✓
	✓		✓	✓	✓	✓		✓	✓				✓	✓
	✓		✓	✓	✓	✓		✓	✓	✓			✓	✓

Special Features at a Glance

Name of Property	Accessible to Guests with Disabilities	Antiques	On the Water	Best Value	Car Not Necessary	Historic Building	Romantic Hideaway	Luxurious	
Rosewood		✓		✓		✓			
The Ryan House		✓		✓		✓			
St. Croix River Inn		✓	✓			✓	✓	✓	
The Scofield House		✓				✓	✓	✓	
Sherman House						✓			
Stagecoach Inn	✓	✓				✓	✓	✓	
Sugar River Inn		✓	✓	✓					
The Swallow's Nest				✓					
Trillium		✓		✓			✓		
Ty-Bach			✓	✓					
University Heights Bed and Breakfast		✓			✓	✓			
Victorian Garden		✓		✓		✓	✓		
Victorian Swan on Water		✓		✓		✓			
Victoria-on-Main		✓		✓		✓			
Viroqua Heritage Inn		✓		✓		✓	✓		
Washington House Inn	✓	✓				✓	✓	✓	
Water's Edge			✓				✓		
Westby House		✓				✓			
The Whistling Swan		✓				✓	✓		
The White Gull Inn	✓	✓				✓	✓		

Pets Allowed	No Smoking Indoors	Good Place for Families	Boating Nearby	Beach Nearby	Cross-Country Ski Trails	Golf Within 5 Miles	Fitness Facilities	Good Biking Terrain	Skiing	Horseback Riding	Tennis	Swimming on Premises	Fishing Nearby	Hiking Nearby
	✓		✓					✓					✓	✓
	✓	✓	✓	✓	✓	✓		✓	✓				✓	✓
			✓	✓	✓	✓		✓	✓				✓	✓
	✓		✓	✓	✓	✓		✓					✓	✓
		✓	✓	✓	✓	✓		✓	✓	✓			✓	✓
	✓		✓	✓	✓	✓		✓	✓	✓	✓		✓	✓
	✓		✓	✓	✓	✓		✓	✓			✓	✓	✓
	✓		✓	✓	✓	✓		✓	✓				✓	✓
		✓	✓	✓	✓	✓		✓	✓				✓	✓
	✓	✓	✓	✓	✓			✓				✓	✓	✓
	✓		✓	✓	✓	✓		✓					✓	✓
	✓	✓	✓	✓	✓	✓		✓	✓				✓	✓
	✓		✓	✓	✓	✓		✓	✓		✓		✓	✓
	✓		✓	✓	✓	✓		✓	✓	✓			✓	✓
	✓	✓	✓	✓	✓	✓		✓	✓		✓		✓	✓
			✓	✓	✓	✓		✓	✓	✓	✓		✓	✓
	✓		✓	✓	✓	✓		✓	✓	✓		✓	✓	✓
		✓	✓	✓	✓	✓		✓	✓				✓	✓
	✓		✓	✓	✓	✓		✓			✓	✓	✓	✓
	✓	✓	✓	✓	✓	✓		✓			✓	✓	✓	✓

Michigan

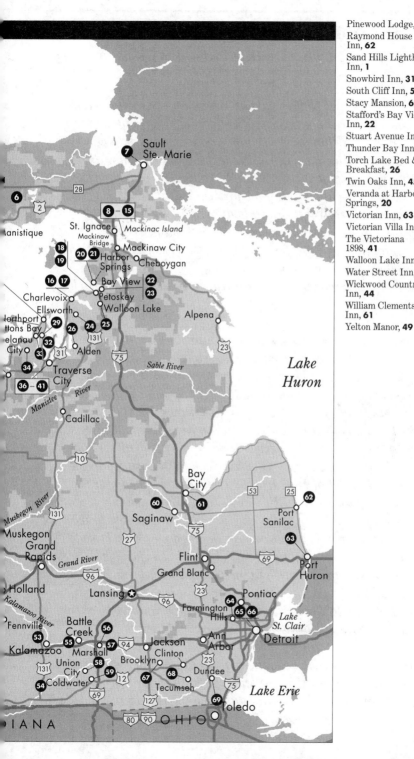

Southeastern Michigan
Including Ann Arbor and Detroit

First-time visitors to this part of Michigan are surprised to find there's more here than postindustrial forests of cold smokestacks. Although the region's two major urban centers, Detroit and Flint, struggle with the same socioeconomic problems that afflict other Rust Belt cities, no other part of the state offers a greater mix of natural, cultural, and recreational resources. Row a boat on a quiet lake in the morning, browse through rural antiques shops in the afternoon, take in a professional sporting event, and dine at a world-class restaurant in the evening, even visit another country for a nightcap—all usually within an hour's reach of your lodging.

Although one-third of the state's population lives here, an excellent network of freeways and secondary roads allows travelers to zip easily out of city centers and into the surrounding countryside. If you find shopping in the cavernous Renaissance Center in downtown Detroit frustrating, drive north on I–75 to Troy's Somerset Collection, where designer boutiques rival New York's Madison Avenue and Chicago's Oak Street. Or head even farther north to the charming hamlet of Holly, a pastoral pocket of old stores. Port Huron is an hour from Flint or Detroit, and once there, you can watch freighters pass by so close you can almost touch them. Port Huron is at the base of the largely rural Thumb region (the lower peninsula of Michigan is shaped like a mitten), honeycombed with farms, sleepy ports, and superb county and state parks. U.S. 25 traces the thumb's outline from Bay City to Port Huron and affords exquisite views of Lake Huron and Saginaw Bay.

Detroit, of course, anchors the region. The Motor City, ringed by some of the most affluent suburbs in the country, is dissected by three major interstate highways. Interstate 75 will take you to Monroe (home of General George Custer) in the south and to Bay City, a port town on Saginaw Bay, to the north. Interstates 96 and 94 will carry you west to Lansing and Jackson, respectively. Running north from the Ohio border, U.S. 127 strings these two cities together and forms a logical western boundary to the region. Urban sprawl is minimal here, and the little there is blends easily into miles of open country.

Despite its lunch-bucket reputation, Detroit actually has a cosmopolitan feel befitting the oldest city west of the Appalachians. The flags of three nations—France, Britain, and the United States—have flown over this onetime trading post. As a chief port of entry for settlers heading for the interior in the mid-1800s, then later as a magnet drawing a multitude of immigrants, Southerners, and Latin Americans to its booming auto plants, Detroit has always been a melting pot. At one time an exasperated Henry Ford was obliged to post work signs in eight languages in his factories.

Today, this diversity is evident in the scores of ethnic restaurants sprinkled throughout the region. Many are in such ethnic enclaves as Hamtramck, a separate town largely of Polish-Americans found within the Detroit city limits, and Dearborn, a western suburb that has the largest Arab population outside the Middle East. A growing colony of transplanted Japanese—a sign of the increasing interdependence between U.S. and Asian carmakers—has materialized, resulting in a wave of Asian restaurants and karaoke bars. The village of Frankenmuth, an hour's drive north of Detroit, remains more German than American and is famous for its family-style chicken dinners and its cavernous, year-round Christmas store.

To add to the mix, Canada is just a short bridge or tunnel ride away. Americans and Canadians freely move back and forth; passports are not necessary for citizens of either country (though you will need some form of identification, such as a driver's license). Spectacular annual events, such as the Detroit Grand Prix auto race, the Montreaux Detroit Jazz

Festival (the largest free jazz fest in the world), the Port Huron–Mackinac Island sailing regatta, the North American International Auto Show, the Gold Cup powerboat races, and the International Freedom Festival, draw hundreds of thousands of people each year and help to maintain the region's international flavor.

Countless chain motels and luxury hotels have been built to handle the business and convention trade. As a result, historic inns and bed-and-breakfasts are not nearly as numerous in southeastern Michigan as in other parts of the state. Those that do exist, however, have been around for a long time and are typically very good; their owners have learned to weather the boom-and-bust cycles that are so much a part of this area's history.

Places to Go, Sights to See

Ann Arbor. Home to the University of Michigan, this leafy, liberal community is a 45-minute drive from downtown Detroit via westbound I–94. Ann Arbor is the quintessential university town: drowsy neighborhood bookstores and funky street performers peacefully coexist with respected arts centers and world-class research facilities. Sidewalk cafés operate past midnight, and the 101,000-seat Michigan Stadium, the nation's largest college-owned stadium, makes Ann Arbor a great place for tailgate parties on autumn football weekends.

Auto Racing. The Detroit Grand Prix (tel. 313/393–7749), held each June since 1981, has evolved into a three-day weekend party interrupted periodically by the main event and support races. The Michigan International Speedway (tel. 517/592–6671), 60 miles west of Detroit on U.S. 12 in Brooklyn, features NASCAR and Indy-style races.

Detroit. Once the nation's fifth city, Detroit has lost half its population since the 1950s. The shrinking tax base has caused one of the country's truly great museums, the **Detroit Institute of Arts** (5200 Woodward Ave., tel. 313/833–7900), to juggle hours of operation, so call ahead. But while the core city has struggled, as jobs and people have moved elsewhere, downtown and surrounding suburbs continue to offer first-class shopping, dining, cultural, and entertainment experiences. **Belle Isle** (tel. 313/267–7115), a 1,000-acre island park, sits in the Detroit River, 3 miles from the heart of the city, connected by a bridge to the mainland. The multipurpose park—designed by Frederic Law Olmsted, the same landscape architect who laid out New York City's Central Park—has facilities for baseball, golf, swimming, cycling, hiking, basketball, tennis, and many other recreational activities. Other attractions are an aquarium, a zoo, a nature center, a conservatory, and the Dossin Great Lakes Museum. The Detroit Grand Prix is held here in June. The lavishly restored **Fox Theatre** (2211 Woodward Ave., tel. 313/983–6611), which opened in 1928 as America's largest movie palace, today showcases big-name musical acts and large-screen movies. The **Henry Ford Museum & Greenfield Village** (Village Rd. and Oakwood Blvd., Dearborn, tel. 313/271–1620) are two world-famous collections of Americana in the western suburb of Dearborn. Especially noteworthy is "The Automobile in American Life," a lavish, upbeat collection of chrome and neon devoted to the evolution of the automobile and roadside culture. Detroit's chapter of the American Dream comes alive in a tour of **Historic Homes of the Auto Barons** that includes several mansions that once belonged to auto pioneers such as Henry and Edsel Ford and the Dodge brothers. The **Motown Museum** (2648 W. Grand Blvd., tel. 313/875–2264) is in the unassuming two-story house on West Grand Boulevard where Berry Gordy, Jr., started the "Motown Sound" in the late 1950s. It's stuffed with memorabilia, including album covers, costumes, gold records, and, yes, one of Michael Jackson's gloves. You can squeeze into the small recording studio where such acts as the Temptations, Smokey Robinson and the Miracles, and Diana Ross and the Supremes cranked out hit after hit. The Detroit Tigers and their predecessors have been playing baseball at the corner of Michigan and Trumbull streets in **Tiger Stadium** (tel. 313/962–4000) since 1896, making this spot professional sports' oldest address. Prices are reasonable, and acquiring tickets is almost never a problem, making it easy to enjoy a summer game. Do it soon, however, as the classic ballpark may soon be replaced with a newer facility.

Frankenmuth. "Little Bavaria," founded by German immigrants in 1845, sits just off the I–75 corridor between Flint and Saginaw. The town markets its heritage through scores of gift shops, lodgings, and restaurants that groan under the weight of flower boxes and gingerbread trim. The village's most popular attractions are Bronner's Christmas Wonderland (25 Christmas La., Frankenmuth, tel. 517/652–9931), where more than 50,000 lights and ornaments are for sale year-round, and the Zehnder's and Bavarian Village restaurants, which both serve thousands of family-style chicken dinners each year.

Port Huron. At the confluence of the St. Clair River and Lake Huron, the hometown of inventor Thomas Edison has changed very little since he was a youth there. The 1858 Grand Trunk Depot, where he got on Detroit-bound trains to sell newspapers, has been restored in a riverside park. In Port Huron, visitors get incredible close-up views of freighters from all over the world passing through a narrow, quarter-mile-wide passageway. Other maritime treats include the 152-foot-high Blue Water Bridge, from which pedestrians can enjoy panoramic views while waiting for freighters to pass underneath; and the Lighthouse Park complex, which includes an 1874 light keeper's dwelling, a white clapboard Coast Guard station, and the oldest surviving lighthouse in Michigan.

Tecumseh. This town, about 30 miles east of Jackson on Route 50, is the antiques center of the region. Founded in 1824, it has three antiques malls among its many historic buildings and restored train depot. One of the state's largest antiques fairs is held on the third Sunday of every month from April to November.

Boating

Michigan has more registered boat owners than any other state, so the Great Lakes and inland waters become crowded playgrounds in warm weather. Most county and state parks offer boat and canoe rentals and have beaches with supervised swimming. Bay City, a freighter port on Saginaw Bay, has speedboat and offshore powerboat racing and other water sports. River cruising is gaining popularity. You can dine while enjoying the breezes of Lake St. Clair on the 100-foot yacht the *Infinity* (tel. 313/778–7030).

Fishing

With almost 100 lakes in the metro Detroit area alone, you'll never be far from a fishing hole. The Detroit River, especially around Belle Isle, is popular with anglers. Generally, the waters throughout the region are rated good to excellent for trout, yellow perch, bluegills, crappies, bass, walleye, panfish, and northern pike. Charter-boat fishing for salmon, walleye, and lake trout is available on Lakes Huron, St. Clair, and Erie.

Golf

Michigan's golf season stretches from April through October and to meet the growing demand, new courses continue to spring up. Some of the more recent additions include Marion Oaks Golf Club (2255 Pinkey Rd., Howell, tel. 517/ 548–0050), halfway between Lansing and Detroit on I-96. Desmond Muirhead designed the course at Bay Valley Inn (2470 Old Bridge Rd., Bay City, tel. 517/ 686–5400, and Cascades Golf Course (1992 Warren Ave., Jackson, tel. 517/ 788–4323) is considered one of the best golf values in the state. In the Thumb, Verona Hills (3175 Sand Beach Rd., Bad Axe, tel. 517/269–8132), with an excellent layout, is just east of Bad Axe on Route 142. For a complete listing, contact RSG Publishing for a 304-page guide ($19.95; tel. 800/223–5877) to the state's public courses—there are more than 900 of them!

Skiing

Downhill resorts can be found just off I–75 north of Detroit at Pine Knob Ski Resort (tel. 810/625–0800), in Clarkston, and Mt. Holly (tel. 810/582–7256), in Holly. Mt. Brighton Ski Area (tel. 810/229–9581), in Brighton, and Alpine Valley (tel. 810/887–4183), in Milford, are also popular. Many county and state parks, as well as a growing number of golf courses, have groomed trails for cross-country skiing.

Restaurants

There is no lack of good restaurants in the region. The cavernous **Bavarian Inn** (713 S. Main St., tel. 517/652–9941), in Frankenmuth, specializes in hearty, homemade chicken dinners. Ann Arbor's most popular restaurant, the **Gandy Dancer** (401 Depot St., tel. 313/769–0592), serves fresh seafood dishes in an old fieldstone train station. Some of the favorites in Detroit include downtown's **Fishbone's Rhythm Kitchen Cafe** (400 Monroe St., tel. 313/965–4600), home of New Orleans–style gumbo and whiskey ribs; the classically Italian **Roma Cafe** (3401 Riopelle St., tel. 313/831–5940), the city's oldest restaurant; and the **Whitney** (4421 Woodward St., tel. 313/832–5700), where American food and music are served inside a pink stone mansion that once belonged to lumber baron David Whitney. The **Lark** (6430 Farmington St., tel. 313/661–4466), in suburban West Bloomfield, is famous for its crisp service, superb Continental cuisine, and genuinely warm hospitality. World travelers Jim and Mary Lark have transformed their interestingly decorated country inn into the best dining experience on this side of the state. North of the city in St. Clair is the **River Crab** (1337 N. River Rd., tel. 810/329–2261), known for its fresh seafood and great views of Lake St. Clair.

Tourist Information

The umbrella organization for the entire state is the **Michigan Travel Bureau** (333 S. Capitol Ave., Lansing, MI 48933, tel. 800/543–2937). For information on boating, fishing, and hunting, contact the **Michigan Department of Natural Resources** (530 N. Allegan St., Lansing, MI 48933, tel. 517/373–1204). Site-specific tourist information can be found through the **Ann Arbor Convention and Visitors Bureau** (120 W. Huron St., Ann Arbor, MI 48104, tel. 313/995–7281); **Flint Area Convention and Visitors Bureau** (400 N. Saginaw St., Flint, MI 48502, tel. 810/232–8900); **Frankenmuth Chamber of Commerce** (635 S. Main St., Frankenmuth, MI 48734, tel. 517/652–6106); **Greater Lansing Convention and Visitors Bureau** (119 Pere Marquette, Box 15066, Lansing, MI 48901, tel. 517/487–6800 or 800/648–6630); **Metropolitan Detroit Convention and Visitors Bureau** (100 Renaissance Center, Suite 1950, Detroit, MI 48243, tel. 313/259–4333); **Port Huron/Marysville Chamber of Commerce** (920 Pine Grove Ave., Port Huron, MI 48060, tel. 810/985–7101); and the **Saginaw County Convention and Visitors Bureau** (901 S. Washington St., Saginaw, MI 48601, tel. 517/752–7164).

Montague Inn

Robert Montague was a respected businessman and civic leader when he built his 12,000-square-foot Georgian house—all of handmade brick—in 1929 in Saginaw's historic Grove District. To help preserve important landmarks of the district—once an enclave of stunning residences—the city bought Montague's home in the early 1960s and demolished several of the more rickety surrounding properties. Then a group of five entrepreneurial-minded couples bought it from the city in 1985. Eight months later, they reopened the restored mansion and the adjacent carriage house as the Montague Inn. Not only has the three-story brick mansion been named to the State Register of Historic Places, but it is also considered one of Michigan's best inns, a designation that's hard to dispute.

The inn's location on 8 gently rolling acres overlooking Lake Linton is a mixed blessing. There is usually a lot of activity on the grounds, and on days when the city park across the water is staging a concert or a raft race, there can be a large volume of traffic in the area. Caveat noted, the inn is still a champion. A winding staircase connects the three floors of guest rooms. The Georgian-style quarters typically contain four-poster beds and wing chairs and are tastefully decorated in subtle hues and patterns. The most compelling—and at $140 per night, the most expensive—is the elegant two-room Montague Suite, which features a fireplace, green Pewabic tile, and great views of the impeccably landscaped grounds. Other interesting accommodations are in the former chauffeur's quarters and the cleverly renovated five-car garage.

Guests enjoy a Continental breakfast of oatmeal, cereals, juice, and baked goods in either of two dining rooms, one of which has a welcoming fire on cold mornings. Lunches and candlelight dinners are first-class affairs, too, with an expansive (and expensive) menu and wine list. After meals—everything from asparagus ravioli to honey-marinated quail—logs are lighted in the fireplace of the main-floor library, and guests can look for the hidden cabinets inside the library walls, where Montague stashed his expensive liquor during Prohibition (by special request, you can even dine in a secret alcove behind a bookcase). Other guests choose to wander in the extensive herb and flower garden, participate in one of the inn's exciting events (Independence Day picnic, black-tie New Year's Eve dinner, or summer herb-garden luncheons), or just pen a postcard at the antique writing desk. Those who scrawl "Wish you were here" know what they're talking about.

🏨 *1581 S. Washington Ave., Saginaw, MI 48601, tel. 517/752-3939, fax 517/752-3159. 16 double rooms with baths, 2 doubles share bath, 1 suite. Restaurant, air-conditioning, phone and TV in rooms. $65–$140; Continental breakfast. AE, MC, V. Smoking in library only, no pets.*

Raymond House Inn

As the inn's owners, Shirley and Ray Denison, enjoy pointing out, there is no McDonald's in Port Sanilac. The retired couple do what they can to keep the golden arches at bay by heading a movement to have this old port village declared a Historic Maritime District, thereby limiting commercial development.

Port Sanilac sits halfway up the eastern edge of the Thumb region on Route 25, about 30 miles north of Port Huron and less than two hours from Detroit. It was one of Lake Huron's first ports of call during the heyday of steamship lines. Its colorful history includes lumberjacks, lake storms, rum-running, and forest fires that more than once destroyed the town. The port's history is honored in the newly opened shipwreck and maritime center.

The background of this comfortable, impressive Victorian house, which is listed on the State Register of Historic Places, is a little calmer but nevertheless significant. In 1850, Uri Raymond, the original owner, opened what is reputed to be the first hardware store in the state (Raymond Hardware, just a block down the road, is still in business). Raymond built his two-story brick residence in 1871, adorning it with classic Victorian touches: elaborate moldings and a winding oak staircase inside and outside a gingerbread facade with dripping white icicle trim. It stayed in the family for the next 112 years until Ray and Shirley—he's a retired Washington lobbyist for the AFL-CIO, she's an artist and conservation expert who in 1976 reframed the Constitution for the Bicentennial—bought it in 1983 and moved here from Washington, D.C.

The house, set on an acre planted with trees and gardens of wildflowers, was in good condition and is now full of family heirlooms, antiques, and numerous examples of Shirley's considerable artistic and restorative skills. She has recaned the chairs, restored the frames that hold a collection of old family photos in an upstairs hallway, and designed the clock in the dining room (she also designs and crafts artistic dolls). The upstairs quarters are authentically furnished, down to crocheted lacework on the window shades, handmade quilts, and hand-crocheted rugs. Lake Huron, a block away, can be spied from upstairs.

▥ *111 S. Ridge St., Port Sanilac, MI 48469, tel. 313/622–8800 or 800/622–7229. 7 double rooms with baths. Air-conditioning; fireplace, cable TV, and phone in parlor, radio/cassette player in rooms. $65–$75; full breakfast. AE, D, MC, V. No smoking, no pets, closed Jan.–Mar.*

The Stacy Mansion

The story of one of the state's grandest homes can be gleaned from a quick look inside its first-floor library. On a desktop, the 1874 *Historical Atlas of Lenawee County* is opened to a sketch of the four-story brick mansion as it looked when Judge C. A. Stacy owned it. Directly above the open book hangs a buffalo head, provided by the current owners, Sonny and Joyce Lauber, who, among their other business interests, run one of the few bison farms in the country.

Stacy, newspaper publisher, businessman, and the first probate judge in the county, built the 8,000-square-foot house in the mid-1850s in anticipation of using it as the governor's residence. He lost the gubernatorial election but held on to the house, which has fine examples of 19th-century craftsmanship such as a foyer with marbled wood and a rare cantilevered staircase.

"Sonny drove past the house for 25 years and always talked about buying it," says Joyce. When the badly neglected building on the outskirts of Tecumseh came on the market in 1988, the Laubers didn't think twice. The house had been stripped of nearly everything—from the furnishings to the brass doorknobs and gingerbread trim—so restoration has been a slow, expensive process. To their credit, they have taken time to research—and have spent the money necessary to recall its 19th-century ambience. They tore out the carpeting, restored the floors and woodwork, and replicated the plaster-work. They also researched historical wallpapers and were even able to buy back some of the furniture from former owners and area real-estate agents. All told, the house "is about 95% antiques," says Joyce. One bedroom has a double-mirrored wardrobe, another an 8½-foot-high, ornately carved walnut head-board. The only incongruous item is the water-filled mattress in the master bedroom. "We couldn't find a mattress that would fit the odd-sized mahogany full-tester bed," she explained.

During your stay, a morning "wake-up" tray of tea, coffee, juice, and home-made coffee cake is brought to your door, followed later by a full gourmet breakfast in the formal dining room.

The 1¼-acre site is expertly land-scaped. Judge Stacy, who owned a local brickyard, would certainly approve of the 45,000 bricks the Laubers used to create the paths that wind through the yards and gardens. A 150-year-old pine tree shades a formal garden often abloom with annuals and perennials and accented with wrought-iron garden furniture, while old-fashioned street lamps and red maple trees flank the circular drive and help to make the outdoors an appealing retreat in itself.

🏠 *710 W. Chicago Blvd., Tecumseh, MI 49286, tel. 517/423–6979. 5 double rooms with baths. Air-conditioning, phone in sitting room. $85–$120; full breakfast. MC, V. No smoking indoors, small pets only. Children welcome; $10 additional per child.*

Victorian Inn

L ynne Secory and Vicki Peterson were neighbors busily renovating their own homes when they got the impulse to breathe new life into what was once one of Port Huron's most magnificent houses, the old James A. Davidson residence. Davidson, founder of a large furniture and dry goods company that bore his name, had built the elaborate Queen Anne house in 1896 and lived in it until his death in 1911. In 1983, Lynne and Vicki persuaded their husbands to buy the property. Enlisting the aid of many preservation-minded friends, relatives, and craftsmen, and working from the architectural plans and spec sheets, they managed to accomplish their mission by the end of the year. Halfway through the project, the house was placed on the State Register of Historic Places. The result of their efforts is a harmonious combination of luxurious lodging and fine dining in a neighborhood of well-maintained Victorian-era buildings that has become a travel destination in itself.

Immediately to the right of the foyer as you walk in is the parlor. Its green velvet valances, antique lace window curtains, green-and-gold floral wallpaper, pincushion settee, and hurricane lamps are invitingly elegant. The second-floor guest rooms are similar blends of antique furnishings and little flourishes: a needlepoint headboard, a papier-mâché picture frame. Two rooms have modern private baths, while the Victoria and Edward rooms share a pedestal sink, claw-foot tub (no shower), and pull-chain toilet.

Guests can eat breakfast in the main-floor 50-seat restaurant, also open for lunch and dinner Tuesday through Saturday. The service is attentive, the staff is immaculately attired in crisp white uniforms, and the mainly American menu is well executed. The inventive soups and desserts are especially popular.

The inn is just a couple of blocks from the St. Clair River, which carries freighter traffic and cool breezes. The Museum of Arts and History is one block over, on Court Street, and houses one of the finest collections of marine lore in the state. Travel the dozen or so blocks to the Fort Gratiot Lighthouse, the first one on the Great Lakes, and return to the inn and wet your whistle at the stone-walled Pierpont Pub. Originally a cellar, it features an old red oak bar that used to be a dry goods counter.

🏠 *1229 7th St., Port Huron, MI 48060, tel. 810/984–1437. 2 double rooms with baths, 2 doubles share bath. Air-conditioning, room service, fireplace in parlor, restaurant, pub. $65–$75; Continental breakfast. AE, D, MC, V. No pets.*

William Clements Inn

This gray Queen Anne–style mansion in Bay City is what eccentric Great-Aunt Emily's house always looked like, at least in the movies: Ornately carved staircases and ceilings, heavy oak furniture, and voluminous velveteen drapes establish the look. The house was built in 1886 for William Clements, a local lumber baron and a collector of rare books who donated his impressive collection to the University of Michigan library in 1920.

Today, his love of books is still felt in the inn, where each suite is named after a writer or fictional character—from Louisa May Alcott and Emily Brontë to Henry David Thoreau and Charles Dickens. This is just one of the lovely touches the owners, Brian and Karen Hepp—a local couple with a great appreciation of history—brought to the inn when they purchased it in 1994. The two most lavish accommodations are the Ernest Hemingway Suite, a two-room whirlpool suite with a working fireplace, sitting area, French doors, a king-size bed and an in-room shower for two, and the Alfred Lord Tennyson Suite, which is actually the 1,200-square-foot former ballroom, now outfitted with a kitchen, living room, dining room, and queen-size bed. Second-floor guest rooms are spacious and filled with period furnishings, including iron or brass beds, marble-top tables, and oak armoires. One bathroom is particularly gracious, featuring china tiles bordered with hand-painted morning glories.

As the quintessential 19th-century man of industry and culture, Clements also exhibited a respect for music, equipping the music room with a magnificent Steinway grand piano. But Clements's true passion was books, and a few volumes from his former collection remain in the richly paneled main-floor library. Guests, however, are more likely to be found in the screened-in back porch, shaded by a 200-year-old beech tree. There they play cards and talk of the sea captains and lumber barons who built the other grand mansions that fill this historic district.

🏨 *1712 Center Ave., Bay City, MI 48708, tel. 517/894–4600, fax 517/895–8535. 4 double rooms with baths; 3 suites. Air-conditioning, TV, phone, and toiletries in rooms; fireplace in 4 rooms, whirlpool bath in suites. $70–$175; Continental breakfast by candlelight, evening refreshments. AE, D, MC, V. No smoking, no pets.*

Blanche House Inn and the Castle

When interior designer Mary Jean Shannon sold her suburban house in 1986 to buy a run-down mansion in Detroit, no one thought a bed-and-breakfast could make it anywhere in the Motor City. Today, there are two other downtown inns, but the Blanche House and its sister B&B, the Castle, are the best examples of Detroit's grand past and an inspiration for the ongoing renaissance of the center-city area.

Designed by Louis Kamper and built in 1905, the Colonial Revival–style Blanche House was once a prep school attended by Henry Ford II, former governor G. Mennen Williams, and other local notables. The Shannons bought the adjacent late 19th-century building known as the Castle (it once served as a religious commune) several years after making a success of the Blanche House Inn. Recently, they have purchased a nearby cottage-style house (boasting 150 neighboring feet of waterfront) for guests who plan extended stays.

Mary Jean and her son, Sean, have done a commendable job restoring the three structures. Highlights include towering porch pillars, 10-foot etched-glass doors, oak woodwork and floors, and ornate paneling and plasterwork. The guest rooms, all named after someone who has figured in the inn's history, are fitted with antiques, including an 1850s brass British army bed in the Bell Parker Room. There is a back porch where guests can relax in hammocks that overlook a marina and the Stanton Canal. Inquire about the Shannons' special Spa Night package, which includes deluxe accommodations, a massage, and more.

🏨 *506 Parkview Dr., Detroit, MI 48214, tel. 313/822–7090. 13 double rooms with baths, 1 suite. Air-conditioning, cable TV, and phone in rooms, hot tubs in 4 rooms. $60–$125; full breakfast. AE, D, DC, MC, V. No smoking, no pets.*

Botsford Inn

The unofficial motto of Michigan's oldest continuously operating inn, built as a stagecoach stop in 1836, is "History never goes out of style." So says Creon Smith, a North Carolina native who purchased the National Historic Landmark in late 1993 and has lovingly maintained its high ranking among preservationists and lovers of fine cuisine. Today the inn features a total of 63 rooms, 14 in the original historic building.

At one time the inn was owned by Henry Ford, whose wife, Clara, stocked the place with such antiques as a spinet piano that once belonged to General Custer's sister, Abraham Lincoln's writing desk, a Simon Williams grandfather clock, and original Currier & Ives prints. However, the restaurant and banquet facilities are the main attraction today. The hearty meals are based on American heritage recipes, and Smith insists the full breakfast include extra-thick bacon and Triple-A eggs. So you can burn off those calories, the inn hosts ballroom or country dances on a cushioned floor designed by Ford himself.

The rooms are decorated traditionally (four-poster beds, quilts) with an eye toward modern practicality (coffeemaker, cable TV).

🏨 *28000 Grand River, Farmington Hills, MI 48336, tel. 810/474–4800. 14 historic double rooms; 49 modern rooms, all with baths. Air-conditioning in certain rooms, restaurant, cable TV, coffeemaker, and phone in rooms. $65–$75; full breakfast. AE, D, DC, MC, V. No pets.*

Chicago Street Inn

If you like water sports, you can hardly do better than stay at this bed-and-breakfast in touristy Irish Hills. Its central location is within 15 minutes of more than 50 lakes. Then, of course, there are the antiques malls, glorious public gardens, and the Croswell Opera House, the oldest opera house in the state.

Innkeepers Bill and Karen Kerr prefer to keep the tone casual, letting authenticity take a backseat to comfort. Aluminum siding and a contemporary veranda do nothing for the Queen Anne–style house, especially when compared with the beautifully restored brick residence next door. Your stay, however, is made pleasant by the easygoing atmosphere and an interior graced by hand-wrought oak moldings and fretwork, stained-glass windows, a striking cherry-wood and ceramic-tile fireplace, and original electric chandeliers. Guest rooms are a bit feminine but tastefully done. Shades of rose, teal, cinnamon, peach, and cream bring out the best in the antique beds and accessories. Recently, the inn added two suites—complete with Jacuzzis—in the 1920s bungalow on the property.

🏨 *219 Chicago St., Brooklyn, MI 49230, tel. 517/592–3888, fax 517/ 592–9025. 3 double rooms with baths, 2 doubles share bath, 2 suites. Air-conditioning, cable TV in sitting room, phone in entranceway, fireplace in sitting room. $65–$165; full breakfast. MC, V. No smoking, no pets.*

Corktown Inn B&B

After a visit to downtown Detroit's Corktown Inn, you might believe the legendary luck of the Irish had something to do with this B&B's existence. Innkeepers Richard Kokochak and Chet Allen had long dreamed of starting a luxury inn in Corktown, which is Detroit's most historic neighborhood and had been originally settled by the Irish. After being turned down by the banks three times, their luck finally changed and they were given the go ahead.

Visitors will be glad they did, for this is now a welcoming and lush oasis, housed in Detroit's oldest brick residence—a three-story, 1850 Federal-style structure built by 19th-century beer baron John Mason. Public rooms as well as each of the lavishly decorated four bedrooms—named Earth, Air, Fire, and Water—are filled with one-of-a-kind works by local artists as well as impressive antiques, including a desk once owned by Edwin Stanton, Abraham Lincoln's Secretary of War, along with souvenirs from Richard and Chet's travels around the world. Extra-nice touches include daily delivery of the *Wall Street Journal* and the weekend *New York Times*, a silk kimono for visitors' use, a help-yourself cookie jar, and a private courtyard with a pergola, a perennial and herb garden, and a koi pond.

In summer, the gardens are the perfect place to enjoy the inn's signature "Only in Detroit" breakfast specialties, which include ethnic-inspired dishes such as Huevos corktowners, Greek Toast Soufflé, Eggs Maltaise, and, of course, imported Irish oatmeal.

🏨 *1705 6th St., Detroit, MI 48226, tel. 313/963–6688, fax 313/964–3883. 4 double rooms with baths. Air-conditioning, TV, VCR, and phone in all rooms, extensive video library, exercise room in basement. $125; full breakfast. AE, MC, V. No smoking, no pets.*

Dundee Guest House

The greatest asset of Karen and Jerry Glover's gingerbread-trimmed brick house in Dundee is its location. The sleepy village sits on the river Raisin, near wineries, historic sites, and a meandering stream, and is just 15 miles west of Monroe, home of General George Custer. Dundee is also near the university towns of Ann Arbor (where both innkeepers work during the day) and Ypsilanti and is 20 miles north of Toledo, Ohio.

The Glovers bought the 121-year-old house, built by a local lumber baron, in 1989. They enjoy running a friendly establishment, taking the time on weekends to linger over what is truly a bottomless cup of coffee. The decor is mainly Victorian with such authentic touches as crocheted lace curtains, a bentwood cradle (it once rocked Karen's father), a carved oak staircase, and Karen's collection of porcelain dolls. The popular Thoma Room has a view of the flower gardens and charming gazebo; Anita's Suite has an adjacent sitting room with fireplace. Guests often remark on a good feeling here—the kind of unhurried pleasantness thought to characterize this country back when it was a collection of small towns like Dundee.

🏠 *522 Tecumseh St., Dundee, MI 48131, tel. 313/529–5706. 1 double room with bath, 1 suite with bath. No air-conditioning. Croquet and gazebo in backyard. $55–$95; Continental breakfast. MC, V. No smoking, no pets.*

Southwestern Michigan
Including Battle Creek, Grand Rapids, Kalamazoo, and Saugatuck

The southwest quadrant of Michigan offers travelers a wide range of diversions, from a leisurely afternoon drive to pick raspberries in the country to a week of carefully orchestrated relaxation at one of the area's tony lakeside retreats. In fact, thanks to growing media attention, which has resulted in a number of travel-magazine pieces, the region is fast becoming recognized as a four-season vacation region. This "discovery" would have amused such old-time aficionados as Al Capone and L. Frank Baum, who knew the Lake Michigan shoreline as a salve for troubled spirits. Baum wrote some of his Wizard of Oz *books here; perhaps Scarface came here to sort out his thoughts about Bugs Moran or the Purple Gang.*

The advent of air-conditioning and affordable air travel to more exotic places made some of the area's features less compelling. But southwestern Michigan's cool summers and mild winters are starting to draw visitors again, thanks to a blossoming of individual entrepreneurs and increasingly promotion-minded communities. Along the Red Arrow Highway, which runs north from the Indiana border through towns like New Buffalo, Union Pier, and Lakeside, cottages and storefronts are finding new life as bed-and-breakfasts, art galleries, and antiques shops.

Farther up the coast, nearly everything revolves around sand and water, from beach volleyball and kite-flying tournaments to breakneck dune-buggy rides. Such upscale ports as South Haven and Saugatuck do land-rush business from Memorial Day to Labor Day, with a 50-50 mix of Chicagoans and Michiganders vying for space in the harbor inns and B&Bs. Saugatuck is particularly trendy, with a large number of fine restaurants and shops. The combination of berthed sailboats, ancient shade trees, and old houses reminds visitors of New

England coastal villages, and its thriving gay community sets it apart from the more conservative towns typical of the area. A few miles north is the delightful city of Holland, noted for its tulip farms and its streets that undergo daily scrubbing.

Inland, orchards parade across the gently rolling, fertile terrain. Spring produces an explosion of fragrance and color—and numerous festivals. July ushers in picking season. You can drive down just about any back road and come across a U-Pick farm, cider stand, or winery. In the fall, the orange globes of pumpkins and squash splash the roadsides with color. During the winter, cross-country skiers glide silently up and down the mild, undulating hills, later heading for inns that are nearly always empty in midweek.

The countryside is a jumble of farms, small manufacturing centers, and a few crossroads communities that have yet to recover from the decline of the railroad. If you're lost, don't be afraid to approach someone for directions. Even in the larger cities—Kalamazoo, Grand Rapids, and Battle Creek—people are unmistakably, hospitably Midwestern. Not only do they talk to you; they listen. And those traveling the area's highways should know strangers are trusted enough that rest rooms at gas stations and elsewhere require no key for entry.

Places to Go, Sights to See

Battle Creek. Dubbed the "Cereal Capital of the World" because the Post Cereals, Ralston Purina, and Kellogg companies here, Battle Creek is host to a pair of fun annual events: Every June thousands participate in what is described as the world's largest breakfast; in July some 200 hot-air balloonists compete in the weeklong International Balloon Championship (tel. 616/962–0592). Ten miles to the east is the well-preserved town of Marshall, whose Historical Society presents a tour of nationally recognized 19th-century homes every September (tel. 616/781–5163).

Cherry County Playhouse. A fixture in Traverse City for many years, the theatrical company moved to the Frauenthal Theater in downtown Muskegon in 1991. Summer-stock productions include children's plays, musicals, comedies, and celebrity concerts. Call 616/727–8000 or 800/686–9666 (after April 15, 1997) for the schedule.

Flower Festivals. Every spring 30 communities work together to produce the Blossomtime Festival (tel. 616/926–7397), which includes a floral parade through Benton Harbor and St. Joseph. More than 400,000 people attend the Tulip Time Festival (tel. 616/396–4221) in Holland, a 10-day celebration every May, when the blooms are at their peak.

Grand Rapids. The state's second-largest city is a clean, well-ordered manufacturing community 30 minutes east of Lake Michigan. It has an amazing number of churches per capita and is a conservative, friendly place with quite a few things to see. The Gerald R. Ford Museum (303 Pearl St. NW, tel. 616/451–9290) traces the life and times of the 38th president. Self-guided walking tours of Heritage Hill (tel. 616/459–8950), a historic district of some 1,300 buildings east of the rejuvenated downtown, are popular, as is the exotic John Ball Zoological Gardens (1300 W. Fulton St., tel. 616/336–4300).

Kalamazoo. This pleasant college town, roughly halfway between Chicago and Detroit on I–94 and just an hour's drive from Lake Michigan, is popular as a way station or as a destination in itself. The immaculate Kalamazoo Aviation History Museum (3101 E. Milhan Rd., tel. 616/382–6555) features rare, operational World War II aircraft, memorabilia, and restoration work of vintage planes. Aircraft buffs and casual visitors flock to the Michigan International Air Show (tel. 616/381–8237), which attracts more than 100,000 people every June.

Michigan's Adventure Amusement Park (4750 Whitehall Rd., off U.S. 31, tel. 616/766–3377), 8 miles north of Muskegon, is the state's largest amusement and water park with more than 20 thrill rides, 10 water slides, a wave pool, a children's activity pool, shows, games, food, and the only roller coasters in Michigan.

Paw Paw. A dozen miles west of Kalamazoo, the village has several wineries, including St. Julian Winery (tel. 616/657–2964) and Warner Vineyards (tel. 616/657–3165), two of Michigan's largest vintners. Each offers free tours and samplings.

Saugatuck and Douglas. A thriving arts colony has developed in these two lakefront communities, which sit on opposite sides of the mouth of the Kalamazoo River. The Ox-Bow Art Workshop in Saugatuck is the Midwest's oldest summer school of painting, but artists are in evidence everywhere—from the tasteful downtown shops and galleries to the boardwalk pier, one of the Great Lakes' longest. Picturesque beaches and the area's relaxed lifestyle have helped create one of the state's most fashionable vacation spots.

SS *Keewatin*. One of the last of the Great Lakes' classic passenger steamboats is permanently docked in Douglas and is now a maritime museum (south of the Saugatuck-Douglas Bridge, tel. 616/857–2107). Guided tours of this luxuriously appointed 1907 vessel are available from Memorial Day through Labor Day.

Veldheer Tulip Gardens/DeKlomp Wooden Shoe & Delft Factory. Two million bulbs exhibit their color every spring at Veldheer's (12755 Quincy, at U.S. 31, Holland, tel. 616/399–1900), making it one of the premier attractions for

Holland-area visitors. At the DeKlomp factory next door, visitors can watch workers carve wooden shoes and paint the famous blue-and-white Delftware.

Beaches

The best beaches are in state parks such as Grand Haven, Holland, and Van Buren. The state's longest stretch of beach—2½ miles—is at Warren Dunes State Park (Red Arrow Hwy., tel. 616/426–4013), south of Bridgman. However, because of eroding shorelines, some of the area's public beaches may be partially restricted.

Boating

No one in Michigan is ever more than 6 miles from a lake or stream, so you won't have to work hard to find a place to either launch or rent a boat. Marina activity, particularly in major yachting and sportfishing ports like South Haven and Muskegon, is frenzied through the peak summer months but slows down considerably with the cool weather. For those who prefer to leave the driving to someone else, you can cruise the Kalamazoo River and Lake Michigan aboard the *Queen of Saugatuck* (tel. 616/857–4261), a 67-foot-long stern-wheeler, or the *City of Douglas* (tel. 616/857–2107), a 60-foot yacht.

Fishing

Whether you cast your line from a boat or off a pier, southwestern Michigan offers some *reel* opportunities. The waters hold panfish, trout, walleye, bass, northern pike, bullhead, catfish, and, especially, yellow perch. Visiting anglers will find some of Michigan's finest fishing in the center of Grand Rapids, where the Grand River is kept stocked with chinook, steelhead, and coho salmon. Also worth noting are Reeds Lake in East Grand Rapids, which has bluegills, crappies, and northern pike, and the Muskegon River, popular for its annual perch and salmon runs. Charter fishing on Lake Michigan is available at marinas up and down the shoreline.

Golf

The state is known for its large number of fine courses, many on the "Golf Coast" of Lake Michigan. You can play 18 holes among dunes and pines at the Grand Haven Golf Club (17000 Lincoln Rd., Grand Haven, tel. 616/842–4040), rated one of the country's top public courses. Clearbrook (6494 Clearbrook Dr., Saugatuck, tel. 616/857–1766) is the southwestern shoreline's only complex with championship public golf *and* fine dining. Tee off at Winding Creek Golf Course (4514 Ottogan St., Holland, tel. 616/396–4516) or Grand Island Golf Ranch (6266 W. River Dr., Belmont, tel. 616/363–1262), in Grand Rapids. A complete listing of all public golf courses in the state is available through RSG Publishing, which offers a 304-page guide for $19.95 (tel. 800/223–5877).

Restaurants

A favorite in downtown Grand Rapids is **Schnitzelbank** (342 Jefferson St., tel. 616/459–9527), where German fare and paneled rooms transport you to the Old World. In Macatawa, just west of Holland, the sophisticated but unpretentious **Sandpiper Restaurant** (2225 S. Shore Dr., tel. 616/335–5866) offers a full range of reasonably priced American cuisine and a gull's-eye view of the harbor. Orchard country farther south offers more than just roadside cider stands. In Bridgman, sautéed chicken breast with chopped pecan crust is a specialty of the **Tabor Hill Winery Restaurant** (185 Mt. Tabor Rd., tel. 616/422–1161), which overlooks the surrounding vineyards. And "monster" Reuben sandwiches and chunky wedges of homemade pie make **Wick's Apple House** (52281 Indian Lake Rd., tel. 616/782–7306), in Dowagiac, a delicious detour.

Tourist Information

The **Michigan Travel Bureau** (Box 3393, Livonia, MI 48151, tel. 800/543–2937) has statewide tourist information. To learn more about boating, fishing, and hunting opportunities and regulations, contact the **Michigan Department of Natural Resources** (530 W. Allegan St., Lansing, MI 48933, tel. 517/373–1204). The following cover more specific areas: **Battle Creek Area Visitors and Convention Bureau** (34 W. Jackson St., Battle Creek, MI 49017, tel. 616/962–2240); **Grand Rapids Area Convention and Visitors Bureau** (140 Monroe Center NW, Grand Rapids, MI 49503, tel. 616/459–8287); **Holland Area Convention and Visitors Bureau** (272 E. 8th St., Holland, MI 49422, tel. 616/394–0000); **Kalamazoo County Convention and Visitors Bureau** (128 N. Kalamazoo Mall, Kalamazoo, MI 49007, tel. 616/381–4003); **Muskegon County Convention and Visitors Bureau** (349 W. Webster Ave., Muskegon, MI 49443, tel. 616/722–3751); **Saugatuck/Douglas Chamber of Commerce** (303 Butler St., Saugatuck, MI 49453, tel. 616/857–5801); **Lakeshore Convention and Visitors Bureau** (Box 890, South Haven, MI 49090, tel. 616/637–5252); **West Michigan Tourist Association** (136 E. Fulton St., Grand Rapids, MI 49503, tel. 616/456–8557).

Chicago Pike Inn

Parental love is the simple story behind this large yellow inn, which sits on U.S. 12 halfway between Detroit and Chicago. Looking to lure their daughter Becky back to Michigan, Harold and Jane Schultz dangled a carrot: They would buy one of Coldwater's most elegant mansions and convert it into a B&B if she would come home to run it. Becky, who had studied hotel management in college and was working at a plush Florida resort at the time, immediately agreed.

The 7,500-square-foot mansion was built in 1903 by local mercantilist Morris G. Clarke, who hired Asbury Buckley to design it. The Chicago architect was responsible for many of the fine homes built on Mackinac Island in the 1890s. Although the mansion was being used as a boardinghouse when the Schultzes bought it, it was still in remarkably fine condition. Today, such elegant touches as the built-in mirrored buffet in the cherry-paneled dining room, the double-mantel fireplace in the reception room, and the oak parquet floors can make you feel almost guilty about showing up in jeans and a T-shirt.

Guest rooms in the main house are appointed with period wall coverings and Victorian antiques such as marble-top tables. All but one are on the second floor; the exception is the Clarkes' Own Room (as it was labeled on the original architectural drawings). Off the library—a restful refuge with a marble fireplace and century-old tea table—this room is furnished with an ornately carved, lace-covered canopy bed. At the top of the stairs is Miss Sophia's Suite, the inn's most popular room, which has a yellow-tile fireplace with an oak mantel and a private balcony. The velvet sofa and large table make private breakfasts here a favorite option. A gambrel-roofed, two-story carriage house contains the two newest rooms. Decorated in the same style as the main house, these lodgings also include air-conditioning, whirlpool baths, refrigerators, and private balconies. All rooms reveal the innkeepers' attention to detail and include extra-nice touches such as individual thermostats and four pillows—two hard, two soft.

The antiques centers of Allen and Marshall are nearby, and northern Indiana—home to the famous Shipshewana auctions and a thriving Amish community—is just a half hour's drive away. Or you can hop on one of the inn's bicycles and explore Coldwater, a drowsy town filled with 19th-century statuary and Victorian-era homes.

🏨 *215 E. Chicago St., Coldwater, MI 49036, tel. 517/279-8744. 5 double rooms with baths, 3 suites. Air-conditioning in 2 rooms, cable TV, fireplace, and phone in common area, fireplace in 1 room, refrigerator and whirlpool bath in 2 rooms, bicycles. $80–$165; full breakfast, afternoon refreshments. AE, MC, V. Smoking in common areas only, no pets.*

Crane House

Bob and Lue Crane are fourth-generation Fennville fruit farmers whose sprawling homestead comprises a restaurant, a 120-year-old farmhouse painted white with green shutters, and 310 acres of apple, cherry, raspberry, blueberry, and peach orchards. The farmhouse is a large, two-story wooden structure that Bob and Lue bought from Bob's cousin and renovated seven years ago. "The place was empty and ready to fall down," says their daughter, Nancy Crane-McFarland, who today serves as innkeeper. "To help defray some of the costs of fixing it up, we decided to turn it into a bed-and-breakfast."

In many ways, the Cranes seem as if they've stepped right off a *Saturday Evening Post* cover—along with the house. The interior is a pleasant mix of farm antiques, Americana, and primitive art. The upstairs guest rooms have stenciled walls, ceiling fans, and wooden, iron, and brass beds, each with a handmade quilt and a feather mattress. The rooms overlook the orchards—a truly splendid sight in the spring and fall. The parlor boasts a curved-glass oak curio that belonged to Nancy's grandmother and a 1900 stove, and the breakfast room has a pine hanging dry sink. "The only other time I've seen one was in an old episode of *Bonanza*," says Nancy, whose own young family lives in the house.

The Cranes are genuine, neighborly, family-centered, and industrious. They also have a fair amount of business savvy. Across the highway from the house is their Pie Pantry Restaurant, which Bob and Lue started as a way to earn an income when American agriculture suffered reverses in the early 1970s.

The restaurant, in an old barn, is a cheerful jumble of worn chairs and tables under a folksy burlap-sack ceiling, with an antique stove and a wall of framed Charles Lindbergh memorabilia. In summer, the gravel drive is as congested as a subway turnstile during rush hour, as pleasure drivers take time out to pick fruit, buy cider, or sample some of the outstanding sandwiches, soups, and fruit pies. The orchards, restaurant, and B&B are truly a family operation, with three generations of Cranes pitching in wherever they're needed.

6051 124th Ave., Fennville, MI 49408, tel. 616/561–6931. 3 double rooms with baths, 2 doubles share shower. No air-conditioning, TV and phone in den. $75–$95; full breakfast. AE, D, MC, V. No smoking indoors, no pets.

Kingsley House

David and Shirley Witt tout their impressive Queen Anne house in tiny Fennville as being "as American as apple pie," an example of truth in advertising if ever there was one. It was built in 1886 by Harvey Kingsley, who introduced fruit trees to this area around Lake Michigan. Tipping their caps to Kingsley, the Witts have placed his picture in the living room and named each of the guest rooms after a variety of apple. An oak stairway leads to six second-story chambers, two of which are dubbed McIntosh and Golden Delicious. The most interesting is the Jonathan Room, formerly a stable boy's quarters, with a century-old bed and an 1850s platform rocker. Nestled in the tower is the Dutchess Room, which, with five windows, is the brightest, and is regally decorated in cranberry-hued wallpaper and antique lace. Immediately above it is Northern Spy, a honeymoon suite, which features an electric fireplace, a whirlpool bath, and a tower sitting room, with a calming view of miles of rolling countryside.

Shirley, who was born in the Netherlands, runs the household with smooth efficiency and simple elegance. The guest rooms and common areas are spacious and immaculately clean. The furnishings are a tasteful blend of oak and cherry antiques that harmonize with such family ornaments as the shadowboxes the Witts made.

A Continental breakfast buffet is served during the week. On weekends, breakfast is a fancy affair, served on linens and Royal Doulton china in the formal cherry-wood dining room. The Delftware and silver are typical of Dutch touches throughout the house. Five menus are rotated, but meals usually include country ham, farm-fresh eggs, hash browns, and home-made muffins and bread. Coffee and the morning paper are set out by 7:30, and tea, cold drinks, cookies, and snacks are available all day.

With busy Route 89 close at hand, traffic noise can be a problem in the front rooms. To escape, hop on one of the four 18-speed bikes the Witts provide and pedal 8 miles south to the Allegan State Game Area, famous as a rest stop for geese and other migrating waterfowl. Once there, you can hike, canoe, swim, cross-country ski, or pick wild blueberries, strawberries, and other fruit.

🏠 *626 W. Main St., Fennville, MI 49408, tel. 616/561–6425. 1 king-size room, 1 queen-size room, four double rooms, all with baths, 3 suites. Air-conditioning, TV, phone, fireplace, and whirlpool tub in suites, 2 phones in common areas. $65–$145; full breakfast on weekends, buffet breakfast weekdays, refreshments all day. AE, D, MC, V. No smoking, no pets.*

National House Inn

More than a smooth-running and magnificently preserved hostel from another period, the National House Inn is a centerpiece of what many consider the finest cross section of 19th-century architecture in the country. The oldest inn in the state opened as a stagecoach stop in 1835, two years before Michigan was admitted to the Union. For many years it served double duty as one of the final stops on the Underground Railroad, which spirited escaped slaves to Canada, 120 miles to the east. In 1878, it was converted into a wagon and windmill factory. The inn was drawing its final breath as an apartment house when a consortium of local businesspeople bought and restored it for the nation's Bicentennial.

For the past 14 years, innkeeper Barbara Bradley has watched a parade of tourists, business travelers, and honeymooners pass through the rustic entryway, which is warmed by a massive beam-and-brick open-hearth fireplace. The rough-hewn ceiling beams and aged plank floors are the framework for the particular selection of country antiques found in each room. There are punched-tin chandeliers; Windsor, ladderback, and herringbone wing chairs in the living room; spindle-leg tables and hurricane lamps in the dining room; and gilt-framed oil portraits throughout. Thanks to a unique fireplace set into handcrafted paneled cabinets, the upstairs lounge is comfortable and inviting, although in

warmer weather guests prefer moving to the back porch and gardens.

Guest rooms are attractively wallpapered and carpeted, with the decor ranging from country style to the Victorian-era design of the Ketchum Suite, which overlooks a handsome garden and the village circle. There's plenty of elbow room in the dining room, where a Continental breakfast of boiled eggs, bowls of fruit, wheat bread, coffee, and a wide variety of fruit juices and teas is served.

Marshall is right off I–94, 10 miles east of Battle Creek. In 1991, the village— frequently referred to as "the Williamsburg of the Midwest"—was designated a National Historic Landmark District. The district encompasses some 850 structures (and nearly 50 historical markers), including striking examples of Queen Anne, Italianate, and Gothic Revival architecture.

🏠 *102 S. Parkview St., Marshall, MI 49068, tel. 616/781–7374, fax 616/ 781–4510. 16 double rooms with baths. Air-conditioning, cable TV, and phone in rooms. $66–$120; Continental breakfast. AE, MC, V. No-smoking rooms available, no pets.*

Pebble House

"Serenity is our goal," says Jean Lawrence, who, along with her husband, Ed, owns the relaxing Pebble House. Chicago expatriates, Jean was an art therapist and Ed a real estate investment analyst when they fell in love with the 1912 concrete-block and river-rock house on the shores of Lake Michigan. The Lawrences decided to furnish the inn in mission-style furniture because it seemed to fit and at the time, it was still relatively inexpensive. Today, the Pebble House is one of the few B&Bs faithful to the revolutionary early 1900s style that preached a return to handcraftsmanship. The Lawrences, who also own East Road Antiques in town, have meticulously furnished all the guest rooms and public areas with distinctive, clean-lined mission-style furniture and accessories, including hand-hammered copper bowls and green lead-glass lamps. Even Jean's Scandinavian-style breakfasts of baked Finnish pancakes and homemade coffee cakes are served on Roycroft Revival china.

The Lawrences work hard to make this a true retreat: There are no phones in the guest rooms and nary a television in sight. As an alternate pleasure to the electronic age, more than 2,000 books, including volumes of fiction, travel, and design, are tucked all about. Needless to say, their collection of books on the Arts and Crafts movement is a connoisseur's delight. If you're looking to explore the area's bountiful antiquing, you're in luck:

Ed's even written a guidebook to the region's shops. For those who prefer more active relaxation, a tennis court and nearby beach also beckon.

⊞ *15093 Lakeshore Rd., Lakeside, MI 49116, tel. 616/469–1416. 3 double rooms with baths, 3-bedroom Coach House with bath, 2-bedroom Blueberry House with 2 baths. Air-conditioning, phone in guest rooms on request, phone in main lounge, kitchenette and wood-burning stove in Blueberry House. $90–$140, $220 for Blueberry House; full breakfast, refreshments. D, MC, V. No smoking indoors, no pets, closed Dec. 24.*

South Cliff Inn

S even years ago, Bill Swisher left behind a decade-long career as director of the Cassopolis, Michigan, Probate Court and opened the South Cliff Inn. "I grew up in the area, and I suppose I was always looking for an excuse to come back," Bill says.

In the pre-air-conditioning days of the early 1900s, St. Joseph (or St. Joe, it's sometimes called) and its sister city, Benton Harbor, were among the Midwest's most popular lakefront summer resorts. The collapse of the area's manufacturing base led to a decline of its fortunes in the 1970s, especially in Benton Harbor, always the more blue-collar of the two. South Cliff Inn, a salmon-color brick English cottage, is a small but important representative of an economic renaissance that once again is capitalizing on the therapeutic breezes of Lake Michigan.

The 82-year-old inn is perched on a bluff, giving all but one of the seven guest rooms superb views of the water. The largest room, the Sunset Suite, is perhaps the most popular. The queen-size bed, sofa, and wing chair are dressed in complementary English chintz fabrics; the private bath features a custom-designed marble tub. In the Harbour Room, guests can lie back in a bubbling whirlpool bath and watch the sun melt into the lake in the evening. Two rooms now have balconies overlooking the lake. The entire place is decorated in English country style (not surprisingly, a perennial garden was added last year), with plenty of bold prints, chintz fabrics, and a large number of antiques. One of the guest rooms houses an imposing 150-year-old oak armoire that is so large it had to be hoisted through the windows.

The trouble was worth it: The inn is comfortable, sun-filled, and, with just one part-time staffer to assist Bill, commendably unhurried. The Continental breakfast includes juice, homemade bread, muffins, coffee cakes and—after all, this is orchard country—plenty of fresh fruit. That's enough carbohydrates to fuel a short walk to the downtown of this pleasant harbor town, whose turn-of-the-century storefronts and monuments, landscaped brick streets, and Lake Michigan backdrop combine to make it perhaps the most picturesque in the entire state.

🏠 *1900 Lakeshore Dr., St. Joseph, MI 49085, tel. 616/983-4881, fax 616/983-7391. 7 double rooms with baths. Air-conditioning, cable TV in den, fireplace in 2 rooms, whirlpool bath in 2 rooms. $75–$150; Continental breakfast, refreshments all day. AE, D, MC, V. Smoking in den only, no pets, 2-night minimum weekends, 3-night minimum holidays.*

Wickwood Country Inn

Guests at Saugatuck's oldest bed-and-breakfast are in for a treat, both figuratively and literally. The owner, Julee Rosso-Miller, is the coauthor of the *Silver Palate Cookbook*. With 2 million copies of her gourmet masterpiece sold, only the *Joy of Cooking* has kept it from being the best-selling cookbook of all time.

Julee came to her new career as innkeeper in much the same way she became a well-known gourmet writer: serendipity. Her mother's heart attack in 1986 forced her to reappraise her own hectic lifestyle as co-owner of one of the first-ever gourmet take-out shops in the country, New York's Silver Palate. She moved to Saugatuck and fell in love with the sunsets over Lake Michigan—and with Ray Miller, a local builder. They married, then persuaded their neighbors to sell what has long been regarded as the best B&B in town. Of course, the location doesn't hurt: It's two blocks from downtown's many fine shops and restaurants and a short walk from the beach and other lakefront attractions.

With its brick floors, cedar walls, and vaulted ceilings, the circa-1940 inn resembles one of those small toasty hotels that dot the English countryside. The main-floor rooms, filled with overstuffed chairs, French and English antiques, fresh flowers, and original art, surround a courtyard blooming with perennials, roses, and herbs. The guest rooms have individual themes but are uniformly captivating, with plenty of antique lace, Ralph Lauren and Laura Ashley fabrics, and cabbage-rose patterns on the walls and beds.

Guests are pampered from daybreak to dusk. A buffet breakfast is served and a newspaper supplied weekday mornings on the old English pine buffet table in the dining area, which is filled with antique toy trains, boats, and trucks. On weekends, a hearty brunch is prepared. Hors d'oeuvres, which might include a light salmon mousse, bruschetta, Chinese ribs, and crudités with low-fat dip, are put out at 6 PM. As if this weren't enough, candies and jars of spiced nuts are placed in each room. Calorie counters can relax, though: most items are selections from Julee's recent low-fat cookbook, *Great Good Food*.

🏨 *510 Butler St. (Box 1019), Saugatuck, MI 49453, tel. 616/857–1097, fax 616/857–4168. 11 double rooms with baths, 2 suites. Air-conditioning, cable TV in library, phone in common room, fireplace in 1 suite. $140–$190; full breakfast, evening refreshments. MC, V. No pets, 2-night minimum on weekends, closed Dec. 24–25.*

Fairchild House

In an area fairly bustling with bed-and-breakfasts, Felicia Fairchild's is one of the most intimate and romantic. The two-story white-stucco inn, built in 1919, has a reputation for thoughtful, personalized service. For Felicia, the phone and TV in the parlor are barely tolerable amenities; her idea of relaxation is classical music filling the house as a backdrop for evening hors d'oeuvres and pleasant conversation in front of the fireplace. Some of that conversation is sure to be about the area's many attractions—during the day, Fairchild runs the Saugatuck Convention and Visitors Bureau.

There are three distinct bedrooms, all tastefully done with fine period antiques, cutwork linens, European feather beds, and down comforters. One bedroom set is a replica of Abraham Lincoln's wedding suite, complete with arched canopy bed and Battenburg-lace linens; another room has an English hunt theme with a headboard converted from an antique mahogany fireplace and a private bath lined in oak paneling that once graced a Chicago mansion. Fresh flowers and plush Turkish bathrobes (on request) are examples of the care that goes into everything here, including the elegant champagne breakfasts served in the formal dining room.

⊞ *606 Butler St., Saugatuck, MI 49453, tel. 616/857–5985. 3 double rooms with baths. Air-conditioning; phone, TV, and fireplace in parlor, bathrobes in rooms. $125; full champagne breakfast. MC, V. No smoking, no pets, 2-night minimum weekends.*

Greencrest Manor

Finding a French Norman–style château on Battle Creek's St. Mary's Lake is an unexpected treat for bed-and-breakfast fans: The city is home to Kellogg and Post cereals and is known more for cereals than châteaux. Con-structed of sandstone, slate, and copper, the gracious 1935 inn sits on 15 acres adorned with formal gardens and European-style fountains. Open since 1989, it has drawn favorable reviews from numerous publications and has become known as one of the most romantic spots in the state.

Looking at the elegant marble floors, spiral staircase, ballroom-size living room, and paneled library, it's hard to imagine the inn's once-dilapidated condition. Originally built for a lumber baron, it served for almost two decades as a Roman Catholic monastery, then remained empty for more than seven years until 1987, when current owners Tom and Kathy Van Daff purchased it—Tom had actually grown up in the area and always admired the unusual structure. At the time the Van Daffs acquired it, the house was just a large concrete shell with no windows, doors, or interior light fixtures; there was a hole in the roof and several inches of water in the basement.

The Van Daffs were lucky enough to locate original blueprints of the house and garden, which guided them throughout the extensive renovation. Today, the 13,000-square-foot mansion is once again outfitted in the style it had been accustomed to, including spacious parlor rooms featuring elegant European antiques, soothing chintz fabrics, silk flowers, and a cosmopolitan country style. Spacious guest rooms decorated in the same manner also sport modern amenities including telephone and cable TV; suites have fireplaces and whirlpool baths. As for breakfast, your Rice Krispies will be served up in Wedgwood china—or you can opt for some delicious homemade muffins.

⊞ *6174 Halbert Rd., Battle Creek, MI 49017, tel. 616/962–8633. 6 double rooms with baths, 2 double rooms with shared bath, 4 suites. Air-conditioning, cable TV, phone in rooms, whirlpool* bath in suites. $75–$170; Continental breakfast. AE, MC, V. No smoking, no pets.

The Inn at Union Pier

In 1983 Chicagoans Mark and Joyce Pitts bought the 1910 main house and two cottages of this lakeside resort that sits on impeccably landscaped grounds and has a light Scandinavian look, with plenty of comforters and watercolor pictures. Comfort and thoughtfulness are the buzzwords here. For instance, towels are provided for those who wish to dip into either the hot tub on the back porch or Lake Michigan, just 200 feet away.

Hikers, bicyclists, and cross-country skiers all find tree-lined Lakeshore Road an attractive conduit to several interesting shops and galleries in neighboring New Buffalo. This is where orchard country meets the shoreline, so sunset cruises and wine tasting are also just a short drive away.

▦ *9708 Berrien St. (Box 222), Union Pier, MI 49129, tel. 616/469–4700, fax 616/469–4720. 16 double rooms with baths. Air-conditioning, cable TV and phone in Great House, fireplace in 12 rooms, hot tub, sauna, beach towels. $115–$185; full breakfast, afternoon and evening refreshments. D, MC, V. No smoking, no pets, 2-night minimum weekends, 3-night minimum holidays.*

Maplewood Hotel

This 1860s Greek Revival has been gradually restored since Catherine Simon bought it in the early 1990s. The elegant structure was originally a private residence but, surprisingly, it has been a hotel for much of its 130 years. Part of the hotel's charm is in its combination of formality and hospitality; it's one of the few in the area that warmly welcomes children. Each of the 15 antiques-filled bedrooms has its own bath (five have whirlpool tubs), and five of the rooms have working fireplaces. Breakfast is served at 14 small, linen-covered tables in the Burr Tillstrom Dining Room (named for the former Saugatuck resident who created Kukla, Fran, and Ollie) and on the screened porch.

Maplewood's central location puts first-rate shops, galleries, and restaurants within shouting distance—literally—so street noise can be a concern. But the spot has the advantage of nearby golf, tennis, boating, and fishing.

▦ *428 Butler St. (Box 1059), Saugatuck, MI 49453, tel. 616/ 857–1771, fax 616/857–1773. 15 double rooms with baths. Air-conditioning, cable TV, phone, fireplace in 5 rooms, whirlpool bath in 5 rooms, lap pool. $85–$155; full breakfast. AE, MC, V. No smoking, no pets, 2-night minimum weekends, 3-night minimum holidays, closed for 3 days at both Thanksgiving and Christmas.*

McCarthy's Bear Creek Inn

In 1942, the noted agricultural inventor Robert Maes built a Williamsburg-style home on a knoll overlooking serene Bear Creek, just 1 mile from the downtown district of Marshall. As soon as he finished his house—Cape Cod in structure—he laid the fieldstone fences by hand to surround the land's centuries-old Burr oak trees and outbuildings. In homage to the property's picturesque meandering stream, he named the estate Bear Creek Farm.

In 1985, Mike and Beth McCarthy purchased the farm and added their name, converting it to the elegant McCarthy's Bear Creek Inn. Today, the inn is known for its gracious guest rooms—seven in the original main house and another seven in the renovated Creek House, formerly the farm's dairy barn. All rooms feature private baths, antique beds, and period-style wallpaper. Newer Creek House rooms are more spacious and also include balconies with French doors. Popular rooms in the main house include the paneled library room, which is now outfitted as a bedroom (with a queen-size brass bed) and a walnut-paneled fireplace; everyone's favorite in the Creek House is the dramatic Sunset Room, with its neoclassical-style bed, love seat, and a vista of the property's lush meadows.

🏠 *15230 C. Dr. North, Marshall, MI 49068, tel. 616/781-8383. 14 rooms with bath. Air-conditioning, TV on request, phone in common area. $65-$98; breakfast buffet. AE, M, V. No pets.*

Mendon Country Inn

Built in 1843 as the Western Hotel, this historic 14-acre inn once housed a bakery, restaurant, church hall, and even a cow barn, before current owners Dick and Dolly Buerkle purchased it and, in 1987, began welcoming guests. Since then, Dick has served as an enthusiastic ambassador for the area's many attractions, including Amish farms, wineries, and antiques (the nearby Centreville market attracts some 600 dealers on weekends).

The inn features 18 rooms, including main-house accommodations, cottage suites, and candlelight lodge suites. Rooms reflect a variety of motifs—from the Hired Man Room, with cozy country furnishings, to the elegant Adams Wakeman Room, with Empire-style furniture and a 12-foot ceiling. A converted house on the property offers Native American–themed suites with whirlpool saunas and fireplaces.

A deluxe Continental breakfast is served in the Puddleburg Room, where old town signs fill the walls. The inn also offers free canoeing from its dock, as well as free bikes for guests

(including a romantic two-seater). Mendon is the only inn in Michigan with its own canoe livery: Be sure to take a spin in the "courting canoe" designed after the 19th-century models once used in New York City's Central Park—it even comes with a parasol for the ladies.

🏠 *440 W. Main St., Mendon, MI 49072, tel. 616/496-8132. 9 double rooms with baths, 9 suites. No air-conditioning, full cedar sauna, rooftop garden, picnic area, bikes, canoes available. $50-$159; deluxe Continental breakfast. AE, D, MC, V. Smoking in game room only, no pets.*

Parsonage 1908

Once a parsonage, this white, classic two-story American four-square, adorned with black shutters, geranium-filled window boxes, and tricolor crescent flags, sits on a little rise in an upscale residential section of Holland. Like so many neighborhoods in this heavily Dutch community, there is a palpable sense of order and serenity in the rows of immaculately kept houses, lawns, and gardens.

Bonnie McVoy-Verwys, assisted by her daughters, Wendy and Heather, is an outgoing hostess and a very capable gardener and cook. She bought the house in 1974 and 10 years later opened it as Holland's first bed-and-breakfast. Through patience and attention to detail, she has restored the Victorian house over the years. The oak woodwork and lead-glass windows are supplemented by less obvious touches of authenticity: lined dresser drawers, each with a sachet; a bedroom closet holding high-button shoes, hatboxes, and other old-fashioned accessories; and more. In the finely landscaped backyard, croquet wickets share space with a fragrant—and rare—mimosa tree. Breakfast is served in a formal dining room or on the outdoor patio.

🏠 *6 E. 24th St., Holland, MI 49423, tel. 616/396-1316. 1 double room with bath; 2 doubles share 1 bath. Airconditioning, TV in sitting room, portable phone in hallway. $90–$100; full breakfast, refreshments. No credit cards. No smoking, no pets, closed last week in Feb.*

Pine Garth Inn

Guests immediately get a good feeling about this comfortably rumpled summer estate, which is as unpretentious as its owners, Russ and Paula Bulin. These transplants from suburban Chicago bought the 90-year-old yellow frame house in 1988 and dressed it up in what Paula calls Country Eclectic—a blend of striped and floral linens and wallpaper and family furniture. Paula is a former nurse; Russ is a professional woodworker who always had a yen to run a bed-and-breakfast. Samples of his handiwork are everywhere inside the inn and in the five adjoining contemporary wooden cottages: log beds, twig furniture, distressed pine armoires. The inn sits on a bluff overlooking 200 feet of private beach. All but one of the guest rooms have a full view of the water; five rooms have private decks. The cottages have kitchens and are good for family gatherings; otherwise, the rooms in the house are more desirable.

🏠 *15790 Lakeshore Rd, Box 347, Union Pier, MI 49129, tel. 616/ 469-1642. 7 double rooms with baths, 5 2-bedroom cottages with baths. Airconditioning, TV and VCR in rooms, phone in library and upstairs, hot tub and fireplace in cottages. $115–$150 double, $195–$225 cottage; full breakfast, afternoon refreshments (inn only). AE, MC, V. No smoking, no pets, 2-night minimum weekends, 3-night minimum holidays.*

Stuart Avenue Inn

The downtown Kalamazoo block that boasts the Stuart Avenue Inn has been likened to the exterior lot of one of those MGM musicals set at the turn of the century. Statuesque Queen Annes, Italianates, American Four-Squares, and other examples of high Victorian style form a colorful chorus line along tree-shaded Stuart Avenue. Modern civilization in the form of Kalamazoo College (a block away) and Western Michigan University (a half-mile walk), are nearby, but you'd never know it.

The Stuart Avenue Inn is actually a group of three houses, all adjacent to each other and grouped around a lovely garden. The showpiece is the spectacular 1886 Eastlake Queen Anne–style Bartlett-Upjohn House—built by newspaper publisher Edgar Bartlett and once home to Upjohn Pharmaceuticals cofounder James T. Upjohn. Next door is the 1902 Arts and Crafts–style Chappel House, site of the VIP suites. A few steps away is a small carriage house, with rooms as well as a miniapartment perfect for extended stays.

Popular accommodations in the Bartlett-Upjohn House include the Mayor's Room, with elegant Bradbury and Bradbury wallpapers, burled walnut accents, and a queen-size bed. Others prefer the spacious VIP suites—complete with Jacuzzis, VCRs, and fireplaces—in the Chappel House (if you opt to stay here, be sure to check out the "secret room" off the back staircase). Carriage-house rooms are more modest—but so is their room rate. All rooms are furnished with family antiques and photographs as well as what the staff charmingly calls "garage-sale relations."

A great place to relax is the adjacent gardens, a vacant lot turned into a city showcase. Formerly the site of a 1920s nationally recognized Shakespearean garden, it now features a gazebo, pergola, fountain, and lily pond and is a favorite spot for area weddings. Now under the stewardship of Mary Lou and Tom Baker, the Stuart Avenue Inn continues to offer a delightful range of options for weary travelers.

🏨 *229 Stuart Ave., Kalamazoo, MI 49007, tel. 616/342–0230. 12 double rooms with bath, 4 suites. Air-conditioning, TV and phone in rooms. $49–$130; Continental breakfast. AE, D, DC, MC, V. No smoking, no pets, 5-day cancellation policy.*

Twin Oaks Inn

Many bed-and-breakfasts eschew the family market, preferring to position themselves as a couples destination or a romantic retreat. Jerry and Nancy Horney, who have owned Twin Oaks since 1989, welcome children with wide smiles and open arms. Rooms have portable cribs; a large basket in the comfortable common room is full of well-loved and well-used toys for kids of all ages. Rates are family-friendly too, about one-third less than other, more expensive, inns in the popular resort town of Saugatuck.

The home, built in 1860, is decorated with both antiques and quality repro-ductions in classic English-cottage style. Guest rooms have queen- or king-size beds covered with Laura Ashley comforters, cable TV and VCRs (another plus: the inn's exten-sive video library has more than 700 titles, including lots of kids' classics). There's even a resident "grandma"— Nancy's mother, Kay, who lives on-site, oversees the property, and looks after youngsters as if they were her own children or grandchildren. Weary par-ents will head directly for the outdoor hot tub, where they can relax after a full day of sightseeing or dune hopping on nearby Lake Michigan beaches.

🏨 *227 Griffith St., Box 867, Saugatuck, MI 49453, tel. 616/857–1600. 8 double rooms with bath, 3 suites, private cottage. Air-conditioning, cable TV and VCR in rooms, phones. $65–*

$95; Continental breakfast weekdays, full breakfast weekends. D, MC, V. No smoking, pets in cottage only.

Victorian Villa Inn

At 13, Ron Gibson was hired to clean out a neighbor's attic—the first step in a lifetime of collecting antiques, which led to owning this redbrick Victorian mansion. Gibson bought the badly deteriorated house in 1978 and opened it as a B&B after a major renovation in 1982. Occupying a tree-shaded corner lot, it was built in 1876 for $12,000 by local doctor William P. Hurd, later known as "Doc Billy." His former bed-chamber, now the Renaissance Suite, is the most sumptuous guest room in the house. Although Gibson and innkeeper Cindy Shattuck have maintained the home's opulent integrity, whimsical touches such as the parlor's mounted-elk hat rack show that they're not above having a little fun. Accordingly, the inn regularly stages Sherlock Holmes Mystery Weekends and other Victorian-themed special events.

Gibson, who clearly knows his way around a kitchen, has built a 50-seat dining room (inn guests receive prior-ity) and deck onto the main house. They blend gracefully with the sur-rounding gardens, which include a giant flag-bedecked gazebo, fountains, and honeysuckle trees. Hobart's tomb-stone stands in the shadows of the car-riage house, allowing him to keep an eye on his old property. He undoubt-edly approves of what he sees.

🏨 *601 North Broadway St., Union City, MI 49094, tel. 517/741–7383 or 800/34–VILLA, fax 517/741–4002. 5 double rooms with baths, 5 suites. Restaurant, air-conditioning in most rooms, phone in common area, fire-place in 2 suites, bicycles built for 2 available. $75–$145; full breakfast, afternoon tea, dinner in adjacent restaurant available. D, MC, V. No smoking indoors, no pets.*

Yelton Manor

A pair of self-styled refugees from the corporate world, Elaine Herbert and her husband, Robert Kripaitif, have turned this rambling 1890 Victorian into arguably the finest bed-and-breakfast in South Haven. The house is done in an elegant turn-of-the-century style, with mostly oak reproduction furnishings. The grounds include Elaine's award-winning perennial and rose gardens as well as the recently built guest house, designed for those desiring a more intimate setting. Each room in the adjacent 1993 guest house features a fireplace, whirlpool bath, and TV; upper-level rooms have balconies and panoramic lake views. Patrons in the main house are served a full breakfast featuring homemade pastries; those in the guest house have a Continental breakfast delivered to their door. The fridge in the separate guest kitchen is kept stocked with juices, homemade cookies, and other goodies.

In the heart of South Haven, the Yelton is only a quarter-block from North Beach access. One mile north is the Kal-Haven Trail, a 38-mile bicycle path that is especially pretty in July when the blueberry fields are in fruit.

🏨 *140 N. Shore Dr., South Haven, MI 49090, tel. 616/637–5220, fax 616/ 637–4957. 17 double rooms with baths. Air-conditioning, cable TV in rooms, 6 guest phones in common areas, fireplace in 7 rooms, whirlpool bath in 11 rooms. $95–$190; full or Continental breakfast, refreshments. AE, MC, V. No smoking indoors, no pets.*

Upper Peninsula

*Even Ernest Hemingway was inspired by the Upper
Peninsula's raw natural beauty. He kept a map of northern
Michigan tacked to the wall of his Paris apartment while
writing* Big Two-Hearted River *in the early 1920s. Who
wouldn't be inspired? The U.P. (as it's commonly called) has a
staggering array of natural resources—a wondrous landscape
of thick pine forests, rushing rivers, crashing waterfalls, and
endless sand beaches. Sandwiched among lakes Superior,
Michigan, and Huron and tethered to the United States only
by the border it shares with Wisconsin, the U.P.'s isolation is
both physical and spiritual. Its fiercely proud residents fondly
refer to it as the "last frontier" and like to point out the
indigenous wildlife population—deer, bears, moose, eagles,
even the elusive gray wolf—vastly outnumbers the human one.
Though geographically larger than Massachusetts,
Connecticut, Rhode Island, and Delaware combined, its
largest city, Marquette, is home to just 23,000 people.*

*The Upper Peninsula was Michigan's consolation prize in a
deal struck with Ohio in 1837. In exchange for admission to
the Union, Congress demanded the Michigan Territory
relinquish the valuable Great Lakes port of Toledo for the
"barren wasteland" of the U.P. Michigan soon realized its good
fortune in acquiring the vast stands of timber and the huge
deposits of copper, silver, and iron discovered under the
peninsula's bedrock. Evidence of this rich mining and
lumbering history fills the museums, ghost towns, and
shipwrecks that dot the region. But the peninsula's real wealth
today comes from its mother lode of stunning natural
resources.*

*Natives of the region, who proudly call themselves Yoopers,
have historically reveled in their isolationism. They are quick
to share their pseudoserious distaste of the mitten-shape
Lower Peninsula of Michigan. When the Mackinac Bridge
opened in 1957, finally linking the two very dissimilar halves
of the state, more than one Yooper suggested dismantling it;*

those living south of the bridge were pretty sure they were kidding. Even today, locals launch sporadic drives to declare sovereignty from the rest of Michigan and create the state of Superior. A local musical group, Da Yoopers, sings, "Dear Mr. Governor, you better turn us loose/We asked you for some rest stops, instead you sent us moose/The honeymoon is over, the declaration's written/We'll take what's above the bridge, and you can keep the mitten."

This is not to say Yoopers aren't an affable bunch. If anything, they're too busy enjoying their surroundings to worry about a visitor's origin. Spring finds the rivers teeming with spawning trout, salmon, and steelhead and the forests thick with wildflowers. During the peak vacation season—from Independence Day to Labor Day—vacationers flock to the U.P. to be quickly dispersed in its vastness. Even on weekends, it's easy to find solitude in a state park or along the shores of a quiet lake. From early September to mid-October, the U.P.'s color show rivals the best New England has to offer. Winter comes early and stays late, which suits the locals, most with Scandinavian heritage, just fine. Heavy snowfalls promise a reliable season of skiing, snowmobiling, snowshoeing, dogsledding, and other pursuits, often well into April. The end of winter is officially declared when students at Lake Superior State University in Sault Ste. Marie ceremonially burn a clothed snowman in effigy.

Although the U.P. has many finely furnished places in which to eat and bed down, the real appeal of the peninsula is what isn't there—crowds, rules, and gussied-up hotels. In the Upper Peninsula, the finest amenities are the ones nature has to offer: wandering the back roads, dangling your feet in a mountain stream, or picnicking beneath towering sand dunes. Most of the region's visitors are looking forward to long evenings discussing trout fishing, not comparing the U.P. with Newport or Martha's Vineyard; their priority—with apologies to E. M. Forster—remains a view with a room.

Places to Go, Sights to See

Isle Royale National Park (tel. 906/482–0984). Stranded in northwestern Lake
Superior, this wilderness archipelago ranks as the least visited park in the
National Parks system, but not for lack of beauty. Ruggedly roadless, 45-mile-
long Isle Royale is a land of unspoiled forests, pristine lakes, rocky cliffs, and
wildlife such as moose and wolves. Its 166 miles of hiking trails attract primarily
backpackers and boaters, who explore the ragged shoreline of Isle Royale itself
and the 200 smaller surrounding islands. The only accommodations—a lodge and
a handful of cabins—are found in Rock Harbor, accessible May through October
by ferry, private boat, or floatplane. Reservations are a must.

Lighthouses. For more than 150 years, Great Lakes mariners have entrusted
their lives to these beacons. More than 40 lighthouses pepper the Upper
Peninsula, guiding boats along its vast stretch of shoreline. While the Coast
Guard has automated most lights over the years, many local organizations have
worked to restore and maintain the historic towers and light keepers' homes.
Some are open to the public, including the 1870 Point Iroquois Lighthouse (tel.
906/437–5272), near Brimley. Owned by the U.S. Forest Service, you can climb
the 65-foot brick tower and tour a small museum in the keeper's home.

Museums. The Upper Peninsula is home to several specialty museums that
highlight the region's unique heritage. The U.P.'s mining-boom days come to life
at the Michigan Iron Industry Museum (73 Forge Rd., tel. 906/475–7857), near
Negaunee. The state-run museum features interactive exhibits and overlooks the
Carp River, where a forge produced the area's first iron in 1848. Nearby
Ishpeming is home to the U.S. National Ski Hall of Fame and Ski Museum (U.S.
Hwy. 41, tel. 906/485–6323), tracing the sport's development. The Great Lakes
Shipwreck Museum (110 Whitefish Point Rd., tel. 906/635–1742) chronicles the
history of Great Lakes transportation and the disasters that sometimes
accompanied it, including the 1975 loss of the *Edmund Fitzgerald*, which
disappeared just 17 miles from the museum. You can explore firsthand the
hundreds of shipwrecks in the area—known as the "Graveyard of the Great
Lakes"—by diving in the cold, clear waters at several underwater preserves,
including the Alger Underwater Preserve (tel. 906/387–4477), in Munising, and
the Whitefish Point Underwater Preserve (tel. 906/492–3445).

Soo Locks (Sault Convention and Visitors Bureau, tel. 800/647–2858). This series
of locks in Sault Ste. Marie tames the 21-foot drop between Lake Superior and
Lake Huron, one of the busiest waterways in the world. Watch the massive,
1,000-foot freighters squeeze through, transporting minerals from Wisconsin and
the U.P. to the industrial centers of the southern Great Lakes. An information
center in Locks Park downtown posts a schedule of expected arrivals, a display
describing how the locks function, and a high observation deck. For an almost
overwhelmingly close-up view of the action, Soo Locks Boat Tours (tel. 800/
432–6301) offers two-hour trips through the locks during the summer months.

Tahquamenon Falls. With more than 250 waterfalls to choose from, it's
impossible to single out the Upper Peninsula's most impressive cascade. But
Tahquamenon (or, Taq) Falls, the second-largest waterfall east of the Mississippi

River, gets many votes. At Upper Tahquamenon, tea-colored water boils furiously over a 200-foot-wide, 50-foot drop. Tahquamenon's fame was first secured in Longfellow's *Song of Hiawatha,* and tourists haven't stopped coming yet. Tahquamenon Falls State Park (tel. 906/492–3415) trails provide easy access year-round.

Fishing

For anglers, the U.P. is a paradise: With its 4,300 inland lakes, 12,000 miles of rivers and trout streams, and access to three of the Great Lakes, how could it be anything less? Lake Gogebic in the western U.P. and Lake Michigan's Little Bay de Noc are famous for large walleyes. Try the pristine lakes of the Sylvania Wilderness and Recreation Area, near Watersmeet, for pike, perch, bass, and trout, as well as walleye. The Great Lakes offer coho, lake trout, steelhead, chinook salmon, yellow perch, northern pike, and smallmouth bass; there are numerous marinas and public-access sites from which to launch or charter a boat. Local advice will steer you to the best cold-water trout streams for brook and brown trout. For more information, contact the Department of Natural Resources (tel. 906/228–6561).

Skiing

Thanks to its hilly terrain and reliable lake-effect snow, the U.P. offers some of the best downhill skiing in the Midwest. Several ski runs are clustered near the western border in Gogebic County, including Indianhead Mountain Resort (tel. 800/346–3426) and the retro Porcupine Mountains (tel. 906/885–5275), which provides skiers with an awesome view of Lake Superior. Well-marked cross-country trails crisscross the entire peninsula. Try state and national forest and park offices, or contact local visitors bureaus for maps and information.

Snowmobiling

Snowmobiling has long been a popular recreation in many parts of the Upper Peninsula, where annual snowfalls regularly top 200 inches. Hundreds of miles of groomed trails traverse the peninsula. Some pass through the centers of towns, while others offer backcountry treks through the wilderness. Contact local chambers of commerce for detailed maps and specific area information. Snowmobile dealers in most communities provide rentals and service.

Restaurants

Stop in at the friendly **Kaleva Cafe** (234 Quincy St., Hancock, tel. 906/482–1230) for a specialty of the U.P.—the miner's pasty (pronounced *pass*-tee, a potpie-type concoction of beef, potatoes, onions, and rutabagas. The **Dog Patch** (820 E. Superior St., Munising, tel. 906/387–9948) is representative of most restaurants in the U.P.: casual and inexpensive, specializing in fresh seafood such as lake trout and whitefish. The **Harbor Haus** (1 block off U.S. 41, tel. 906/289–4502), which overlooks Lake Superior in tiny Copper Harbor, breaks out of the mold with a German menu in addition to fresh-catch specials.

Tourist Information

The **Upper Peninsula Travel & Recreation Association** (Box 400, Iron Mountain, MI 49801, tel. 906/774–5480 or 800/562–7134) is the central source for travel information in the region. The **Michigan Department of Natural Resources** (1990 U.S. 41, South Marquette, MI 49855, tel. 906/228–6561) can answer questions on boating, fishing, and hunting regulations and opportunities. The **Michigan Travel Bureau** (Box 3393, Livonia, MI 48151-3393, tel. 800/543–2937) has statewide tourist information.

Laurium Manor Inn

Dave and Julie Sprenger were working as engineers in San Jose, California, when, as Julie describes it, they "decided to commit corporate suicide" and trade the Golden State's laid-back charms for the ruggedly isolated Keweenaw Peninsula. They shared a dream of owning a mansion they had visited in Laurium, a former copper boomtown. In 1989, they bought the vacant three-story neoclassical house and after three years of restoration work, reopened its heavy oak doors as a bed-and-breakfast.

The Upper Peninsula's largest (13,000 square feet!) and most opulent mansion was built in 1908 by Captain Thomas H. Hoatson, owner of the Calumet & Arizona Mining Company. At a time when miners were toiling 6,000 feet underground for 25 cents an hour, Hoatson spent $50,000 constructing the 40-room mansion and an additional $35,000 furnishing it. The copper magnate had impeccable taste, as lodgers and afternoon tour groups ($3 a head) quickly learn.

Every room is a marvel. Silver-leaf overlay draws your eye to the ceiling of the music parlor. The dining room boasts stained-glass windows and gilded elephant-hide wall coverings, and the kitchen includes a built-in icebox covering an entire wall and made of marble, tile, and oak.

While all the bedrooms were built on an extra-large scale, the Laurium Suite exhausts all superlatives; it covers a majestic 530 square feet and has a hand-carved oak fireplace and private balcony. All the guest quarters feature queen- or king-size beds, handmade flannel quilts, and period antiques.

The National Park Service recently named the inn a "cooperating site" of the new Keweenaw National Historical Park, recognizing its significance in the area's mining heritage. Plan day trips to some of the national park's other historic sites, including the Calumet Theatre (where Sarah Bernhardt, Lillian Russell, and Douglas Fairbanks, Jr., performed) or to one of the ghost towns sprinkled throughout the copper region. Lake Superior is just 4 miles away; Fort Wilkins State Park, a mid-19th-century army post on the northernmost tip of Keweenaw, is a short drive up U.S. 41.

🏨 *320 Tamarack, Laurium, MI 49913, tel. 906/337–2549. 8 double rooms with baths, 2 doubles share bath, 2 suites. No air-conditioning, phone and cable TV in den, fireplace in 2 guest rooms. $49–$109; breakfast buffet. D, MC, V. No smoking, no pets.*

Big Bay Point Lighthouse

Perched high on a rocky point 30 miles north of Marquette, this charming brick lighthouse and light keeper's home has had guided mariners on Lake Superior since 1896. Though the Coast Guard automated the light in 1941, it remains a working navigational aid and one of the few lighthouses open to the public as a bed-and-breakfast inn.

Owners Linda and Jeff Ganble and John Gale were active in historic preservation in Chicago when they discovered the lighthouse and its wooded property, then slated to become a condominium development, were for sale. In 1992, they purchased the lighthouse, several outbuildings, and 43 acres of woods and meadows. Today it houses a large living room with fireplace, dining area with warm exposed brick, and seven double rooms. Most impressive is the Sunset Suite, with cathedral ceiling and spacious sitting room—perfect for watching rosy orange sunsets fade into the lake.

Recreation begins right outside the door: The rugged Huron Mountains stretch to the west, offering hundreds of acres of superb hiking, mountain biking, and fly-fishing. Many guests are content to explore the lighthouse property itself, including 4,500 feet of shoreline. And everyone wants to climb the 60-foot tower for the 360-degree view. On a clear day, you can spot the U.P.'s Keweenaw Peninsula across 45 miles of open water. On rainy afternoons, there are plenty of lighthouse books, blueprints, and other memorabilia to peruse. Or cuddle up with a cup of hot cider and watch the fury of the Great Lake, just like the light keepers did a century ago.

🏠 *3 Lighthouse Rd., Big Bay, MI 49808, tel. 906/345-9957. 7 double rooms with baths. No air-conditioning, sauna. $115–$155 May–Oct., $85–$125 Nov.–April; full breakfast. No credit cards. No smoking, no pets.*

Celibeth House

Widely known as a northern resort town in the 1920s, Blaney Park today is little more than a crossroads. Fortunately, the 22-room Celibeth House has been a constant through the decades and continues the community's long tradition of hospitality. While some guests opt to soak up the silence from a rocking chair on the enclosed front porch, others use the inn as a perfect base for exploring the U.P. About 65 miles west of the Mackinac Bridge, the Celibeth House is surrounded by many of the peninsula's most popular attractions. Pictured Rocks National Lakeshore, Seney National Wildlife Refuge, Fayette State Park, and Tahquamenon Falls are all less than 90 minutes away.

In 1987, Elsa Strom purchased the home and 86 surrounding acres and opened it as a B&B. She filled it with furnishings from the Blaney Park resort era, including a fainting couch and beautiful sleigh bed. Guest rooms are spacious and tidy, often brightened with fresh flowers. A favorite gathering spot is the deck and sunny breakfast room, where a wall of windows overlooks the woods and an array of bird feeders. Hummingbirds, orioles, foxes, coyotes, deer, beavers, otters, and other wildlife are frequent visitors. Guests exploring the property will discover walking trails, a beaver pond, and Lake Anne Louise—perfect for a quiet paddle or an afternoon of fishing.

🏠 *Blaney Park Rd., M-77 (Rte. 1, Box 58A), Blaney Park, MI 49836, tel. 906/283-3409. 6 double rooms with baths, 1 quad. No air-conditioning, telephone in hallway. $48–$53 (4% discount if paid by cash or check); Continental breakfast. MC, V. No smoking, no pets.*

Pinewood Lodge

"I hate drywall," says Jerry Krieg, which explains the rustic warmth of the Pinewood Lodge, a log home resplendent with knotty pine walls and rich maple floors. A masterful woodworker, Jerry and his wife, Jenny, sold their Milwaukee electronics store in 1989 in order to build their dream lodge on the shores of Lake Superior. An addition in 1994 added guest suites and an atrium overflowing with plants, as well as other generous public spaces. A favorite among guests is the great room, with an antique Apollo player piano and a soaring granite fireplace—also built by Jerry, with rocks from the beach.

Twenty-seven miles east of Marquette on Route 28, the lodge sits on a private sand beach the length of a football field. Guests can take full advantage of this enviable location, thanks to an enormous wraparound deck, a maze of boardwalks, a gazebo and an outdoor hot tub. The area offers plenty of recreational opportunities, too, including fishing on nearby Au Train River and Au Train Lake, hiking, and cross-country skiing. Pictured Rocks National Lakeshore is less than a half hour away.

Sweeping scenes of Lake Superior fill the soaring floor-to-ceiling windows in the dining room, where guests enjoy a hearty breakfast that might include baked Finnish pancakes, fresh fruit, and Jenny's homemade strawberry and blueberry preserves. Upstairs guest rooms offer the same magnificent views. Lower-level rooms—outfitted with twin beds—are best for couples (the inn isn't really appropriate for small children) or anyone who wants close proximity to the traditional Finnish sauna.

🏠 *Rte. 28 (Box 176), Au Train, MI 49806, tel. 906/892–8300. 3 double rooms with baths, 2 double rooms with shared bath, 2 suites. No air-conditioning, hot tub and sauna. $75–$150; full breakfast. D, MC, V. No smoking indoors, no pets.*

Sand Hills Lighthouse Inn

Isn't it almost everyone's dream to live in a lighthouse? Well, Bill Frabotta decided to make this fantasy into a reality—and this magical inn is the result. Together with his late wife, Eve, Bill had searched for the perfect structure to acquire and renovate, and in 1960 they found just the place: the 1919 Sand Hills Lighthouse, a cream-colored brick building overlooking Lake Superior on wildly beautiful Keweenaw Peninsula. Perched at the end of Five Mile Point about 25 miles northeast of Houghton, the Sand Hills Lighthouse was the last such manned building on the Great Lakes shore.

Bill spared no energy or expense outfitting the inn. While continuing to run his photography studio in Dearborn, Michigan, he and Eva spent whatever vacation time they could at the property. While much of the original woodwork remains, most of the structure has been completely overhauled. The Frabottas also collected an impressive collection of antiques to furnish the inn, which finally opened as a B&B in 1995. From the ornate crown molding to the velvet drapes in the common room, Sand Hills is bathed in Victorian splendor. Guest rooms feature Victorian dressing tables or chests, and the King Room and several others have massive four-poster beds. Other unique pieces are scattered throughout the inn, such as a lighthouse lens and the 5-foot-high turn-of-the-century coffee grinder tucked against the stairway in the light tower. Many of Bill's photographic portraits decorate the walls.

Still, it's hard to upstage Mother Nature and the majestic lake just outside the door. Guests are welcome to climb the 80 steps to the top of the light tower, which rises 90 feet above the water and offers magnificent views of unspoiled forest and the wide blue horizon of Lake Superior. Water lovers should opt for the Northeast Room or the Northwest Room, both with French doors that open onto private balconies overlooking the lake.

Downstairs, guests relax around the fireplace or curl up on the leather couch and sing along with Bill at the grand piano. Bill uses a late-1800s square grand piano as a sideboard in the dining room, where he serves up a full breakfast that might include "decadent" French toast, apple pancakes, and banana bread. After a hearty meal, guests can explore the rocky shoreline, hike, or ski the trails on the inn's 35 acres, or set off for a day of adventure in the Keweenaw.

🏠 *Five Mile Point Rd, Box 414, Ahmeek, MI 49901, tel. 906/337-1744. 7 double rooms with baths (1 room includes additional single daybed). No air-conditioning, portable phone available for guest use, fireplace in 1 room and common room. $115–$175; full breakfast. No credit cards. No smoking, no pets.*

Thunder Bay Inn

From the wide front porch of the gray clapboard Thunder Bay Inn, guests can gaze down on Lake Independence, picturesquely accented with the tower of an old sawmill peeking above the treeline. It's exactly the view Henry Ford—founding father of the automotive industry—wanted when he purchased the turn-of-the-century general store and warehouse in the 1940s. Ford owned vast holdings throughout the Upper Peninsula, including the old sawmill at Big Bay (not so incidentally, this mill produced the wooden panels for those beloved relics of the '50s and '60s, the Ford "Woody" station wagon).

In 1986, present owners Darryl and Eileen Small purchased and restored Ford's executive retreat and reopened it as the Thunder Bay Inn. They've collected a fascinating array of Ford memorabilia, displayed throughout this comfortable, unpretentious inn. Newspaper clippings in the dining room tell stories of the Ford company towns that peppered the peninsula as early as the 1920s, marvels of modernity with electric lights and indoor running water.

Guests today may not marvel at indoor plumbing, but they will appreciate Thunder Bay Inn's simple comforts and superb location. Guest rooms with period furniture line the wide second-floor corridor. The Henry Ford Executive Suite claims the prime front corner, with a fine lake view and ample sitting areas. Some double rooms have adjoining doors for conversion into suites. On the main floor, guests relax over Continental breakfast in the immense great room, where Ford held summer parties, or settle into wicker chairs on the porch.

But Henry Ford didn't provide the inn's only entry in the history books. The hotel was the setting for the 1959 classic *Anatomy of a Murder*, starring Jimmy Stewart and Lee Remick. Hollywood filmmakers even added the inn's northwoodsy pub, now a favorite among locals for its whitefish, steaks, and terrific homemade pizza. Although the hotel's name in the novel and movie—Thunder Bay Inn—is fictional, the story was based on a true crime, which took place in Big Bay in 1951. Today, Big Bay is a tiny resort area tucked against the Lake Superior shoreline and surrounded by the rugged and remote Huron Mountains. An avid outdoorsman himself, Darryl can direct guests to hiking trails, waterfalls, fishing spots, and other activities.

🏠 *Box 286, Big Bay, MI 49808, tel. 906/345–9376 or 800/732–0714. 5 doubles with baths, 5 doubles with half baths and shared showers, 4 suites. No air-conditioning, television and pay phone on 1st floor. $70–$105; Continental breakfast. MC, V. No smoking on 2nd floor, no pets.*

Water Street Inn

For those infatuated with Great Lakes lore, the Water Street Inn is the perfect place to drop anchor. The sprawling three-story Queen Anne structure sits in the heart of Sault Ste. Marie, the third-oldest city in the United States, just an hour's drive north of the Mackinac Bridge.

The house, bought by retirees Phyllis and Greg Walker in 1991, oozes classic elegance, with a turret, Tiffany windows, and marble fireplaces. The sometimes whimsical decor is a reflection of the Walkers' travels, with a Colombian sculpture of a rain god sharing space with a Mexican stuffed owl. Phyllis serves "a serious Northern breakfast" of lemon bread, apple butter, wild rice pancakes, and other delights. The four second-floor guest rooms are comfortable, tidy, and graced with family heirlooms. Each bed comes topped with a cozy comforter. The front-facing guest rooms offer wonderful views of the river and the twinkling lights of Canada. From the wraparound porch or the gazebo, guests can gaze at the St. Mary River, where massive freighters slowly pass on their way to or from the nearby Soo Locks.

🏠 *140 E. Water St., Sault Ste. Marie, MI 49783, tel. 906/632–1900 or 800/ 236–1904. 4 double rooms with baths. No air-conditioning, shared telephone. $75–$105; full breakfast. D, MC, V. No smoking indoors, no pets.*

Mackinac Island

In 1780, fearful of an American attack during the Revolutionary War, the British moved an entire town from what is now known as Mackinaw City over icy waters to a remote island. The townspeople could never have envisioned the nearly 1 million visitors who today flock to Mackinac Island (pronounced Mac-i-naw, like the city) each year to absorb its rich history and natural beauty.

Mackinac Island is between three of the Great Lakes (Huron, Michigan, and Superior) in the Straits of Mackinac, where Huron and Michigan join. Beginning in the 1600s, the region played a vital role in the northern frontier, long before the island was settled by the British. The Chippewa supplied the French with furs in exchange for such items as blankets, cooking utensils, and weapons. Originally called Michilimackinac, after a Native American word meaning "great turtle," Mackinac Island, with its rising bluffs, looks like the back of a turtle.

In 1815, after more than 30 years of military struggles, Mackinac Island became a permanent part of U.S. territory, and in 1875 Congress created the nation's second national park on the island. The land, which now comprises more than 80% of the island's 2,200 acres, was later transferred to Michigan and became its first state park.

The island's military history and late-1800s culture come to life inside the walls of Ft. Mackinac. This historic fort has been painstakingly restored (14 of its buildings are more than 200 years old), and a tour is one of the best ways to learn about the island. Be forewarned, however; the fort's cannons are fired numerous times throughout the day as part of dramatic reenactments, and although islanders have learned to take this in stride, more than a few visitors have been shaken by the blasts.

Aside from these noises, Mackinac Island has a romantic and timeless tranquility about it, and visiting is akin to traveling back about 100 years. As you approach the island, a foghorn sounds in the distance and magnificent Victorian homes overlooking the harbor come into view. The only signs of the 20th century are the five-seater airplanes that fly over from St. Ignace or the catamaran that ferries you to the island. There are no bridges leading from the mainland. The beautiful Mackinac Bridge, an experience in itself to travel over or look at, connects only Michigan's upper and lower peninsulas.

Three different boat companies operate from the towns on either side of the bridge (Mackinaw City on the Lower Peninsula and St. Ignace on the Upper Peninsula). The ferry lines are comparable in schedule and price, and competition is stiff—so stiff that after exiting I-75, the main highway leading north from central Michigan, you'll start seeing individual ticket booths a good 10 minutes before you get to the docks.

Plan to leave your car behind when you board the ferry since no motorized vehicles are allowed on Mackinac Island (parking is free for day visits and just a few dollars for overnight). Once you've landed, step lightly, since the main mode of transportation is the horse-drawn carriage; more than 600 horses inhabit the island during the summer months. Visitors can also rent bikes or walk to almost anywhere on the island. Bicycle valets will deliver your luggage from the ferry docks, leaving you to peruse the island at your leisure.

Main Street winds along the harbor, and although "downtown" is not exactly peaceful, the sounds of clomping horses and bicycle bells add some charm to the noise of the crowds during peak season (July and August). A wealth of tourist attractions, such as fudge shops (an island specialty and source of the name "fudgie," humorously bestowed on tourists), souvenir and gift shops, galleries, restaurants, bike rentals, and carriage companies, makes this the busiest spot on the island. Watching the hustle and bustle of the ferry handlers is a fascinating reminder of a bygone era, since most everything needed on the island (food, supplies, horses, and so forth) is brought by ferry from the mainland and then delivered by carriage or bicycle to its destination.

The island is only 8.1 miles in circumference, and a paved road circles the perimeter. A bicycle ride or carriage tour around the island is a popular way to enjoy the natural beauty of Mackinac Island State Park, which provides unique limestone formations and breathtaking views of the Great Lakes.

Mackinac Island has an active year-round community of about 600 residents. The tourist season runs from mid-May to mid-October, and most accommodations are booked far in advance for July and August. Known worldwide for events such as the Lilac Festival in June and the Stone Skipping Contest in July, Mackinac attracts an international set. September offers a calmer pace, since crowds have diminished and the weather is still warm during the day but cooler at night, wonderful for sound sleeping. Most of the attractions are only open during the tourist season, and until the whole collegiate workforce arrives on the island, don't be surprised to find your innkeeper still finishing up some last-minute details.

Places to Go, Sights to See

Beaumont Memorial (Market St., tel. 906/847–3328). Dr. William Beaumont is renowned for his landmark experiments on the human digestive system in the 1820s. Educational displays tell of his experiments and discoveries and the conditions under which he worked.

British Landing Nature Center (tel. 906/847–3328). On the northwest side of the island, the center has exhibits that provide information about the night of July 16, 1812, when 36 British soldiers and hundreds of their Native American allies landed and captured Ft. Mackinac without firing a single shot.

Butterfly House (McGulpin St., tel. 906/847–3328). Here you'll find a live display featuring several hundred butterflies encompassing over 80 species from around the world.

Colonial Michilimackinac (tel. 906/847–3328). In Mackinaw City, this is a reconstruction of the original mainland fort and surrounding frontier fur-trading village, which was founded in 1715.

Fort Mackinac (E. Bluff Rd., tel. 906/847–3328). Costumed interpreters demonstrate 19th-century blacksmithing and stage dramatic reenactments. Also of interest are the exhibits, artifacts, and a Discovery Room, where children can try on period clothing and "fire" muskets. Fourteen of the restored buildings are more than 200 years old.

Grand Hotel (Cadotte Ave., tel. 906/847–3331). One of the island's premier landmarks, the Grand Hotel first opened in 1887 and is considered one of the world's finest resorts. Visitors may stroll on its 700-foot veranda, visible from the mainland; partake of afternoon tea; meander through its gardens; peruse the historical photo collection; or even swim in the pool, built especially for the 1946 Esther Williams film *This Time for Keeps*. A special $5 guest pass must be purchased by any visitor who is not a hotel guest.

Indian Dormitory (Main St., tel. 906/847–3328). Native American culture displays and period settings are enhanced by live interpretations of life in the 1800s.

Mackinac Island State Park (tel. 906/847–3328). A tour of the park, from Arch Rock (a natural limestone arch that stands almost 150 feet above the water and 50 feet across) to Wildflower Trail (a small grove of wildflowers that shows a beautiful array of colors) is a must, especially since it encompasses nearly 80% of the island.

Mill Creek (tel. 906/847–3328). On the mainland in Mackinaw City, this is an authentically reconstructed water-powered operating sawmill. Founded in 1790, it supplied lumber for many of the buildings on Mackinac Island.

Stuart House Museum (Market St., tel. 906/847–3783). Housed in John Jacob Astor's American Fur Company warehouse, which was built in 1810, the museum depicts the history of the bygone fur-trading era.

Restaurants

The **Pub Oyster Bar** (Main St., tel. 906/847–3454) serves up seafood chowder, homemade pizza, and, of course, oysters. The elegant 100-foot-long lunch buffet served daily at the **Grand Hotel** (Cadotte Ave., tel. 906/847–3331) includes a large selection of entrées and great desserts; dinner is also served, and a $5 discount to offset the guest pass is applied to the restaurant bill. In the Iroquois Hotel, the **Carriage House** (Main St., tel. 906/847–3321) offers gourmet dining overlooking the water; a specialty is Great Lakes whitefish. At **Horn's Gaslight Bar** (Main St., tel. 906/847–6154), you can enjoy burgers, steaks, and at dinner, Mexican food accompanied by a piano player and dancing.

Tourist Information

Mackinac Island Chamber of Commerce (Mackinac Island, MI 49757, tel. 906/ 847–6418 or 800/454–5227); **Mackinac State Historic Parks Visitors Center** (Main St., Box 370 G, Mackinac Island, MI 49757, tel. 906/847–3328); **Michigan Travel Bureau** (333 S. Capitol, Lansing, MI 48933, tel. 800/543–2937).

Bay View at Mackinac

Owner Doug Yoder's great-great-grandfather, Dr. John R. Bailey, a surgeon at Ft. Mackinac, would be pleased. Doug, who works in the music industry in Nashville during the winter, has painstakingly restored this 1890s house, which has been in his family for more than 100 years. The two-year renovation, which cost half a million dollars, has made the most of the home's elegance.

The sitting room's tin ceiling and fireplace and the refinished wood moldings throughout the house have kept their charm. The wraparound porch is decked out in green and white with skirted glass-top tables. Panoramic views of the water and abundant bright begonias and geraniums make this a perfect place to enjoy late afternoon refreshments.

Guest rooms feel more modern than Victorian as a result of the renovation, but bright new fabrics, skirted tables, and flower-garden wallpaper borders mixed with authentic period pieces, such as an antique inlaid-mahogany headboard, create a nice blend of old and new. Marble floors and ceramic tile in the bathrooms add a classic touch. All the curtains and bedspreads have been handmade for the inn, as was the carpeting in all the hallways and on all the stairs. Three different designs were cut and laid together to create a beautiful rose-colored and flowered carpet.

Newlyweds and chronic romantics will especially enjoy Doug's final additions—three suites, each luxuriously furnished with a whirlpool bath, a television, a CD and video library, a wet bar, and a private balcony overlooking the harbor. There have already been several weddings on those balconies.

Upon arrival you'll discover a sampling of fudge in your room in true Mackinac Island tradition. In the morning you'll awaken to the aroma of Doug's Bay View Blend Coffee and home-baked pastries. Take your breakfast up to the second-floor balcony and start your day off right—with a spectacular view of the Straits of Mackinac.

🏠 *Summer: Main St. (Box 448), Mackinac Island, MI 49757, tel. 906/847-3295. 17 double rooms with baths, 3 suites. No air-conditioning, TV in sitting room on request, ceiling fans in rooms, conference room, gallery and marine supply store, short-term docking facilities. $95–$165, suites $285; Continental breakfast. MC, V. No pets, 2-night minimum weekends, closed Oct.–Apr.*

Haan's 1830 Inn

The charm of Haan's 1830 Inn is not just in its appearance but in the owners themselves. Vernon and Joy Haan share business responsibilities at the inn with their son Nicholas and his wife, Nancy. Even their grandchildren lend a hand by folding napkins before breakfast at the 12-foot harvest table.

The house was built around the foundations of a log cabin that had been dragged over the ice from the mainland during the Revolutionary War. In the mid-1800s, it was the home of Ft. Mackinac officer and onetime island mayor Colonel Preston. The white columns in front give evidence the inn is the oldest Greek Revival home in what was the Northwest Territory; it was also the first B&B on Mackinac Island.

The Haans have turned what could have seemed old and shabby into someplace warm and inviting. Guest rooms are named after figures from the island's past and are tastefully decorated with a variety of antiques, including an elegant burled-walnut headboard. Taller guests should avoid the Reverend William Ferry and Pere Marquette rooms, since the ceilings in that part of the house are unusually low, probably to retain heat in the winter.

A fascinating centerpiece in the sitting room is a large black safe originally used by one of fur trader John Jacob Astor's agents. Original 1830 prints hang on the wall, and there is a large,

dark cherry-wood desk that was built and used in Ft. Mackinac. The second-story porch, tucked under the trees, is a great place to hide out and absorb the island's atmosphere; for those looking for more excitement, the island's downtown is a mere three blocks away.

The Haans clearly enjoy running the inn. The marble-top breakfast buffet brims with delicious coffee cakes, muffins, and jams to be enjoyed at your leisure in front of a crackling fire in the dining room. Vernon is a history buff with a special talent for bringing history to life. In fact, you won't need to spend money on any of the island tours; Vernon is far more interesting and lively. The *Haan* in the inn's name, like the *1830*, is clearly not just for effect.

⌂ *Summer: Huron St. (Box 123), Mackinac Island, MI 49757, tel. 906/847–6244. Winter: 3418 Oakwood Ave., Island Lake, IL 60042, tel. 847/526–2662. 4 double rooms with baths, 2 doubles share bath, 1 housekeeping suite. No air-conditioning, ceiling fans and chocolates in rooms, vouchers for cocktails at local restaurants. $80–$140; Continental breakfast. No credit cards. No smoking indoors, no pets, closed mid-Oct.–mid-May.*

The Inn on Mackinac

Trying to find all 13 colors on the inn's exterior, beyond the easier-to-identify hues of purple, pink, green, and peach, is a favorite pastime of guests. Assistant general manager Kelly Irby says most people can only identify five or six. The bright colors, inspired by Victorian homes like the so-called painted ladies of San Francisco, make the Inn on Mackinac one of the more eye-catching houses on the island.

Built in 1867, with the back section added later, the house used to be called the Chateau Beaumont in memory of the fort's famous army surgeon, William Beaumont. In 1988, the inn was remodeled to emphasize its quaint Victorian charm yet still provide a number of modern amenities.

The larger and more expensive rooms are in the front, which is the older section; they are charmingly furnished with cherry armoires, white shutters in the windows overlooking the street, and white lace swags over the beds. Although rooms in the back section are comfortable and also redecorated, they don't have as good a view and are smaller. Request a room with a bay window (found in both sections) since they add a sense of spaciousness to the room.

Although you are unlikely to meet up with owners Pat and Alice Pulte (they also own the Murray Hotel), a complete staff is on hand to answer any questions about the island or the inn.

Because of its size, the inn may lack some intimacy found at other B&Bs, but it makes up for that in style and convenience. Although not right in the center of town, it is certainly close.

A sense of camaraderie is evident as soon as you step onto the expansive, second-floor wraparound porch, where guests gather throughout the day. In fact, the outdoor areas at the inn are as enjoyable as the rooms. At street level, a lattice-covered arch leads to a charming brick patio surrounded by gardens. This level, which includes the lobby and dining room, was created during the remodeling by digging out the home's basement and adding French doors all the way around. You can eat breakfast inside or on the patio or sample some of the Pultes' homemade fudge, made fresh daily and sold in the lobby.

🏨 *Summer: Main St., Mackinac Island, MI 49757, tel. 906/847–6348 or 800/462–2546. Winter: Box 7706, Ann Arbor, MI 48107, tel. 313/665–5750. 44 double rooms with baths. Air-conditioning, TV in rooms, wheelchair accessible. $74–$175; Continental breakfast. MC, V. No pets, closed Oct. 15–Apr.*

Metivier Inn

You can't miss the Metivier Inn, on a quiet section of Market Street one block from the hustle and bustle of Main Street. Beautiful landscaping and a white picket fence along the front sidewalk make this inn a standout.

The house, built in 1877, was a single-family home until 1984, when it opened as a B&B. Originally it had only 13 guest rooms, but recent renovations have added more on the third floor. One of the new rooms boasts a Jacuzzi and a small deck overlooking the magnificent Grand Hotel and its golf course. A side porch, accessible from four rooms on the second floor, is perfect for a group of people looking for some shared privacy. The front porch runs the full width of the house and is nicely furnished with the owners' personal collection of antique white wicker. In fact, soft colors and antique-style furniture throughout give the inn a simple, clean, and tasteful look.

Various names from Mackinac Island's past adorn the doors to each guest room. Because of its larger size and unique view, the John Jacob Astor Room, in the turret at the front of the house, is one of the nicest. An antique sleigh bed adorns one of the main-floor rooms, or for a romantic night, try one of the four rooms outfitted with a four-poster canopy bed.

A Continental breakfast, brought from a local bakery each morning, is served in the lobby, which is somewhat sparse but comfortable; it is furnished with couches, chairs, and a wood-burning stove that adds atmosphere when stoked up on cooler days or in the evenings.

Metivier is efficiently run and quiet, but it lacks some of the personal touches that can make for a unique stay. Although it is owned by two couples, Ken and Diane Neyer and Mike and Jane Bacon, the inn is professionally managed by George and Angela Leonard, who live on the premises and seem very responsive yet not intrusive to their guests' needs.

Guests can also enjoy a visit to Biddle House, a restored turn-of-the century home right next door.

🏨 *Summer: Market St. (Box 285), Mackinac Island, MI 49757, tel. 906/ 847–6234. 22 double rooms with baths, 1 efficiency suite. No air-conditioning, cable TV in conference room, wood-burning stove in sitting room. $110– $245; $185 for suite; Continental breakfast. AE, D, MC, V. No smoking, no pets, closed Nov.–Apr.*

Bogan Lane Inn

Trish Martin grew up in this home on Bogan Lane, and even though the house shows its age in some areas (it was built around 1850), she has made it so cozy her guests will feel at home as well. The location just off Huron Street, three blocks from downtown, is close enough for visitors to enjoy the island and far enough for them to hear only the foghorns at night.

Of the guest rooms, the Porch Room, with charming quilts and curtains, offers a cozy retreat, although it has only twin beds. The Yellow Room, next door, is furnished with a comfortable antique double bed.

As the only year-round B&B on Mackinac Island, Bogan Lane Inn is perfect for a cross-country ski weekend or midwinter getaway, and Trish's home-baked pastries warm up even the coldest morning. Whether enjoying a fire in the living room, playing one of the many board games kept on hand, or getting the scoop from Trish on the island's secret spots, you'll feel like you're staying at your grandmother's cottage.

🏠 *Bogan La. (Box 482), Mackinac Island, MI 49757, tel. 906/847–3439. 4 double rooms share 2 baths. No air-conditioning, ceiling fans in guest rooms. $55–$65; Continental breakfast. No credit cards. No smoking indoors, no pets.*

Cloghaun Bed & Breakfast

Baskets of bright red begonias adorning both balconies are the first things you see at this Market Street B&B. Inside, century-old family treasures, beamed ceilings, arched windows and doors, the butter churn by the fireplace, and Rosebud china set out for breakfast create the relaxed and charming atmosphere at the Cloghaun (pronounced Claw-hahn).

The original owners, Thomas and Bridgett Donnelly, left Cloghaun, Ireland, during the great famine of 1848 and settled here. The house, built in 1884 for their growing family, is still owned by descendants James Bond and his wife. The property is managed by Leonard and Jane Johnson, who run it in such an inviting manner you'd think it was their own.

All the rooms interconnect and can be turned into suites if desired. Even those without private baths have sinks. The sitting room is full of books, historical tidbits, jigsaw puzzles, games, and even a box of toys for the younger set.

🏠 *Summer: Market St. (Box 203), Mackinac Island, MI 49757, tel. 906/847–3885. Winter: tel. 810/778–9311. 8 double rooms with baths, 2 doubles share bath. No air-conditioning. $70–$110; Continental breakfast. No credit cards. No smoking indoors, no pets, closed Oct. 15– May 15.*

Murray Hotel

The Murray Hotel, dubbed the "centennial bed-and-breakfast inn," has been providing hospitality to visitors for more than 100 years. Owned by islanders Pat and Alice Pulte (they also own the Inn on Mackinac), it has a distinctly Victorian air, enhanced by the wide balustrade staircase and the wicker-filled lobby. The guest rooms are clean but simply decorated with floral wallpaper borders, wicker furniture, and a few antique dressers and headboards.

The Murray is on Main Street, in the heart of Mackinac Island's downtown. This means noise from morning to night during the summer season, but it's a great spot for people-watching and for being at the heart of the comings and goings.

With a professional staff running the daily operations, dining rooms, delicatessen, cocktail lounge, and a more formal check-in procedure, the Murray feels somewhat more like a quaint 19th-century hotel than a B&B retreat.

🏠 *Summer: Main St. (Box 476), Mackinac Island, MI 49757, tel. 906/847–3361 or 800/462–2546. Winter: Box 7706, Ann Arbor, MI 48107, tel. 313/665–5750. 69 double rooms with baths. Air-conditioning and TV in rooms, whirlpool bath in 2 rooms. $74–$175; Continental breakfast. MC, V. No pets, closed Oct. 15–Apr.*

1900 Market Street Inn

Facing Marquette Park, this recently renovated turn-of-the-century house was formerly a private home owned by the Triskett family. Island residents and sisters Sandra and Deborah Orr teamed up to convert it into a B&B in 1991, but they rely on resident manager Bonnie Anderson-Surre to run the inn.

The downstairs guest room is elegant and romantic, with high ceilings, a fireplace, a piano, and a beautiful four-poster bed. The woodwork up the wide staircase leading to the second-floor rooms was beautifully restored, and each room, from the chintz to the wallpaper, carefully adheres to coordinated color schemes, from soft pastels in one to deep burgundy and green in another.

Although very clean and modern, the inn itself is relatively small, with only a sparse lobby and tiny front porch to gather in. Coffee and pastries are served in the lobby each morning; there's also a complimentary Continental breakfast two blocks away at the Pub Oyster Bar that offers more variety.

🏠 *Market St. (Box 315), Mackinac Island, MI 49757, tel. 906/847–3811. 7 double rooms with baths. No air-conditioning, ceiling fan, cable TV in rooms, wheelchair accessible. $85–$140; Continental breakfast. MC, V. No pets, 3-night minimum during boat races, closed Nov.–Apr.*

Grand Traverse Region
Including Traverse City

The Traverse City Convention and Visitors Bureau promotes
Traverse City as "a Great Lakes paradise," a statement that
may not be far from the truth. More than 250 miles of Lake
Michigan shoreline and numerous inland lakes contribute to
this area's natural beauty and recreational opportunities. The
region that Chicago businessman Perry Hannah built as a
lumber empire in the late 1800s has long been a popular
vacation destination for Midwesterners. Over the past 10
years, it has gained national prominence as a convention
area. It is also host to the National Cherry Festival.

Its popularity is most obvious during the summer (May
through Labor Day), when the population swells from just
under 30,000 to 300,000. Traffic jams can be annoying, and
reservations for weekend lodging are a must. Winter also
attracts visitors, since the terrain is perfect for cross-country
skiers, and four of the Midwest's top downhill ski resorts are
within an hour's drive. Luckily, winter crowds are not
overwhelming. Fall, which brings the brilliant foliage to the
hardwood trees, and spring, when cherry orchards are in full
blossom, also offer a special beauty, and crowds are not as
intense.

Three counties—Leelanau, Grand Traverse, and Benzie—
make up what Michiganders refer to as the Grand Traverse
region. It stretches north from Frankfort, up the east side of
Lake Michigan to the tip of Leelanau Peninsula, back down to
Traverse City, and east through a town with the unlikely name
of Acme. The Old Mission Peninsula juts north from Traverse
City, dividing the waters of Grand Traverse Bay into the East
and West bays. Although East Bay is home to a wide variety of
chain motels and restaurants, it also claims some of the
cleanest beaches in the area. The growth of West Bay has been
more carefully monitored, so there are numerous public

*beaches, marinas, parks, and a bike path that stretches the full
width of the harbor.*

*Traverse City, at the foot of West Bay, is considered the
metropolitan hub of northwestern Michigan and is the area's
central destination point. With a year-round population of
just under 30,000, it offers an unusually strong mix of
cultural activities, and a huge selection of shops for a town its
size. Among the city's entertainment offerings are a fine-arts
museum, professional theater, symphony orchestra, zoo,
steam-power passenger train, ski area, active arts council and
community playhouse, and public recreational center
(complete with lighted walking and biking paths, an indoor ice
rink, a swimming pool, and tennis courts); it also has a
college. Traverse City, however, has maintained an appealing
small-town feel: Tree-lined historic neighborhoods, a
downtown waterfront, regularly held open-air block parties
and street sales, and people with a well-deserved reputation
for friendliness help to keep the city bustling, but accessible.*

*Myriad opportunities for fun are not confined to Traverse City.
Touring Old Mission and Leelanau peninsulas is a perfect way
to spend a day. Acres of generations-old farms and wineries
mingle with art galleries, restaurants, shops, antiques stores,
parks, and beaches. The climate is favorable for farming, and
the area boasts abundant orchards and six excellent wineries
offering free tastings and tours. Visitors can also play golf in
the Grand Traverse area, on courses designed by Jack Nicklaus
and Arnold Palmer. The nationally renowned Interlochen
Center for the Arts, just south of Traverse City, hosts a variety
of entertainment, which includes the Canadian Brass, the
Tokyo String Quartet, the Red Star Red Army Chorus and
Dance Ensemble, and Peter, Paul, and Mary.*

Places to Go, Sights to See

Dennos Museum Center (1701 E. Front St., Traverse City, tel. 616/922–1055),
built in 1991, contains three galleries that hold exhibits from around the country
and displays a permanent collection of Inuit art, said to be one of the largest in

the United States. There are also hands-on exhibits for children, a small theater, and a 367-seat auditorium, home to the summer stock Michigan Ensemble Theatre.

Grand Traverse Lighthouse (M201, just north of Northport on Leelanau Peninsula, tel. 616/386–5503) was built in 1858, has been restored, and is now a living museum. Descendants of the former lighthouse keeper live in the front half of the building; the remaining space is devoted to pictures and displays—including a Fresnel lens used in the lighthouse—testifying to the rugged life of a keeper.

Gwen Frostic Prints (5140 River Rd., Benzonia, tel. 616/882–5505) is on a 280-acre nature preserve 30 minutes southwest of Traverse City. The stone studio, library, gift shop, and printing facility were created by popular naturalist, author, and artist Gwen Frostic. Frostic's beautifully simple nature prints and poetry are reproduced in books, stationery, and other paper products and shipped around the world. Visitors may find it fascinating to watch the press at work or take delight in wandering around the grounds.

Interlochen Center for the Arts (Rte. 137, tel. 616/276–9221) has earned international recognition as a leading center for the development and training of talented and gifted students and as an advocate of the arts. It operates as a private high school during the school year, with students from around the world, and hosts a music camp for all ages during the summer. Throughout the year, student and faculty exhibits and performances are held along with those of internationally acclaimed artists. The 1,200 acres of scenic forest that make up the campus are on the edge of Green Lake in Interlochen, just south of Traverse City. The campus is open to visitors year-round.

Leelanau Sands Casino Resort (Rte. 22, just north of Suttons Bay, Peshawbestown, tel. 800/922–2946) is operated by the Grand Traverse Band of Ottawa and Chippewa Indians. Under the provisions of an agreement with the federal government concerning the sovereignty of Native American reservations, the tribe offers the only legal gambling in the region. Visitors can try their luck at anything from blackjack and poker to slot machines, bingo, and roulette.

The **Manitou Islands,** off the coast of Lake Michigan near Leland, offer hiking and camping made enjoyable by the enchanting scenery. Motorized tours are also available. Both North and South Manitou islands are under the jurisdiction of the National Park Service. For information on day trips and evening cocktail cruises leaving from Fishtown, in Leland, call Manitou Island Transit (tel. 616/256–9061 or 616/271–4217).

The **Music House** (Rte. 31, 2 mi north of Acme, tel. 616/938–9300) is an emporium and museum offering a magical experience. Wander through replica villages and listen to the working displays of automated music machines, pipe organs, and jukeboxes as well as to the Amaryllis, a 30-foot-wide dance organ from the Victoria Palace Ballroom in Belgium. Exhibits of record collections, early radios, television sets, and phonographs provide an amusing and lively history of the sounds of music.

Sleeping Bear Dunes National Lakeshore (tel. 616/326–5134), one of the world's largest moving sand dunes, towers over the waters of Lake Michigan and Glen Lakes. The area is part of the National Lakeshore Park and also includes the Manitou Islands. A scenic drive through the park provides spectacular views of the dunes, Lake Michigan, and the Glen Lakes. There's a dune climb, for hearty visitors, and plenty of other areas to explore on foot. The Philip A. Hart Visitors Center on Route 72 in Empire offers park information, a minimuseum, and an excellent multimedia presentation.

Traverse City Opera House (112½ E. Front St., tel. 616/941–8082), built in 1891, is one of only 18 opera houses remaining of the 127 built in Michigan. This Victorian landmark is listed on both the National and the State Registers of Historic Sites. Architecture lovers will appreciate the meticulously restored vaulted ceiling and elaborate decorative moldings. The original curtain is still in place, and vintage advertisements and a landscape mural add considerably to the Victorian ambience. There is no charge to tour the opera house, which is host to a variety of community events.

Traverse Tall Ship Co. (13390 S. West Bay Shore Dr., tel. 616/941–2000) operates daily sailing excursions mid-June through September on West Grand Traverse Bay. Hearkening back to earlier days when sailing vessels dominated the Great Lakes maritime trade, visitors can experience a tall-ship adventure aboard two different Coast Guard–inspected, double-masted ships: the *Malabar* sailing out of Traverse City or its sister ship, the *Manitou*, which is based in Northport and offers windjammer cruises. Both ships are operated by licensed captains and crews. Sailing packages have a variety of options, and private charters can also be arranged.

Beaches

In this region known for its attractive shoreline, the beaches are too numerous to list, but rest assured that there is a beach for everyone and no charge for enjoying it. Such city beaches as **Clinch Park** and **West End,** within walking distance of downtown Traverse City, come complete with lifeguards and refreshment stands, marinas, and nearby establishments renting out boats. At the remote **Pyramid Point** and **Good Harbor** beaches (off Rte. 22, on the southwest side of the Leelanau Peninsula), you can enjoy building a fire while watching the sunset on Lake Michigan. Parks with beaches include **Interlochen State Park** (Rte. 137 via U.S. 31, tel. 616/775–9727) and **Traverse City State Park** (Munson Ave., tel. 616/775–9727).

Restaurants

On the Old Mission Peninsula are two very different restaurants in the same big house: **The Bowery** (13512 Peninsula Dr., tel. 616/223–4333), the more casual of the two, is known for its barbecued ribs and large beer selection, and **Bowers Harbor Inn** (13512 Peninsula Dr., tel. 616/223–4222) offers romantic dining overlooking the bay. Visitors may want to inquire about the resident ghost. **Old**

Mission Tavern (17015 Center Rd., tel. 616/223–7280) is filled with an eclectic collection of works by local artists, which are for sale. In Traverse City, two elegant restaurants that serve regional cuisine with views of the bay are **Top of the Park** (300 E. State St., tel. 616/946–5000), on the 10th floor of the Park Place Hotel, and **Windows** (7677 W. Bayshore Dr., tel. 616/941–0100), 2 miles north of town. For a taste of the old lumbering era, try **Dill's Olde Towne Saloon** (423 S. Union St., tel. 616/947–7534), home in the summer to the musical Golden Garter Revue, or **Sleder's Tavern** (71 Randolph St., tel. 616/947–9213), in Slabtown, where you are presented a gift if you kiss the moose head. On the Leelanau Peninsula, the **Riverside Inn** (302 River St., tel. 616/256–9971), overlooking the Leland River in Leland, offers fresh whitefish, French cuisine, and an extensive wine selection. In Suttons Bay, you can try cozy **Boone's Prime Time** (102 St. Joseph's St., tel. 616/271–6688) for steak, fish, or burgers, or the gourmet **Hattie's Bar and Grille** (111 St. Joseph's St., tel. 616/271–6222), where diners can enjoy an eclectic menu ranging from risotto to veal chops while sitting amidst an art exhibit that changes monthly.

Tourist Information

Lake to Lake Bed & Breakfast Association (19271 S. Lakeside Rd., New Buffalo, MI 49117, tel. 616/756–3445); **Leelanau Peninsula Chamber of Commerce** (105 Phillip St., Lake Leelanau, MI 49653, tel. 616/256–9895); **Traverse City Area Chamber of Commerce** (202 E. Grandview Pkwy., Traverse City, MI 49684, tel. 616/947–5075); **Traverse City Convention and Visitors Bureau** (415 Munson Ave., Suite 200, Traverse City, MI 49684, tel. 800/872–8377, fax 616/947–2621).

Centennial Inn

The Centennial Inn, in the heart of Leelanau County's rolling farmland, was designated a Michigan Centennial Farm by the state's Historical Commission. In the same family for more than 100 years, the farm got its first new owners when Karl and JoAnne Smith bought it eight years ago.

The Smiths have carefully restored the two-story clapboard farmhouse, built in 1865. The original barn and two outbuildings are still in excellent condition. The smaller one has been turned into a gift shop, featuring antiques and folk art created by local artisans, as well as JoAnne's baskets and Karl's reproduction furniture. Since the inn is about 6 miles from the small town of Lake Leelanau, guests will need to drive a short way to find restaurants and shops.

As you approach the house, you'll come across a glistening sundial. The lettering around it reads, "Grow old along with me, the best is yet to be." The Centennial Inn is proof that what is old can also be very good. On the front porch, pots of red-blossomed geraniums are placed around a white bench, creating a colorful frame for the entrance.

The Smiths have decorated the farm in Shaker style, yet their loving attention makes what could seem sparse feel warm and inviting. A scattering of Oriental rugs complement the glow of the refinished, original hardwood floors. A candle chandelier hangs over the rough-hewn pine table in the dining room, and an elaborate pewter collection is displayed above the buffet. The parlor, one of the coziest spots, is perfect for reading, watching TV, or just enjoying the country fireplace.

The guest rooms continue the Shaker theme. The front room downstairs has a four-poster bed with a white lace canopy and homemade white quilt. Every detail harmonizes, down to the blue-and-white checkered curtains in the window and the old crockery on the tables.

A deluxe Continental breakfast is more than enough to fill you up. In the cooler months, breakfast can be enjoyed in the cozy dining room, but during the summer, either of two outside areas makes a perfect eating spot: The deck on the west side overlooks a big birch tree and apple orchards, and, on the east side, there's a redbrick patio with twig furniture. A swing in the back overlooks acres of unspoiled rolling land: The peaceful sight can take you back 100 years.

7251 E. Alpers Rd., Lake Leelanau, MI 49653, tel. 616/271–6460. 3 doubles share bath. Nordic ski trails, bicycling trails. $70; Continental breakfast. MC, V. No smoking, no pets.

Linden Lea

A small and enchanting spot on the shore of a crystal-clear inland lake, Linden Lea is, as one of its owners describes it, reminiscent of scenes in the movie *On Golden Pond*. Country roads wind their way to the bed-and-breakfast, and, once you've found it, you won't want to leave.

In 1979, Jim and Vicky McDonnell bought a small summer cottage built around the turn of the century by three Civil War veterans. Vicky remembers, "The original cottage was a mess—rotting floors and everything—but I just kept looking at the view and saying, 'This is it. This is the place.'" Since then, Jim, a former teacher, has skillfully renovated the building and tacked on an addition; nine years ago the couple opened their multilevel, contemporary home as a B&B.

The living room, complete with a marble and cherry-wood fireplace from the late 1800s, expansive picture windows, high ceilings, and a large, comfortable sectional sofa, is an inviting place to unwind and enjoy the view. With that in mind, the guest rooms have cushioned window seats that overlook the lake. The rooms, separate from the family quarters, also offer a measure of privacy.

The mix of antiques and treasures creates a warm, eclectic atmosphere. Jim began collecting unusual paperweights on a trip to Scotland, and now more than 30 of the colorful glass pieces adorn a table near the stairway. The handmade dolls and the decorative plates scattered throughout the house are gifts Vicky's mother received while serving as an army nurse. A player piano dating from 1871 is a favorite of guests.

The McDonnells and their children, Audrey and Wyatt, are a congenial family. They've been known to offer baby-sitting services and to invite guests to join the family for dinner on cold winter nights when the prospect of curling up in front of the fireplace seems more appealing than braving the elements to find a restaurant.

The breakfast menu varies, and guests may be treated to such delights as quiches, freshly baked peach puffs, chocolate-chip banana muffins, and stuffed French toast. After breakfast, guests can take the rowboat to explore one of Long Lake's many islands.

🏨 *279 S. Long Lake Rd., Traverse City, MI 49684, tel. 616/943-9182. 2 double rooms with baths. Air-conditioning, TV and VCR in living room, private sand beach, rowboat and paddleboat available. $80–$95; full breakfast. No credit cards. No smoking, no pets, 2-night minimum weekends May–Oct.*

North Shore Inn

Originally part of an estate, this rambling, colonial-style home was built in 1946. Sue Hammersley, who has lived in the area for 24 years, bought the house in 1983, remodeled it, and turned it into her family home. Sue was a preschool teacher at the time, but a few years later, with her family's support, she left her job to convert the home on the shores of picturesque West Bay into a luxurious retreat.

The sit-down gourmet breakfast (Continental buffet if you miss the 9 AM meal) is an experience. Sue varies the menu according to the season, and the portions are generous. There is always a selection of muffins, coffee cake or cobblers, fresh fruit and juice, and a main dish such as pancakes, eggs, or a sausage casserole. Many of the herbs she uses in cooking and the fresh flowers found throughout the house are grown in Sue's English garden, whose colorful accent can be seen from the Wedgwood Suite.

The common room is filled floor to ceiling with books, games, and a collection of old movies for the VCR. A bay window stretches the full height of the room and looks out over the lawn and the beach. The musically inclined can tinkle on a grand piano and a Hammond organ. At the south end of the house, a screened-in porch is a marvelous place to enjoy the outdoors, even on an overcast or rainy day.

All the guest rooms are large; the popular Heritage Room, on the main floor, has a private entrance and a kitchen. Another favorite is the Country Rose Room, which has a pink marble fireplace and a private balcony overlooking the beach. Sue made the Whig Rose quilt that adorns the brass bed. All the guest rooms except the Bayshore Room, which is the smallest, have separate sitting rooms with sofa beds, so two couples may comfortably share a suite. The fireplace in each room has wood laid, ready to light when you arrive.

There is much to enjoy on the premises, but a bonus is the inn's location: only a few minutes' drive from either the restaurants and shopping in the quaint town of Northport or the rugged beauty of Northport State Park.

🏨 *12271 N. Northport Point Rd., Northport, MI 49670, tel. 616/386–7111. 1 double room with bath, 2 suites, 1 housekeeping suite. No air-conditioning, morning coffee and tea baskets left outside guest rooms. $135–$145; full breakfast, afternoon refreshments. No credit cards. No smoking, no pets, closed Nov.–Apr.*

Aspen House

Owning a B&B was always a "someday thing" for Paula and Philip Swink. Someday arrived unexpectedly during a trip to northern Michigan in May 1995. After living on the West Coast for over 30 years, the Swinks fell in love with the northwoods region and within three months left a fast-paced San Francisco lifestyle, scouted a variety of B&Bs, moved into their new home, and opened for business.

The Swinks have transformed their 4,000-square-foot 1885 farmhouse into a spacious and elegant B&B reminiscent of old-world European charm. The dining room's dark oak table is elegantly set with antique china and silver. The large living room provides numerous overstuffed sofas and leather chairs, floor-to-ceiling bookcases, and a fireplace; a second-floor common room gives extra room to roam.

While two of the guest rooms are both inviting and very spacious—and feature ample sitting areas—each also offers unique amenities; the Pine Room has a small outdoor deck and the Aspen Room boasts a two-person Jacuzzi. The smaller but popular Victorian Room is elegantly decorated with marble-topped, Belgium walnut furniture, and 1920s artist Harrison Fisher's popular depictions of the Gibson Girls adorn the walls.

Two outdoor garden areas are charmingly set with tables and hammocks. Paula has created a lavish herb garden, and she uses all of the fresh herbs and edible flowers in her gourmet breakfasts. Refreshments are served each afternoon. When dining at night, guests may prefer to wait for the final course; Paula enjoys serving one of her dessert specialties—fruit torte, cheesecake, and peach dumpling—in the evenings. With the Swinks' penchant for spoiling their guests, don't be surprised if you are greeted some cold evening with a steaming bowl of homemade soup and Paula's renowned molasses bread.

A short stroll around the Swinks' property reveals remnants of earlier farming days—an aging cherry orchard and a potato patch—as well as a panoramic view of Lake Michigan. Guests may explore nearby trails owned by a local land conservancy, and the accessible beach—an easy climb down from a nearby bluff—is the perfect place to experience a spectacular Michigan sunset.

🏠 *1353 N. Manitou Trail W (Box 722), Leland, MI 49654, tel. 616/ 256–9724 or 800/762–7736, fax 616/ 256–2777. 3 double rooms with bath. No air-conditioning, terry-cloth robes, TV and VCR in living room, computer in small office. $100–$125; full breakfast. MC. V. No smoking indoors, no pets.*

Bowers Harbor Bed & Breakfast

This 1870 farmhouse in the heart of the Old Mission Peninsula's cherry country is on 200 feet of private sandy beach on the West Bay. Owners Gary and Mary Ann Verbanic named each guest room in the two-story house after the view seen from its windows: The Harbor View Room looks down on Bowers Harbor; the Pine View Room overlooks 100-year-old white pines. Each is decorated in a classic country style, with brass beds, goose-down pillows, and comforters. The living room, which also has a view of the water, contains a large stone fireplace and is a peaceful place to enjoy quiet conversation or a good book.

The house has a wraparound fieldstone porch, a perfect spot to watch northern Michigan's dramatic sunsets or the morning mist as it rises off the water. You might go for a swim at the beach, though the water can be on the chilly side. For a surer bet, play a game at the tennis courts or have a meal at one of the area's best restaurants, Bowers Harbor Inn, both within walking distance.

🏠 *13972 Peninsula Dr., Traverse City, MI 49684, tel. 616/223–7869. 3 double rooms with baths. No air-conditioning, off-street parking. $90–$120; full breakfast. No credit cards. No smoking, no pets, 2-night minimum weekends July–Sept. 15.*

Brookside Inn

Owners Pam and Kirk Lorenz have created a private haven perfect for romantic getaways, and they even promote a couples-only policy to ensure quiet and privacy for their guests.

The guest rooms contain king-size waterbeds, TVs, wood-burning stoves, and whirlpool baths for two. Each also has a different theme: The Garden Room has colorful flowered wallpaper, and the New Orleans Room has wrought-iron window trim and flower boxes.

A full-service restaurant on the main floor of the contemporary, cedar-sided structure offers a large selection of unique dishes, including the popular "stone dinner." Delivered to the table on marble warmed by a square stone heated to 900°, this delicious dish consists of beef or veal, boneless chicken breast, shrimp, and three homemade sauces. A full breakfast is also served in the dining room. The Lorenzes cook all food from scratch, using herbs from their garden and wine from their cellar. Guests are invited to partake in some wine tasting, but alcoholic beverages are not included in the room rate.

🏠 *115 N. Michigan Ave., Beulah, MI 49617, tel. 616/882–7271. 20 double rooms with baths. Air-conditioning, saunas, steam baths, and tanning*

solariums in some rooms. $195–$250; full breakfast and dinner for 2. AE, MC, V. No pets.*

Chateau Chantal

Located atop 65 acres of rolling countryside, Chateau Chantal (named after the owners' daughter, Marie Chantal) easily boasts the most spectacular vista of any area B&B. The inn has views of both the east and west arms of Grand Traverse Bay, which surrounds this unique spit of land known as Old Mission Peninsula.

Owners Robert and Nadine Begin have created, as one guest described it, "the ambience of an exclusive European estate." Their primary business is the on-site winery, which was founded in 1983 and now produces 7,000 cases of wine and champagne annually, but the property's wine-related features coexist happily with the inn.

The two downstairs suites—done in French Country decor—have a private entrance off the main floor. Also downstairs are the public area of the winery and the great room, which has a fireplace, cushioned window seats, and a circular picture window in the ceiling. Stained-glass French doors lead to the bricked veranda overlooking the vineyard—a perfect spot to enjoy sunsets, wine tastings, or a quiet country moment.

🏠 *15900 Rue de Vin, Traverse City, MI 49684, tel. and fax 616/223–4110. 1 double room with bath, 2 suites. Air-conditioning, TV, phone, individual heat and air controls in rooms, winery tours and wine tastings. $95–$125; full breakfast. MC, V. No smoking indoors, no pets, 2-night minimum June 15–Oct.*

Cherry Knoll Farm

Dorothy and Percy Cump recently remodeled this 1885 Victorian farmhouse on 115 acres of beautiful rolling farmland a few minutes from Traverse City. The interior is decorated in true country fashion; older furnishings are mixed with authentic antiques.

The family room, with a fireplace, is shared by guests and the Cump family, and the guest rooms are large enough to provide a comfortable upstairs escape if you need some privacy. The bedrooms may not be elegant, but they are comfortably furnished and include such special touches as a bedspread crocheted by Dorothy's grandmother and several patchwork quilts that are family heirlooms.

An old-fashioned porch runs across the front of the house and is a great place to watch the sun rise or to unwind at the end of the day. Guests are free to walk around the property and pick cherries from the orchard during the summer or look for morel mushrooms in the spring.

🏠 *2856 Hammond Rd. E, Traverse City, MI 49684, tel. 616/947–9806 or 800/847–9806. 3 double rooms share 2 baths. Air-conditioning, restricted-diet breakfasts on request. $65–$70; full breakfast. MC, V. No smoking indoors, no pets, closed Nov.–May.*

Lee Point Inn

Nestled in the woods at the tip of Lee Point on the picturesque Leelanau Peninsula is the home that Fred and Patty Kilbourn built in 1979 and opened as a bed-and-breakfast seven years ago. They manage to blend their family life (they have two school-age children) and their business quite well. Guest rooms, one of which has a king-size water bed (great for a bad back), are upstairs with the family bedrooms. To provide privacy, some areas of the house are designated for guests only, but Patty reports that many a visitor ends up curled up on the couch in the Kilbourns' family room off the kitchen, and that's fine with them. The living

room, on the south side, has a wood-stove and classic country decor.

The dining room leads out onto a multilevel deck, which runs across the back of this large, contemporary home and offers a wonderful view of West Bay. Steps lead down to the private beach, which guests are welcome to use. Cross-country trails start outside the front door, making the inn a great place for beach lovers and ski enthusiasts alike.

🏠 *2885 S. Lee Point La. (Rte. 2, Box 374B), Suttons Bay, MI 49682, tel. 616/271–6770. 1 double room with bath, 2 doubles share bath. Ceiling fans in guest rooms; picnic table, canoe. $85–$115; full breakfast. MC, V. No smoking indoors, no pets.*

Leelanau Country Inn

John and Linda Sisson opened the Leelanau Country Inn in the spring of 1984, placing more of an emphasis on cuisine than on accommodations. The excellent restaurant features a varying menu, drawn from at least 20 appetizers and nearly 50 entrées, ranging from fresh seafood flown in from both coasts to homemade linguine. There's a Continental breakfast, but guests may want to pay a little extra for the elaborate daily brunch, voted "best in the region" by a local magazine.

The inn is across the street from Little Traverse Lake, in the heart of the Leelanau County countryside. The spacious, two-story clapboard house was built in 1891, and an addition was put on four years later. The guest rooms are small but nicely decorated in country style with fresh flowers, plants, quilts, and pine furniture. Request any of the four rooms that are a bit larger than the rest. This is not always the quietest bed-and-breakfast, since you can often hear the restaurant and bar well into the night, but memories of your meals may well make up for it.

▦ *149 E. Harbor Hwy., Maple City, MI 49664, tel. 616/228-5060. 4 single and 2 double rooms share 2 baths. No air-conditioning, off-street parking. $35-$55; Continental breakfast. AE, MC, V. Smoking in restaurant only, no pets, open weekends only Nov.-Apr., closed Mar.*

Neahtawanta Inn

In the early 1980s the Neahtawanta Inn started to establish itself as a center for peace research and now houses the nonprofit Neahtawanta Research and Education Center, focusing on "peace, community, sustainable use of resources, and personal-growth issues." Innkeepers Sally Van Vleck and Bob Russell maintain a healthy, informal, and quiet environment for the inn's guests. Sally leads a weekly yoga class, where guests are welcome.

The three-story inn was built around the turn-of-the-century as a summer hotel called the Sunrise Inn. Antique beds and dressers from the hotel's early days are still used to furnish the guest rooms, and original washbasins with marble counters are found in two of the rooms. The common area on the first floor is open and airy but almost cluttered with books, newspapers, magazines, and tapes. The room's centerpiece is a sunken fieldstone fireplace.

The inn sits on a bluff overlooking Bowers Harbor on Old Mission Peninsula, about 12 miles north of Traverse City. Lush woods add to its natural, peaceful appeal.

▦ *1308 Neahtawanta Rd., Traverse City, MI 49684, tel. 616/223-7315. 4 double rooms share bath, 1 double room with bath. No air-conditioning, sauna, private beach. $70-$120; Continental breakfast. MC, V. No smoking, inquire about pets.*

Old Mill Pond Inn

Michigander David Chrobak has spent his winters running a florist business in the Virgin Islands for more than 20 years, but in the summers, this eccentric innkeeper heads back north to live in and operate the Old Mill Pond Inn. Built in 1895, the three-story wooden house is tucked away in a beautiful setting and accented by gardens galore, all of them designed by David. The biggest is the side garden, which displays several larger-than-life statues. There is also a thriving rose garden.

An usual collection of David's treasures makes up the interior decor. In one room you might find Marilyn Monroe memorabilia mingled with fine crystal; in another, South American tapestries hang next to original 20th-century masterpieces. Even the guest rooms have a relaxed personality all their own. Since David believes that most guests seldom use dressers, he has replaced them with comfortable chairs to give each room a cozy sitting area.

David, an excellent cook, serves a wide variety of food: vegetable quiche, eggs with herbs and mushrooms, crepes, and fresh fruit.

▦ *202 W. 3rd St., Northport, MI 49670, tel. 616/386-7341. 5 double rooms share 2½ baths. No air-conditioning, bicycles. $70-$90; full breakfast. MC, V. No pets, closed Nov.-May.*

Omena Shores Bed and Breakfast

Omena is one of the many quaint, sleepy villages that dot Northern Michigan's picturesque Leelanau County, and it just seems to attract special people. Tim Allen, the star of television's popular comedy *Home Improvement* recently purchased a large parcel of land there, and over 100 years ago, the noted Reverend Peter Dougherty came to establish the area's first Presbyterian Church near the shores of Omena Bay. Now, Mary Helen and Charlie Phillips—who, fans state, are truly special when it comes to gracious hospitality—have moved back to Omena for a third time to the renovated barn that was once part of that church's parsonage.

A warm complement to the careful renovation (which has nicely kept the barn's batten siding and hand-hewn beams intact) are Mary Helen's colorful, handmade quilts; they are everywhere—on the walls, over tables, and covering guest beds. A large outdoor deck overlooks the garden, expansive lawn, and shimmering Omena Bay.

The living room is smartly furnished with wing-back chairs and an overstuffed couch and love seat. Hummel figurines, family photos, and a menagerie of reading material round out this downstairs common area. Upstairs, the large Gathering Room is filled with games, books, menus from area restaurants, and unique collections—including birdhouses and antique toys—which all mingle together in a classy blend of country folk art and antiques.

A pencil-post bed adorned in a blue-and-crimson quilt is the focal point of the Colonial Room, which is accented with country samplers, an antique cabinet and dresser, and kerosene lamps. The more whimsical Teddy Bear Room, although smaller, is great for families with children who are sure to be delighted by the dozens of bears of varying shapes, sizes, and personalities. The Bridal Room on the main floor is uniquely sentimental with an array of wedding photos next to the large picture window and an early 1900s wedding dress hanging in the corner.

Hearty breakfasts are served on the Phillips's colorful collection of

Fiestaware and often include Mary Helen's signature dish—spinach pie—as well as cherry pecan sausage, a fresh fruit cup, and a selection of homemade muffins and breads. A silver tray of coffee and tea is left early each morning outside every guest room, and a winter evening is often warmed by hot cider and popcorn.

🏨 *13140 Isthmus Rd. (Box 154), Omena, MI 49674, tel. 616/386–7313. 3 double rooms with baths, 1 double shares bath. Ceiling fans in rooms, TV and VCR in living room, terry-cloth robes, croquet set outdoors. $70–$95; full breakfast. No credit cards. No smoking indoors, no pets, 2-night minimum weekends May–Oct.*

Open Windows Bed & Breakfast

When an antique sampler in one of the guest rooms reads, "Give to the world the best you have, and the best will come back to you," and antique wooden alphabet blocks strategically placed along a stairway ledge spell out, "Have a great day," pleasant hospitality is sure to follow. And here, at the Open Windows, it certainly does. Although there aren't really any vast open windows to speak of (as the name might imply), the ambience and quaint setting—apart from the other neighboring homes on a small hill, the B&B is surrounded by a white picket fence and overlooks the charming village of Suttons Bay and its harbor—gives this in-town B&B a relaxed, country feel that is quite appealing.

That appeal caught the attention of owners Don and Norma Blumenschine when they visited the B&B as guests several years ago. Shortly after that, in 1994, they decided to buy it and relocate from Toledo, Ohio, their home of 35 years.

The Blumenschines are a talented pair; Norma's culinary skills are recognized in the area, and she has conducted B&B cooking classes at the local college as well as hosted gourmet weekends. After relaxing in the Adirondack chairs on the porch, it's nice to discover they are custom made by Don, and he is more than happy to take custom orders for his handcrafted deck furniture.

Breakfast includes coffee cakes, stuffed French toast, fresh fruits from nearby orchards, and homemade jams and jellies, which along with Norma's special vinegars are available for purchase under the Open Windows label.

The three guest rooms are all upstairs and share a second floor common area, although guests are also welcome to enjoy the downstairs living room and dining area. The Rose Garden Room features a brass bed, a rose-covered Oriental rug, and a small sitting area. The largest room is Helen's Room, which is charmingly decorated with white wicker furniture, rich blue carpet, and country-style tab curtains. The Sunshine Room lives up to its name with yellow and white gingham, an antique white brass bed, and a marble-top dressing table.

Open Windows' downtown location also puts guests within easy walking distance of Suttons Bay's unique shops, galleries, and restaurants.

▥ *613 St. Mary's Ave. (Box 698), Suttons Bay, MI 49682, tel. 616/271–4300 or 800/520–3722. 3 double rooms with baths. Air-conditioning in Rose Garden Room, ceiling fans in the others, TV and VCR in common room, croquet set. $75–$105; full breakfast. No credit cards. No smoking indoors, no pets, 2-night minimum holidays and weekends May–Oct.*

Snowbird Inn

Everything about the Snowbird Inn is eclectic and romantic—the history, the decor, even the setting. The inn is shaded by ancient black walnut trees and situated on 18 acres consisting of both woods and open meadows, a secluded pond, private access to Lake Michigan, a working cherry orchard, and colorful flower gardens.

The entire estate first operated as a dairy farm in 1885, and the original outbuildings and barn still surround the farmhouse, which was built in 1917. Guests can explore a colorful piece of history by walking to a neighboring cottage used as a hideaway in the late 1920s by infamous gangster Scarface Al Capone; the 30-foot gun tower manned by his sentries also still stands.

Over the last five years, it is innkeepers Martha Sintz and Joe Psenka's penchant for the eclectic that has helped created the charm inherent in this country retreat. Guests enjoy browsing the unique collections displayed in the living and dining room areas, ranging from hatboxes, dolls, and oil lamps to candles, dishes, and folk art. A grapevine tree bathed in white lights stands in an upper hallway window overlooking the front wraparound porch and operates year-round as a festive nightlight.

The library adjacent to the living room is a book lover's dream—floor-to-ceiling bookshelves are literally overflowing with everything from Joseph Wambaugh thrillers and historical biographies to popular paperbacks, physics textbooks, and coffee-table art books. A cabinet next to the overstuffed couch is filled with an array of jigsaw puzzles and games, including a cute wooden cow and milk-can tic-tactoe board, reminiscent of the inn's earlier days. Guests are also welcome to enjoy music from the owners' collection of over 300 compact discs.

Touted as Leelanau's "Grand Lady," it's not surprising that the Inn's four guest rooms are named after different women in the family and comfortably decorated in an array of flowered wall-paper, pinstriped curtains, and checkered comforters. In Thelma's Room—named after Joe's mother—the bird's-eye maple headboard and dresser are accented by a delightful custom-painted mirror and table, courtesy of Joe's daughter.

Martha's desire to "feed people well and make them feel comfortable" is augmented by her hearty breakfasts, which may include corned beef hash, egg casseroles, homemade bread, and fresh fruit.

🏠 *473 N. Manitou Trail W (Box 1124), Leland, MI 49654, tel. 616/256-9773, fax 616/256-7068. 2 doubles with bath, 2 doubles share 1½ baths. No air-conditioning, fireplace in dining room, ceiling fans in all rooms. $85–$125; full breakfast. No credit cards. Smoking on porch only, no pets, 2-night minimum weekends Memorial Day–Oct.*

The Victoriana 1898

Although the name dates this gracious Victorian home, innkeepers Flo and Bob Schermerhorn provide the intimate elegance. Before opening the B&B in 1987, they enjoyed, as Flo describes it, "people professions"—she was a teacher and he a hospital administrator. Their love of people carries through in their hospitality and lively conversations at breakfast—a big affair offering anything from Flo's Norwegian pastries to waffles with strawberry-rhubarb sauce.

The house, which sits in a historic neighborhood just two blocks from downtown and public beaches, displays its magnificent craftsmanship with two ceramic-tile fireplaces, an oak staircase, and original fretwork throughout. The parlor and library are furnished with an eclectic mix of antiques and family heirlooms, including a framed wreath made with pieces of hair from members of Flo's family. A functional 1912 Seybold Pipe Organ, salvaged from a Catholic Mission Church, sits in the library. An artesian well, drilled in 1898, is still flowing in the back of the house; the gazebo was originally the bell tower for the area's first high school.

🏠 *622 Washington St., Traverse City, MI 49684, tel. 616/929-1009. 2 double rooms with baths, 1 suite. Air-conditioning, fireplace in parlor. $60–$80; full breakfast, evening refreshments. MC, V. Smoking on porch only, no pets.*

Little Traverse Bay Region

*About five hours north of Detroit and seven hours from
Chicago lies the small but lively area around Little Traverse
Bay. The two-lane highway running through the region (U.S.
31) winds along the rugged Lake Michigan shoreline,
providing constant glimpses of the water. The towns of
Charlevoix, Petoskey, and Harbor Springs dominate the area,
largely made up of rolling terrain, picturesque farms and
orchards, numerous inland lakes, and sleepy summer-resort
towns with names like Walloon Lake and Boyne City.*

*The region has had a varied history. Since the late 1800s, it has
served as a lumbering mecca, as an escape from law and order
for the likes of Al Capone, and as a playground for elite
families from Chicago and Detroit. Ernest Hemingway spent
most of his childhood summers at a family home on Walloon
Lake and in the small town of Horton Bay, which provided the
background for some of his early short stories, most notably
the Nick Adams stories and "Up in Michigan."*

*Today the region has evolved into one of northern Michigan's
finest resort areas. Visitors enjoy beaches, golf, and culture
galore during the summer months, and crackling fireplaces,
magical winter landscapes, and some of the Midwest's best
alpine and Nordic skiing in the winter. Nearby ski areas
include Boyne Highlands, Schuss Mountain–Shanty Creek
Resort, Nubs Nob, and Boyne Mountain. A variety of annual
festivals and art fairs are held throughout the year as well.*

*From Memorial Day weekend through Labor Day, the area is
crowded with tourists from all over the country and around
the world. Art galleries and exclusive shops mix comfortably
with the delights of small-town Americana: Petoskey's
concerts in the park; Charlevoix's colorful Petunia Mile, a
stretch of Main Street lined with flowers planted by residents
each spring; and evening strolls in town parks and along
beaches. Harbor Springs, often referred to as the "Newport of*

the Midwest," boasts a deep natural harbor and attracts a world-class boating community as well as a growing colony of artists.

Places to Go, Sights to See

The **Bay View Association,** founded by the Methodist Church in 1875, is a well-preserved summer community occupying 400 acres just north of Petoskey. Beautiful turn-of-the-century cottages are part of this historical landmark where resort life is still enjoyed. Excellent cultural and musical programs abound during the summer months and are open to the public; a full schedule is available at the Petoskey Chamber of Commerce (tel. 616/347–4150).

Beaver Island, settled by descendants of Irish fishermen, is a rustic island with 400 year-round residents. Its claim to fame is its former status as a kingdom. Mormon leader King James Jesse Strang broke away from the church in the 1850s and took some 2,000 followers with him to the island. He was later assassinated by one of his own dissatisfied followers. For information on the two-hour ferry ride from Charlevoix, contact Beaver Island Boat Company (tel. 616/547–2311).

The **Earl Young Houses** were designed and built by the Charlevoix real-estate agent and self-taught architect. These eccentric homes, made of natural stone and cedar shakes, have an almost magical look. Their mushroom cap–shaped roofs, low ceilings, and tiny doorways belie conventional construction methods and make them look like houses for gnomes. Most are now privately owned. You can obtain a map showing their location from the Chamber of Commerce (tel. 616/547–2101).

The **Gaslight District,** named after the gaslights lining the streets of Petoskey's renovated downtown, has more than 75 distinctive shops and art galleries, most of them open year-round.

Little Traverse Historical Museum (100 Depot Ct., Petoskey, tel. 616/347–2620) occupies the now-defunct 1892 Chicago and West Michigan Railroad depot. Converted into a delightful museum, it features 100-year-old handcrafted Ottawa quill boxes, a passenger-pigeon display, and information on Ernest Hemingway's ties to the region. It is open from May to November.

Petoskey Stones are pieces of fossilized coral that are millions of years old and now look like greenish gray stones. Their distinctive designs can be seen only when held underwater. You can buy these popular stones in stores or search for them along the beach, which can be the most satisfying way to obtain this souvenir unique to northern Michigan.

Thorn Swift Nature Preserve and Beach (Rte. 119, just north of Harbor Springs, tel. 616/526–6401) is 30 acres of beach, dunes, and fragrant cedar swamp offering hiking trails and panoramic views of Little Traverse Bay. Naturalistrangers give guided tours from Memorial Day through October, but you can call ahead for permission to enter during the rest of the year.

Beaches

Visitors will discover many beautiful beaches along this stretch of Lake Michigan and Little Traverse Bay. Two state parks, **Petoskey State Park** (Rte. 119, 1½ mi north of U.S. 31, tel. 616/347–2311) and **Fisherman Island State Park** (U.S. 31, outside Charlevoix), offer larger beaches and rugged shoreline. Smaller downtown beaches include **Michigan Avenue** and **Lake Michigan beaches** (off Grant St., Charlevoix); **Pennsylvania Park** (off U.S. 31, Petoskey), complete with an old-fashioned band shell used throughout the summer for free concerts; and **Zorn** and **Ford parks** (1 block east of Main St., Harbor Springs). These town beaches offer calmer water in protected bays and may provide picnic areas and playgrounds. A drive through neighboring Antrim County will reveal the small public beaches and boat launches of northern Michigan's pristine **Chain of Lakes** (including Torch Lake). It encompasses 163 miles of shoreline and includes a 65-mile inland waterway.

Restaurants

In the town of Ellsworth, about 10 miles southeast of Charlevoix, are two of Michigan's finest restaurants: the **Rowe Inn** (603 E. Jordan Rd., tel. 616/588–7351) and **Tapawingo** (9502 Lake St., tel. 616/588–7971). They are recognized nationally for their gourmet regional cuisine and use of such local delectables as whitefish and morel mushrooms. At the **Arboretum** (7075 S. Lakeside Dr., tel. 616/526–6291), in Harbor Springs, you can enjoy good steaks, chops, and seafood—and get your car washed at the same time. In Charlevoix, **Juillerett's** (131 8th St., tel. 616/526–2821) is known for its whitefish dinners, and **Stafford's Pier** (102 Bay St., tel. 616/526–6201), overlooking Little Traverse Bay in Harbor Springs, offers elegant Continental cuisine. Charlevoix's **Great Lakes Whitefish Company** (411 Bridge St., tel. 616/547–4374) serves Michigan's most popular catch in classic fish-and-chips style, while **Willie's Up North** (1273 S. Advance Rd., tel. 616/536–2666), 2 miles north of East Jordan, may have the best barbecued ribs in the region.

Tourist Information

Boyne Country Convention and Visitor Bureau (Box 694, Petoskey, MI 49770, tel. 800/845–2828); **Charlevoix Area Chamber of Commerce** (408 Bridge St., Charlevoix, MI 49720, tel. 616/547–2101); **Michigan Travel Bureau** (333 S. Capitol, Lansing, MI 48933, tel. 800/543–2937); **Petoskey Regional Chamber of Commerce** (Main St., Petoskey, MI 49770, tel. 616/347–4150).

Belvedere Inn

After 22 years of marriage, Tim and Karen Watters felt the time was right to act on what began as Karen's dream—to own an inn on the west shore of Michigan. Following a two-year search, they discovered this stately Victorian home, built in 1887 as a "cottage" in Charlevoix's elite summer colony; later it was operated as a hotel and then a boarding house. In three months the couple completely restored the house—adding everything from porcelain faucets and dual showerheads to new tile, carpet, and Victorian furniture—before opening in March 1994. They have more plans for the interior as well as outside, where they have started a multitiered flower garden and added a picnic area.

Their love of antiques is evident throughout the house. The upright grand piano in the parlor belonged to Tim's great-grandmother, and Karen's grandmother received the curved mahogany shelf, now holding brochures of area attractions and restaurant menus, as payment for cleaning rooms when she was 16 years old. A dining-room shelf sparkles with an eclectic collection of crystal and glassware that Karen purchased at auctions over the years. Tim laughingly explains, "I kept asking Karen why she was always buying this stuff, but now I realize that she had a plan."

Romantics will enjoy the king-size canopy bed in the Spring Room; it is completely surrounded by a floor-to-ceiling white lace curtain. One guest delightedly recalled, "It was like waking up in a cloud." Bathrooms for guests in the Spring and Autumn rooms are off the hallway, but bathrobes have been thoughtfully provided. The Rose Room has twin beds and is on the main floor. The noisiest room is probably the Winter Room; it faces the street and the Grey Gables Inn, a restaurant next door (where Belvedere Inn guests receive a special discount). The efficiency apartment boasts a private entrance and full kitchen, but it is the only area not decorated in the crisp, fresh style of the rest of the house.

Guests are served a complete breakfast that includes such specialties of Karen's as praline- or blueberry-stuffed French toast and sausage, or a strata of baked egg, ham, and cheese. An extra treat is the homemade dessert—which could be anything from cherry pie to strawberry shortcake to warm peanut butter cookies—served each evening in the parlor or living room, or on warm nights, on the spacious front porch.

306 Belvedere Ave., Charlevoix, MI 49720, tel. 616/547–2251 or 800/ 280–4667. 5 double rooms with baths, 1 suite, 1 efficiency. No air-conditioning, cable TV and fireplace in parlor, ceiling fans in rooms. $60–$115; full breakfast. MC, V. Smoking on porch only, no pets.

The Benson House

As a former Chamber of Commerce executive transplanted from downstate, Rod Benson knows how to make people comfortable; he and his charming wife, Carol, make an unbeatable team when it comes to hosting a bed-and-breakfast. The Bensons go out of their way to help you enjoy your stay by providing area restaurant menus, a travel planner, and chocolates in each guest room.

Set in a quiet, tree-filled neighborhood in Petoskey, the Benson House has an enviable location. As the locals tell it, when it opened in 1879 as the Ozark Hotel, people were aghast that anyone would put such an establishment so far from downtown. Nowadays, however, guests are only a few blocks' walk from the shopping and entertainment of the Gaslight District and minutes by car from first-class golf and skiing, but they still feel—what bliss!—miles away.

The two-story wood-frame house has been thoroughly renovated to provide modern amenities while still retaining elements of its Victorian history: high ceilings, wood moldings, pocket doors, old gas fixtures, floral prints, hardwood floors, and area rugs. The spacious guest rooms have individual themes, from the cathedral ceiling, dark wood, and fruitwood four-poster bed of the Grand Master Suite to the white wicker and original wooden water closet in the bathroom of the Wicker Room.

Adjacent to the large living room is a game room, complete with an elegant parquet floor, entertainment center, backgammon and cribbage boards, puzzles, books, and a cozy couch, where the Bensons say they often discover guests relaxing and taking a short nap.

The most popular gathering spot is the 80-foot veranda, which wraps around two sides of the house and overlooks Little Traverse Bay. Furnished with white wicker and ablaze with colorful hanging plants, it is the perfect place to enjoy Carol's hearty breakfasts during the warmer months. Her menu varies and includes a shrimp quiche she calls Neptune's Delight, Irish Cream bread, and sticky-bun French toast. And, after a long day of shopping or recreation, you can return to the veranda, where the Bensons' afternoon hors d'oeuvres quell those hunger pangs and make you feel at home once again.

🏠 *618 E. Lake St., Petoskey, MI 49770, tel. 616/347–1338. 4 double rooms with baths. No air-conditioning, fireplace in living room, turndown service with chocolates. $89–$125; full breakfast. MC, V. No smoking indoors, no pets, 2-night minimum weekends, 3-night minimum holidays.*

House on the Hill

As part of their early retirement plan, lifelong Texans Buster and Julie Arnim considered opening an art gallery in the Southwest, but after a tour of New England bed-and-breakfasts, they decided to open their own. Selling their Houston suitcase business in 1984, the Arnims moved north to see the turn-of-the-century farmhouse they had purchased, sight unseen, after an eight-state hunt for the perfect rural setting. A real-estate ad stated it was "near a gourmet restaurant"; Julie was convinced their B&B would be a success if good food was at hand. Indeed, two of northern Michigan's finest restaurants, Tapawingo and the Rowe Inn, are within two blocks.

After some hard work during the renovation process, the Arnims have made their House on the Hill a successful and elegant B&B. The carefully restored gray-and-white Victorian (including an addition used as their private quarters) sits on a hill near the little village of Ellsworth, overlooking 53 acres of countryside and the St. Clair Lake. Guests are free to hike or ski cross-country around the property and even borrow the boat docked at the lake. A spacious veranda wraps around the house and is filled with white wicker furniture and rocking chairs.

Inside, a curved staircase leads to the guest rooms upstairs. They are all spacious, immaculate, and pleasantly decorated. Each has its own thermostat, fresh flowers, candy, ice water, and bedside lights. A favorite is the Pine Room, with its cathedral ceiling, custom-built four-poster bed draped in white lace, and peaceful view of the woods behind the house. Antiques and such touches as a 200-year-old hand-carved ebony Oriental desk, Julie's rose-colored glass collection, and Japanese-style porcelain could make you nervous about kicking back and really relaxing, but the Arnims make you feel at home with a perfect blend of friendliness and reserve.

Julie and Buster serve a marvelous hearty breakfast on their large oak table, complete with fine china and silver. A culinary whiz, Julie rotates 65 different breakfast menus; for early risers, she puts out a basket filled with home-baked muffins, juice, and coffee, which goes beyond yum to yum-yum.

9661 Lake St. (Box 206), Ellsworth, MI 49729, tel. 616/588–6304. 7 double rooms with baths. No air-conditioning, cable TV in parlor, ceiling fans in rooms. $115–$125; full breakfast. MC, V. Smoking on porch only, no pets.

Kimberly Country Estate

The Greek Revival architecture and the gracious hospitality of the Kimberly Country Estate recall the genteel era of the Old South, but the interior is an elegant, gracious re-creation of an English country estate. Regardless of either impression, it's a treat to discover this 8,000-square-foot house in the heart of northern Michigan.

Owners Billie and Ronn Serba spent more than a year carefully remodeling this 30-year-old home in an effort to enhance its architecture while adding some modern conveniences. They put in new fireplaces, an updated kitchen, recessed lighting, and traditional mullion-style windows to take the place of the modern casements. In the living room, they replaced the sliding glass doors leading to the terrace with more graceful French doors. This attention to detail is evident throughout the house.

The Serbas moved from the Detroit area to Harbor Springs in the early 1980s, after owning a flower shop as well as restoring and decorating three homes together. Once in Harbor Springs, they first opened the shop Kimberly's Nest; the bed-and-breakfast followed in 1989. Throughout their 40-year marriage, they have been avid antiques collectors, acquiring such treasures as a Dutch pin armoire, a cast-iron chandelier, four-poster beds, and numerous chairs and accessories.

Floral chintz mixed with stripes and plaids creates a warm, romantic look, as do the fresh flowers, overstuffed sofas and chairs, Oriental rugs, and Battenburg lace bedspreads in the guest rooms. The B&B has become a very popular place for weddings; the entire house is often rented out on these occasions (or for the occasional executive retreat).

All the guest rooms are very spacious. The two largest rooms are the Lexington, with a fireplace, sitting area, and separate study, and the Verandah, which opens to a private terrace and has a fireplace and whirlpool bath. Guests are free to use the main-floor library; with its North Carolina black walnut paneling, fireplace, English-style armchairs, and paisley fabric–covered ceiling, it has the feeling of an old club—an old club founded on the grounds of a stately southern plantation.

▦ *2287 Bester Rd., Harbor Springs, MI 49740, tel. 616/526–7646. 5 double rooms with baths, 1 suite. No air-conditioning, baby grand piano in living room, swimming pool. $135–$250; Continental breakfast, afternoon tea. MC, V. No smoking, no pets, 2-night minimum weekends, 3-night minimum holidays, closed Apr.*

Stafford's Bay View Inn

It's hard to miss Stafford's Bay View Inn, set just off the main road running through Petoskey's historic Bay View District. A popular dining spot for both tourists and residents as well as a bustling inn, the imposing three-story Victorian was built in 1886; it served as lodging for summer visitors coming north via the now-defunct railroad to enjoy Bay View's cultural programs.

Owners Stafford and Janice Smith met and fell in love while working at the inn for the previous owner. They purchased it during the early 1960s and have now been joined in running the inn by their son and daughter-in-law, Reg and Lori, who are the day-to-day innkeepers. Over time, they have redecorated and added onto the inn—including five new suites—while retaining its comfortable charm. Furnishings in the second- and third-floor guest rooms include canopy and four-poster beds, richly colored wallpapers, antique dressers, wicker furniture, and such details as handmade eyelet and ribbon pillows.

The Smiths renovated the third floor in 1987, including adding a sitting room. Ever mindful of maintaining the house as a haven for young families, they provided this room so parents could enjoy stepping out without venturing too far from sleeping young ones. Children can often be seen happily romping in the first-floor common areas while parents finish their meal at a leisurely pace.

What the Bay View Inn may sometimes lack in quiet, it makes up for in its delicious food and the unending hospitality of its hosts. Open and airy, the main dining room is decorated with chandeliers, draped tables with fanback chairs, fresh flowers and plants, and white lattice dividers between booths. Sometimes it may feel as though the restaurant crowd has taken over the inn, but a trip to the third floor or a stroll down to the water offers a good escape for overnight guests. The menus include such specialties as steaming bread pudding with raisins and cream. A splendid buffet awaits guests for Sunday brunch; selections may include ham, turkey, whitefish, chicken, biscuits, and scrumptious desserts. Although the inn does not serve alcoholic beverages, guests are invited to bring their own wine to dinner.

🏨 *613 Woodland Ave., U.S. 31, Petoskey, MI 49770, tel. 616/347–2771 or 800/456–1917. 17 double rooms with baths, 14 suites. Air-conditioning, cable TV in sunroom and library, gas fireplace and whirlpool bath in 5 suites. $79–$195; full breakfast. AE, MC, V. No smoking in 3rd-floor guest rooms, no pets.*

Bear River Valley

Russ and Sandra Barkman, avid bicyclists and cross-country skiers, moved north a few years ago and created a marvelous, year-round rustic retreat. Sandra used to manage the VIP Guest House at the University of Michigan, and her experience contributes to the relaxed aura at Bear River Valley. Sitting on 2 acres of natural woodlands south of Petoskey, the contemporary cedar-sided home is nestled among birches, maples, and pines. Skiing and boating are just minutes away, and the country roads are perfect for cycling.

Porches and decks surround three sides of the home. The open living room has vaulted ceilings, lots of windows, and a fireplace, ideal for the Barkmans' cozy après-ski refreshments. Guest rooms are not large, but they are clean and comfortably decorated in a Scandinavian country motif. A wood-fired Finnish sauna will relax you instantly.

Freshly squeezed juices and wholegrain cereals are standard breakfast fare, but Sandra's signature recipe is wild blackberry oatmeal muffins.

🏠 *03636 Bear River Rd., Petoskey, MI 49770, tel. 616/348-2046. 3 double rooms share 2 baths. No air-conditioning, TV and VCR in common room, terry-cloth robes. $60–$75; Continental breakfast. No credit cards. No smoking, no pets, 2-night minimum weekends.*

The Bridge Street Inn

Although just a block from downtown on Charlevoix's busy main street, this 1895 three-story Colonial Revival house, with a tulip-lined walkway and a wraparound porch, has a cozy, calm air. John and Vera McKown moved from California four years ago to run the inn. John has been in the hotel business for 26 years.

Maple floors and artistic touches—a Renoir reproduction over the living-room fireplace and stained glass in the front window—lend an elegance to the inn. Guest rooms vary, however. Some look worn and in need of refurbishing, while others, like the Bridal Suite and the Garden View Room, offer a pleasant Victorian getaway, complete with four-poster beds, lace curtains, washstands, floral carpets, and, in the case of the Evening Glow Room, a beautiful view of the sunset.

Belgian waffles, homemade strawberry bread, and raspberries from his garden are a few of John's breakfast specialties.

🏠 *113 Michigan Ave., Charlevoix, MI 49720, tel. 616/547-6606, fax 616/547-1812. 3 double rooms with baths, 6 doubles share 3 baths. No air-conditioning, ceiling fans in some rooms, baby grand piano in common area. $65–$115; full breakfast, afternoon and evening refreshments. MC, V. No smoking, no pets, 2-night minimum weekends July–mid-Oct.*

The Gingerbread House

Sisters Mary Gruler and Margaret Perry have avoided making this renovated pink-and-white 1881 Victorian cottage too cute, despite what the name implies. Surrounded by hedge roses, morning glories, and an English garden, the cottage is right in Bay View, enabling guests to take advantage of all its activities.

Inside are spacious rooms like the Country Blues Room, with a hand-painted iron bed and white wicker, and the Classic Rose Room, whose ruffled, rosebud-patterned window seat offers a view of Little Traverse Bay. The Victoria, decorated in the style of an English rose garden with floral fabrics and more wicker, has a sitting area, daybed, and French doors leading to a private balcony. The large dining and sitting area downstairs provides a welcome place for guests to gather, peruse the bookshelves, or enjoy their breakfast.

Mary and Margaret are delightful hostesses who share a marvelous sense of humor and a sincere interest in their guests' well-being but operate with a nice respect for privacy.

▦ *205 Bluff St. (Box 1273), Bay View, MI 49770, tel. 616/347-3538. 3 double rooms with baths, 1 housekeeping double with bath, 1 housekeeping suite. No air-conditioning, private outside entrances to guest rooms. $55–$100; Continental breakfast. MC, V. No smoking, no pets, closed Nov.–Apr.*

Torch Lake Bed & Breakfast

With a full view of—and only a short walk from—Torch Lake (once named one of the world's most beautiful lakes by *National Geographic*), this turn-of-the-century clapboard house has been lovingly restored by its owners, Patti and Jack Findlay.

An oak staircase, handcrafted by a local carpenter, leads to the second-floor guest rooms. The Violet Room has a private bath and overlooks the lake; crisp white linens of lace and eyelet on the brass-and-iron bed make it clean and fresh. Stained-glass windows and Australian sheepskin rugs add to the room's distinct personality.

The parlor, which has lace curtains and bright prints, has a country feel; and the front porch, which of course has a view of the lake, is outfitted with rocking chairs for friendly, Findlay-style relaxation. Patti is an excellent cook; her breakfast specialties include sausage-filled crepes, raisin scones, French toast with pecan-praline syrup, and locally made fruit preserves.

▦ *10601 Coy St., Alden, MI 49612, tel. 616/331-6424. 1 double room with bath, 2 doubles share bath. No air-conditioning, ceiling fan in rooms. $65–$85; full breakfast. No credit cards. No smoking indoors, no pets, closed mid-Sept.–Memorial Day weekend.*

Veranda at Harbor Springs

Owners Doug and Lydia Yoder, from Georgia, brought a bit of their Southern hospitality north when they opened the Veranda in 1995. Window boxes overflowing with colorful blooms and the crisp yellow-and-white exterior first catch your eye, but it is the glass-enclosed veranda—for which this elegant B&B is named—that is truly the focal point. Here guests enjoy a glimpse of Little Traverse Bay while eating breakfast or an afternoon treat of pink lemonade and homemade cookies. Glass-top tables and armchairs upholstered in an array of peach and green florals mingle nicely with white wicker atop the ceramic-tile patio.

Decorated by Lydia in a distinct mix of garden-style fabrics and antique mahogany and oak furniture, each guest room boasts a private balcony and exudes a quiet, refreshing air. A true delight is the front suite, where a Jacuzzi is tucked into the Tudor-style window overlooking the water.

The Veranda's downtown location also puts guests within easy walking distance of Harbor Spring's upscale shops, galleries, and restaurants.

▦ *403 E. Main St., Harbor Springs, MI 48740, tel. 616/526-7782. 4 double rooms with baths, 1 suite. No air-conditioning, TV and phone in rooms, fireplace in sitting room, refrigerator and ice machine for guests. $95–$175; full breakfast. MC, V. Smoking on guest balconies only, no pets.*

Walloon Lake Inn

Some inns are recognized for their ambience or their hosts, and although Walloon Lake Inn is up to snuff in both areas, it is the food that's truly remarkable here.

Innkeeper David Beier is an accomplished chef, and even though a delicious Continental breakfast is included with a guest room, dinner is the most popular meal. Regional specialties include fillet of brook trout smoked on the premises; venison covered with a sauce of prosciutto, Madeira, and thyme; morel sauce over breast of chicken; strawberry-almond duck; and daily veal specials. That's not to mention the desserts, which include homemade ice cream and pastries. A special children's menu makes for perfect family dining.

The cottage-style two-story home was built nearly 100 years ago, and the guest rooms were completely renovated in 1986. They are clean and comfortable, although at times noise from the restaurant can be disruptive. No worry, just head to the common area that overlooks Walloon Lake or down to the dock to dangle your feet in the water.

🏨 *4178 West Rd. (Box 85), Walloon Lake Village, MI 49796, tel. 616/ 535–2999. 5 double rooms with baths. No air-conditioning, restaurant, beach and dock access on lake. $50–$70; Continental breakfast. MC, V. No pets.*

Minnesota

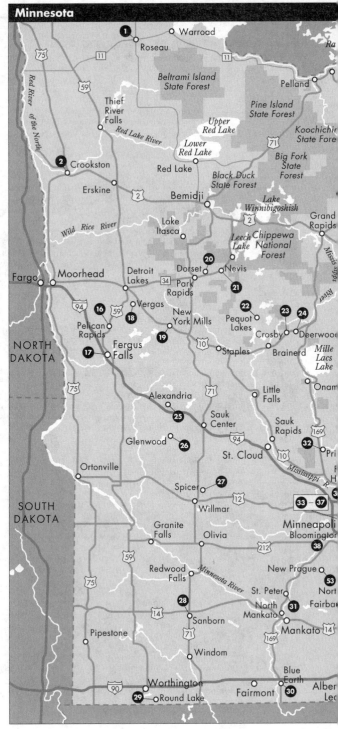

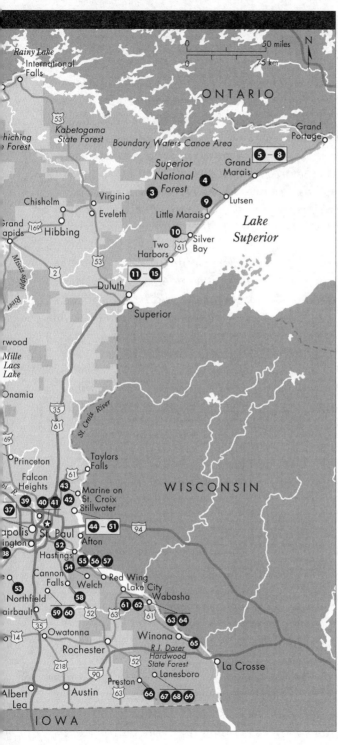

Twin Cities Area

*Hollywood certainly knew what it was doing when it placed
Mary Tyler Moore's fictional television character Mary
Richards in the Twin Cities area. Like Mary, the twin cities of
Minneapolis and St. Paul can still be cosmopolitan while
wearing sensible shoes. A good example of this blend of style
and practicality is the area's clean and efficient mass-transit
system, which includes an extensive network of climate-
controlled glass skyways that allow citizens to spend an entire
day downtown without once setting their galoshes outdoors.*

*Minneapolis was formed in 1872 when the lumbering village
of St. Anthony, which sat on the east bank of the Mississippi,
joined hands with a hamlet on the west bank. Its name derives
from a Sioux word for water (minne) and the Greek suffix for
city (polis). St. Paul, on the other hand, had an uproarious
past. The original settlement was called Pig's Eye, the
nickname of a French trader Pierre Parrant, an evil-eyed
villain who sold whiskey to Native Americans. Presumably as
an act of repentance, the name was changed in 1841 to honor a
log chapel dedicated to St. Paul.*

*Over time, railroad and steamboat traffic transformed St.
Paul into a booming truck, rail, and shipping transportation
center. Meanwhile, flour mills in Minneapolis—such as
General Mills, Pillsbury, and Cargill—grew into giant
corporations, creating a boom in employment. As a result,
hundreds of thousands of immigrants settled in the area in the
19th and early 20th centuries.*

*Like a long-married couple, these geographical partners are
beginning to look more and more alike, although St. Paul is
still considered the more traditional of the two; it's typical of
the cities' differing styles that the flamboyant rock star
formerly known as Prince hails from Minneapolis. The entire
metro area, however, enjoys a rich and varied popular music
scene and has evolved into the cultural center of the Upper
Great Lakes. Besides many thriving music and dance groups,*

the Twin Cities has the Walker Art Center; the St. Paul Chamber Orchestra, the only full-time one of its kind in the country; more than 90 theaters, including the renowned Guthrie Theater; and a large art-gallery district in Minneapolis.

Both communities have masterfully blended the old with the new. State-of-the-art research facilities and glass-walled skyscrapers tastefully coexist with turn-of-the-century neighborhoods and historic commercial districts. Summit Avenue in St. Paul, for instance, has a 5-mile stretch of Victorian homes, including the house where F. Scott Fitzgerald wrote This Side of Paradise.

For a metropolitan area of some 2 million people, the cities remain delightfully small-town in character, due in no small part to the Minneapolis park system, thoughtfully designed by farsighted urban planners of an earlier era. You can stroll or bicycle along the river or a lake just blocks from the center of downtown. Minneapolis alone has 22 lakes and 153 parks, giving it a lush appearance in summer and a romantic Dr. Zhivago–style setting when the snow falls. And the winters here are not nearly as severe as legend and the popular St. Paul Winter Carnival might have you believe. The average daily temperature in February is 26°F, certainly comfortable enough to enjoy the cross-country skiing and ice-skating available right in the cities.

Although it's easy to get around the Twin Cities, it's also easy to get turned around. To the frustration of outsiders, the interlocking grid of highways and streets often appears to be as organized as a bag of spilled pretzels. Blame it on the mighty Mississippi, which not only divides the cities but also cuts through sections of each, including the center of St. Paul. The Big Muddy actually takes several turns, forcing streets to run on the diagonal and baffling unwary tourists hoping to use the river as a north–south compass. Make sure to carry a good street map. Inconvenience aside, generations of locals, from Pig's Eye Parrant to Mary Richards, would undoubtedly

*attest that there is hardly a more pleasant place in which to get
lost.*

Places to Go, Sights to See

Mall of America (I–494 and 24th Ave. S, Bloomington, tel. 612/883–8800), dubbed
the Mega Mall, is the nation's largest shopping and entertainment complex.
Twenty minutes south of downtown Minneapolis, it features over 420 stores,
Knott's Camp Snoopy indoor amusement park, 20 full-service restaurants, and
nine nightclubs. Its newest attraction, Underwater World, is an aquarium
featuring 15,000 fish, as well as sharks and stingrays.

Minneapolis's Parks and Lakes. Minneapolis has an extensive park system,
with bike and walking paths that meander past and along Minnehaha Creek, the
Mississippi River, and six lakes (Cedar Lake, Lake of the Isles, Lake Calhoun,
Lake Harriet, Lake Hiawatha, and Lake Nokomis). At Lake Harriet (W. Lake
Harriet Pkwy., tel. 612/661–4800), be sure to catch a free summer concert at the
band shell, visit the rose garden, take a boat ride, or ride the old streetcar line
between Lake Harriet and Lake Calhoun.

Minnesota State Capitol (Cedar and Aurora Sts., St. Paul, tel. 612/297–3521),
built on a hill overlooking downtown, was designed by renowned St. Paul
architect Cass Gilbert in 1905 and contains more than 25 varieties of marble,
sandstone, limestone, and granite. Near the south entry are cases displaying
Minnesota's two constitutions and artifacts from early statehood years. Take time
to walk around the exceptionally beautiful grounds. Free 45-minute tours are
given daily (weekdays 9–4, Sat. 10–3, and Sun. 1–3).

A half hour south of the Twin Cities, the **Minnesota Zoo** (13000 Zoo Blvd., Apple
Valley, tel. 612/431–9200) was built to resemble the natural habitat of the wild
animals that reside there. The zoo contains some 2,300 animals and more than
2,000 plant varieties. Other features include a zoo lab, bird and animal shows,
pony rides in summer, and daily films and slide shows. Among the amenities are
eating facilities, picnic areas, rest areas, and stroller rentals.

Mississippi River Cruises (Padelford Packet Boat Co., tel. 612/227–1100). Daily
sightseeing tours, Sunday brunch, and weekday and weekend dinner tours of the
Mississippi from both St. Paul and Minneapolis are offered aboard the *Anson
Northrup, Betsey Northrup, Josiah Snelling, Jonathan Padelford,* and *Harriet
Bishop,* modern paddle wheelers modeled after 19th-century Mississippi
riverboats. Excursions last 1½ hours and leave from Harriet Island, St. Paul, or
Boom Island Park, Minneapolis.

Riverplace (43 Main St. SE, tel. 612/378–1969) and **St. Anthony Main** (125 Main
St. SE, tel. 612/378–1226), neighbors on the historic east bank of the Mississippi,
are complexes with horse-drawn carriage rides, movies, waterfront restaurants,
and cafés. Two excellent walking paths, the Mississippi Mile and St. Anthony
Falls Heritage Trail, detail many historical highlights, including an 1883 Stone

Arch Bridge built by railroad magnate James J. Hill. This area is especially popular in the summer months.

Summit Avenue, long one of St. Paul's most prestigious addresses, runs 4½ miles from the Cathedral of St. Paul, built in 1915, to the Mississippi and is home to the nation's longest row of intact residential Victorian architecture. F. Scott Fitzgerald lived at number 599 in 1918 while writing *This Side of Paradise.* Mount Zion Temple, home of the oldest Jewish congregation in Minnesota (founded in 1856), is at number 1300. Number 240 is the James J. Hill House (tel. 612/297–2555), the 19th-century mansion home of the famous railroad baron; tours include a visit to a skylit art gallery with changing exhibits. On Saturdays from June through September, a 90-minute guided walking tour is also offered, which details the history and architecture of the Summit Avenue District.

Walker Art Center (725 Vineland Pl., Minneapolis, tel. 612/375–7600) was founded in 1879 by Thomas Barlow Walker and was established at its current location in 1927. It has been described by the *New York Times* as "one of the best contemporary art exhibition facilities in the world." The permanent collections are strong on 20th-century American and European art, especially paintings, sculpture, prints, and photography from the past two decades. The center offers regular programs of dance, theater, music, and film. In autumn 1988, the Walker opened the Minneapolis Sculpture Garden, the largest urban sculpture garden in the nation. The garden contains about 40 works, including Claes Oldenburg's mammoth *Spoonbridge and Cherry* (1987–88)—an icon of the Minneapolis skyline. The adjoining **Guthrie Theater** (tel. 612/347–1111), celebrated for its balanced presentation of both classics and avant-garde productions, offers tours that include dressing rooms, prop rooms, backstage, and other areas. Reservations are not necessary; meet the tour guide at the ticket office in the lobby on Saturday mornings at 10.

Warehouse District (call the MC Gallery, tel. 612/339–1480, for dates and gallery guides). More than a dozen art galleries, cafés, an eclectic range of shops, and avant-garde theater companies are clustered in Minneapolis's three-block Warehouse District, just north of downtown.

Restaurants

Thanks to an influx of immigrants, restaurants in Minneapolis and St. Paul offer a diverse range of cuisines—including Thai, Vietnamese, and Sri Lankan—that belie the stereotype of bland Midwestern cooking.

In Minneapolis, the bohemian **Loring Cafe** (1624 Harmon Pl., tel. 612/332–1617), which overlooks Loring Park, is near the Guthrie Theater and Walker Art Center on the edge of downtown Minneapolis. It features pastas and fish with creative sauces, and salads; in the summer, you can relax and dine on an unusual alley patio accompanied by the sounds of a saxophone player. The **Nicollet Island Inn** (95 Merriam St., tel. 612/331–1800), with large windows overlooking the Mississippi River, specializes in regional cuisine that uses such local produce as walleyed pike and wild rice. The **Black Forest Inn** (1 E. 26th St., tel.

612/872–0812), with its trellised outdoor *biergarten,* is perfect for a relaxing summer dinner. Specializing in German and European cuisine, such as Wiener schnitzel and sauerbraten, the restaurant also offers an appropriately wide selection of German beers.

If you're looking for elegant dining in St. Paul, try the **St. Paul Grill** (350 Market St., tel. 612/224–7455) in the newly restored St. Paul Hotel. For a more casual meal, check out **W. A. Frost & Co.** (374 Selby Ave., tel. 612/224–5715), a restored turn-of-the-century landmark; American-style food is served by the fireplaces or out on a large patio. **Café Latté** (850 Grand Ave., tel. 612/224–5687) is a modern restaurant serving sandwiches, salads, and coffee cafeteria style in the heart of the popular Grand Avenue shopping area. For food with a view, try the **No Wake Cafe** (Pier One, Harriet Island, tel. 612/292–1411) aboard a restored towboat on the Mississippi River.

Tourist Information

Greater Minneapolis Convention and Visitors Association (4000 Multifoods Tower, 33 S. 6th St., Minneapolis, MN 55402, tel. 612/661–4700); **Minneapolis Park and Recreation Board** (200 Grain Exchange, 400 S. 4th St., Minneapolis, MN 55415-1400, tel. 612/661–4800 or 612/661–4875); **Minnesota Office of Tourism** (100 Metro Square, 121 E. 7th Pl., St. Paul, MN 55101-2112, tel. 612/ 296–5029 or 800/657–3700); **St. Paul Convention and Visitors Bureau** (102 Norwest Center, 55 E. 5th St., St. Paul, MN 55101, tel. 612/297–6985).

The Ann Bean House

The Ann Bean House was an eight-unit apartment building when proprietors Victoria and Bruce Brillhart bought it. Converting it to a country inn was a challenge, but they had a lot to work with. Their 1880 Victorian Stick–style house is a graceful one, with many bay windows and towers and turrets of varying heights. The interior is filled with woodwork that reflects Minnesota's lumbering past, including a beautiful carved oak banister and cherry, oak, and walnut parquet flooring in the vestibule. The abundance of large windows makes the house light and airy.

Two of the five bedrooms, the Guest Room and Ann and Albert's Room, measure a luxurious 400 square feet. The Guest Room has a brass sleigh bed, an enormous bay window, and a working fireplace with a carved oak mantel. Ann and Albert's Room has a north-facing bay window, as well as a bath with a tempting whirlpool that fits into the shorter of the building's towers. Cynthia's Room has a whirlpool 6 feet in diameter and a fireplace embedded with teal-colored marble tiles.

Even more impressive, perhaps, is the whimsical pink Tower Room, with a slanted ceiling and a white cast-iron bed. A few stairs up, you'll find a delightful white wicker table for two, perfect for morning coffee or wine in the evening. Up another flight of stairs at the top of the tower is the star attraction—a spacious aerie with windows on four sides offering spectacular views of hilly Stillwater and the St. Croix River. On its way to becoming the most popular room, however, is the newest addition, Jacob's Room, with its carved-mahogany furniture and sunny window seat.

The house's charm is accentuated by the Brillharts' hospitality, especially Victoria's cooking. When you check in, you're offered homemade herb bread, cheeses, and hot artichoke dip, along with a glass of wine. Breakfast is a mélange of four or five of Victoria's fruit-and-yeast breads, fresh fruit, sausage rolls, hot dishes such as eggs Florentine—and some guests just can't wait for a helping of Victoria's homemade ice cream. After breakfast, your hosts can tell you about paddle-boat trips, hot-air ballooning, and antiques hunting in the area.

319 W. Pine St., Stillwater, MN 55082, tel. 612/430–0355 or 800/933–0355. 5 double rooms with baths. Air-conditioning, fireplace in 3 rooms, whirlpool tubs in 4 rooms. $79–$129 weekdays, $99–$159 weekends; full breakfast, afternoon refreshments. AE, D, MC, V. Smoking on porch only, no pets.

Asa Parker House

On a rainy day, the Asa Parker House, in the tiny historic village of Marine on St. Croix, looks like something out of a British TV miniseries. Extensive grounds, elaborate flower gardens, a tennis court, and a gazebo make the setting of this Greek Revival B&B one of the finest in Minnesota. The house, built in 1856 by lumber-industry pioneer Asa Parker, was distinctive enough to tempt owners Connie and Chuck Weiss to venture into the B&B business, with the hope of providing a "romantic respite for people in love."

The public and guest rooms are all airy, bright, and predominately floral. The two downstairs parlors are done in a most attractive pink, with stylish accents of white wicker and chintz. The "receiving" music room has dried-flower wreaths, delicate furniture, and an organ, while the adjacent Gentlemen's Parlor offers plush leather reading chairs and a wooden chessboard.

If you can get past the frills, the guest rooms can be quite lovely—especially those bouquets of fragrant flowers. Truly luxurious is the rose-and-dusty-green Isabella Parker Room, with white wicker furniture, a claw-foot tub, and spectacular river valley views from its corner spot. The Alice O'Brien Suite, tucked under the eaves, has gabled windows, a large bath with a whirlpool tub, and a private deck with white Adirondack chairs and views of the flowering lawns—perfect for a reclusive weekend of romance or solitude. A screened porch downstairs overlooks a rock garden and fountain.

Connie uses the freshest fruits (her husband is in the produce business) to top off her hearty breakfasts, which include such favorites as baked peach pancakes and Grand Marnier French toast. She'll also encourage guests to reserve the screened gazebo for a private afternoon barbecue, or to enjoy a hike in William O'Brien State Park, just down the road. The park has miles of hiking, biking, and cross-country ski paths. There's also a marina a couple of blocks away, where you can rent canoes. But the sweeping views of the St. Croix River are so beautiful—particularly once the leaves begin to fall— that guests may just want to relax on the lawn.

🏠 *17500 St. Croix Trail N, Marine on St. Croix, MN 55047, tel. 612/ 433-5248 or 888/857-9969. 3 double rooms with baths, 1 suite. Air-conditioning, whirlpool bath in suite, stove in 1 bedroom, tennis court, screened gazebo. $99–$159; full breakfast, afternoon refreshments. D, MC, V. No smoking, no pets.*

Covington Inn

On Harriet Island across from downtown St. Paul, this may be the only B&B with a true view of the Mississippi River. In fact, the inn is a towboat on the river itself. Wanting to provide people with an opportunity to experience life on the Mississippi, owners Tom Welna and Ann Reeves opened the No Wake Cafe on the boat in 1987. The success of the restaurant led to renovating the remaining portions of the towboat into an elegant B&B. The result might please even Mark Twain.

Originally named the *Codrington*, the boat's unique engine set the standard for the transport of liquid cargo, still in effect today. However, little remains of its industrial past. Anne and Tom drydocked the boat to restore the hull and gutted the interior before artfully rebuilding it using mostly recycled materials. The result is an elegant yet nautical B&B with pine wainscoting and unusual portholelike wall lamps.

The one common space is a bright salon on the main level of the boat; the salon is also a wine bar open to the public on weekend nights. The salon's furniture is a mixture of antiques and clever touches, such as paddle-wheel ashtrays and boat-shaped cribbage boards. Plush couches and chairs surround a fireplace below a huge clearstory skylight. Guests can also stroll along the many outer decks, weather permitting.

The guest rooms are all creatively designed, with TV/VCRs hidden away in decorative wall cabinets and small—remember, this *is* a boat—but efficient, bathrooms. The two-level Pilot House Suite is the most spectacular. It has a bedroom with a corner fireplace made from hand-painted Portuguese tiles. A short climb up a private narrow staircase leads you to the original pilothouse, now the suite's comfortable sitting room. Completely encircled with windows, it has soft futon sofas and a large brass helm, which once controlled the rudders and engines. From here, or out on a private fir-wood deck, the entire St. Paul skyline can be seen aglow on a starry night. The bright and airy Master's Quarters also has a private deck, a fireplace, and pine and cedar woodwork.

A warm breakfast of fruit, coffee cake, an egg dish, and coffee is served in the salon, or you can have it brought to your room. Ann and Tom want their guests to feel like part of the crew—a boating etiquette manual can be found in each room—but there is no swabbing of the deck to be done here. Guests can just relax and enjoy the views and the gentle swaying of the mighty Mississippi.

🏨 *Pier One, Harriet Island, St. Paul, MN 55107, tel. 612/292–1411. 3 double rooms with baths, 1 suite. Air-conditioning, TV/VCR, phone in rooms, fireplace in 2 rooms. $95–$155 Oct.–Apr., $120–$180 May–Sept.; full breakfast. MC, V. Smoking on decks only, no pets.*

Elephant Walk

Don't be surprised if you are summoned for breakfast at this delightful B&B by a gong—one that is attached no less to a beautiful and elaborately carved teakwood dragon embedded with glass and mica. From that first morning call, you'll know that Rita Graybill's Elephant Walk provides a refreshing alternative to the standard Victorian B&B. On the outside, one sees a stick-style pale-yellow-and-salmon Victorian home, complete with a cozy porch swing on a wraparound porch. One step inside, however, and you could almost believe you've made a detour to the Raffles Hotel in Singapore.

Rita spent 20 years traveling with her husband—he worked for the navy—mostly in Asian countries, and collected hundreds of spectacular and exotic items that now decorate the downstairs and guest rooms. In fact, the B&B's name comes from Rita's realization while unpacking boxes that the majority of her treasures were elephant keepsakes of various sizes and materials. She arranged them tastefully throughout the house, proceeded to add three bathrooms, three fireplaces, and four whirlpool baths, and opened for business in 1993.

Elephants are not the sole decor emphasis. There are other intriguing artifacts to discover, and better yet, there is an interesting story behind each and every one. Each of the bedrooms highlights a different country or region, and all are luxuriously fitted with whirlpool tubs and fireplaces. The Rangoon Room, done in cinnamon-and-gold tones, has mosquito netting over the four-poster teakwood bed, a hand-forged copper sink—formerly a candy kettle from Spain—and ornate Balinese masks. The Raffles Room has a unique whirlpool tub with an ivy trellis; the water trickles into the tub from the surrounding stone wall—reminiscent of a natural hot spring.

Most spectacular is the two-room Cadiz Suite, named for the city in Spain where Columbus set off to discover the new world. The spacious and bright window-lined suite is decorated with centuries-old hand-carved cathedral doors from Cadiz, a double-sided gas fireplace, a whirlpool surrounded by lush plants and hanging orchids, and an Indian rosewood sitting bench, which has hand-carved elephant armrests—of course. The suite leads to a private sundeck overlooking Rita's fish- and lily-filled water gardens.

Topping off this memorable experience are Rita's ample breakfasts and consistent hospitality. This B&B is as elegant as the more traditional Victorian fare but will fill you with dreams of travels to come.

🏠 *801 W. Pine St., Stillwater, MN 55082, tel. 612/430–0359, fax 612/351–9080. 3 double rooms with baths, 1 suite. Air-conditioning, gas fireplace, whirlpool bath, ceiling fan, and radio in rooms. $129–$189; full breakfast. MC, V. Smoking on porch only, no pets.*

Le Blanc House

L e Blanc House is an elegant piece of the 19th century tucked into a modest and modern Minneapolis neighborhood. The 1896 Queen Anne is a striking structure with a delicate lavender exterior. In summer, its banks of petunias and walls of morning glories and nasturtiums are famous in the neighborhood. Add sparkling stained-glass windows and inviting front and back porches—the latter with the traditional swing—and you could be back in the days when the original owner, William Le Blanc, returned home each evening from the grain mills along the Mississippi.

Current owners Barb Zahasky and Bob Shulstad now run the inn full time, and have kept the decor faithful to the inn's period and named the three guest rooms after the daughters of its former owners. Both Zofi's and Amelia's rooms have great views of the city skyline. Zofi's Room, a corner room with a bay window and a private bath—perfect for weekday business travelers—is furnished with a 19th-century high-topped walnut bed and matching marble-top dresser. Marissa's Room, the smallest of the three, is invitingly cozy. It has an antique brass bed, oak furnishings, handmade quilts and linens, and an unusual porthole window. All rooms have colorfully patterned Victorian reproduction wallpaper.

You'll awaken to the aroma of Bob's homemade breakfasts wafting from the dining room. Dishes include "heav-

enly" Belgian waffles, spinach-pistachio quiche, French toast stuffed with jelly and cream cheese, and filled crepes. Barb's sister owns a St. Paul bakery, and many mornings she brings over fresh muffins and pastries.

Le Blanc House is just blocks from the many attractions of the Minneapolis riverfront, where you'll find the restaurants of St. Anthony Main and Riverplace, as well as Boom Island Park, which offers paddle-boat cruises, the River City Trolley, and an extensive riverfront walk. The area is quite culturally diverse, so you'll also find a wide variety of restaurants—Japanese, Italian, Lebanese, and Polish—within walking distance.

🏠 *302 University Ave. NE, Minneapolis, MN 55413, tel. 612/379-2570. 1 double room with bath, 2 doubles share bath. Air-conditioning, TV available, off-street parking. $85–$105; full breakfast. AE, MC, V. Smoking on front porch only, no pets.*

The Rivertown Inn

I n 1882, wealthy Stillwater lumber baron John O'Brien built what is now the elegant Rivertown Inn. In 1987, Chuck and Judy Dougherty were searching for a change. They considered opening a restaurant, but after seeing this imposing Queen Anne Victorian, they realized they had found their calling. Although the mansion was designed as a stylish home for the O'Brien family, the Doughertys thought its wraparound porch and its site—on a hill near the St. Croix River—would be perfect for a B&B. After major renovations—seven bathrooms were added—the Rivertown Inn opened for business.

The downstairs has kept its turn-of-the-century character, with four-wood parquet floors, stained-glass windows, and ball-and-stick wooded archways. There are many impressive antiques, as well as smaller knickknacks reminiscent of the Victorian love for detail. The most notable of the larger furnishings, a matching dining-room table and buffet, came all the way from a castle in England. There is also an ornate Ben Franklin stove, which serves as the centerpiece of the parlor. In the summer, guests can relax in the gazebo or on a screened porch with a wicker swing.

The guest rooms are named after former residents. Julie's Room, done in blues, has a high walnut bed and dresser and once the leaves have fallen, a lovely view of the river.

Faith's Room, in peach and blue, has an enormous black-walnut half-tester bed, a fireplace, and a double whirlpool bath. The rooms on the third floor are smaller, some under dormered eaves, but pleasantly cozy nonetheless. All floors have sitting areas with books, games, and plush reading couches.

Breakfast, either served downstairs or brought up to the rooms, consists of an assortment of homemade pastries, flans, an egg dish, and sometimes even champagne. The Doughertys now also run the Cover Park Manor across town, which offers more modern accommodations.

🏠 *306 Olive St. W, Stillwater, MN 55082, tel. 612/430–2955 or 800/ 562–3632, fax 612/430–0034. 8 double rooms with baths (1 bath is nonadjoining). No air-conditioning, ceiling fan and whirlpool bath in 5 rooms. $69–$169; full breakfast, afternoon wine, hors d'oeuvres. AE, D, MC, V. No smoking, no pets, 2-night minimum fall and holiday weekends.*

The William Sauntry Mansion

The William Sauntry Mansion is a meticulous restoration of an enormous 1890 Queen Anne home. The work done in the parlor—which was re-created down to the wall beading and corner ornaments—was so accurate that a visiting former resident remarked to owners Duane and Martha Hubbs on how well the wallpaper had held up. Some things *are* original: the parquet flooring laid in four woods and the parlor's oil-on-canvas ceiling, as well as light fixtures, fireplaces, and special stained-glass windows.

The Hubbses have restored houses in both Chicago and St. Louis. When they moved to Stillwater in 1988, they found the 25-room mansion converted to apartments and deteriorating. In 1991, after a two-year restoration in which the second floor was stripped down to the studs, they opened it as a bed-and-breakfast.

Aiming to remain true to the period not only in architecture and design, but in mood as well, the Hubbses provide such authentic touches as piano playing in the parlor during the afternoon social hour. The bedrooms, which have large windows and fireplaces, are also done in a Victorian style, with Asian and floral motifs and the richly hued paints favored by 19th-century builders.

Beltram's Room, with its south-facing tower bay window overlooking the gardens, green-tiled fireplace, spoon-carved cherry bedroom set, and private bath, is especially pleasant. For a Japanese ambience, try William's Room, which has crown dentil molding and is papered in an exotic pattern of gold, blue, and rust. Eunice's Room, in rose and blue, has an antique headboard, parquet floor, and a delicate oak fireplace ringed by the original rose-and-cream ceramic tiles. Its private bath, down the hall, has a galvanized-tin tub dating from the 1860s.

Sauntry, an Irish immigrant turned lumber baron, had maverick ideas about home construction: He sent his architects as far as the Alhambra Palace in Spain to gather details. Behind his home he built a recreation facility complete with ballroom, bowling alley, and swimming pool, and connected it to the house with Minnesota's first skywalk. The skywalk is gone, and the building is owned by another family, but Sauntry's spirit lives on in his enormous house.

 626 N. 4th St., Stillwater, MN 55082, tel. 612/430–2653 or 800/ 828–2653. 7 double rooms with baths (2 nonadjoining). No air-conditioning, fireplace, double whirlpool in 4 rooms, bathrobes. $89–$149; full breakfast, early morning coffee, afternoon refreshments. AE, D, DC, MC, V. No smoking, no pets.

The Afton House Inn

This 1867 hotel, just a few miles south of I–94 in the old town of Afton, stands on the edge of the St. Croix River.

The hotel's guest rooms, all rather dark, have a reproduction country look, with print wallpaper, carpeting, pine furniture, bedspreads patterned to look like patchwork quilts, and lots of wood carvings of ducks. Rooms 44, 45, and 46, on the first floor, are the nicest, with pine or cherry four-poster beds, whirlpool baths, gas fireplaces, tiny skylights over the beds, and sliding glass doors leading to small patios.

Hotel owners Gordy and Kathy Jarvis offer dinners and Sunday brunches in the Wheel Room, which is accented by wood carvings from local artists and has a view of the river. The bar, which serves more casual lunches and dinners, specializes in catfish caught in the St. Croix, just out the back door.

▦ *3291 St. Croix Trail S (Box 326), Afton, MN 55001, tel. 612/436–8883, fax 612/436–6859. 15 double rooms with baths, 1 guest cottage with 2 bedrooms. Restaurant, bar, air-conditioning, TV and phone in rooms, gas fireplace in 8 rooms, double whirlpool bath in 10 rooms, private balcony in 4 rooms. $60–$140; Continental breakfast. AE, D, MC, V. No smoking in some bedrooms, no pets.*

Bluff Creek Inn

Just 30 minutes south of the Twin Cities, this impeccable B&B serves as the perfect romantic getaway. While near most of the Twin Cities' major attractions, the Bluff Creek Inn stands amid a nature oasis of pastures, wildlife, and bounteous English gardens. Anne and Gary Delaney bought the quaint inn from a good friend in 1987 and have tended it as if it were a work of art: with great care and dedication.

The property was originally granted to a veteran of the War of 1812, but it wasn't developed until 1854, when Josef and Veronica Vogel emigrated from Germany and built their Prairie-style house using hand-kilned bricks made out of Mississippi River Valley clay and trees milled on the property. In the oldest building in Minnesota still in daily operation, guests will find several fascinating historical artifacts in the dining room, including the original property deed—signed by Abe Lincoln himself.

The downstairs parlor maintains a country-Victorian feel, with cornflower-blue sofas, antiques, and dried-flower arrangements. There are also two appealing porches. The white one has plenty of rocking chairs; the screened-in side porch—originally an old-time summer kitchen—is where, in the summertime, of course, Anne and Gary serve their gourmet four-course breakfast on pleasantly decorated tables for two. They're particularly proud of their java, which they call "the best B&B coffee in the world."

It is difficult to describe the rooms in detail, for they alternate among no fewer than six different seasonal decorating themes. Anne has limited Gary to six, although he would prefer more. In the spring, guests may see a plenitude of stuffed or porcelain bunny rabbits in evidence, while in the wintertime, 134 Christmas trees of varying sizes decorate the house with holiday cheer.

Upstairs, Emma's Room, with hunter-green-and-red accents, has a hand-carved Norwegian pine bed. The Victorian Elizabeth's Room has an exposed-brick wall and richly hued green accents. Perhaps the best room is Hollyhock Cottage, housed in the upper portion of an adjacent barn replica. The floors, walls, and ceiling of this bright L-shaped suite are knotty pine, and dormer eaves enclose a king-size bed. A two-side Italian marble fireplace looks onto the bed as well as onto the gigantic whirlpool tub—with terry-cloth robes provided as a gracious touch.

🏠 *1161 Bluff Creek Dr., Chaska, MN 55318, tel. 612/445-2735 or 800/ 307-0019. 5 double rooms with baths. Air-conditioning, whirlpool bath in 3 rooms, fireplace in 1 room. $75–$130 weekdays, $85–$150 weekends; full breakfast, afternoon wine and hors d'oeuvres. AE, D, MC, V. No smoking, no pets.*

Chatsworth B&B

New owners Neelie Forrester and Casey Peterson, lifelong residents of the Twin Cities, returned to their native St. Paul to purchase this 1902 Victorian home in a quiet area. Previously extensive business travelers, they understand the needs of the weary traveler and aim to create a calming atmosphere for those traveling for pleasure as well as for business—they have a basement sitting-room with a NordicTrack, TV/VCR, and a fax machine and copier available to guests.

The first floor has leaded-glass windows and glowing birch woodwork, with an especially lovely birch buffet in the dining room, and all the oak floors have recently been stripped of carpet and immaculately refinished.

Each of the five guest rooms has a theme. The Victorian Room has an antique carved-walnut dresser and bed and large bay windows with table and chairs in front of them. The corner Scandinavian Room, with pine furniture, is done in soothing roses and blues. The Garden Room—with African knickknacks, beaded curtains, and a modern black-and-peach whirlpool bath—strikes an unusual decorating note but has the advantage of a private deck.

🏠 *984 Ashland Ave., St. Paul, MN 55104, tel. 612/227-4288, fax 612/ 225-8217. 3 double rooms with baths, 2 doubles share bath. Air-conditioning, whirlpool tub in 2 rooms, private deck in 1 room, NordicTrack, exercise bike. $65–$125; Continental breakfast on weekdays; full breakfast on weekends. D, MC, V. No smoking, no pets.*

Elmwood House

Elmwood House was named for the wilderness of elm trees surrounding the property when the house was built in 1887 as the family residence of prominent liturgical architect Henry Wild Jones. Present owner Bob Schlosser grew up in the impressive Normandy-style château, with distinctive circular corner towers and conical roofs. While renovating the house as a gift for his parents, Bob and his wife and co-owner, Barbara, saw its potential as a B&B. In a five-year process, they replaced the exterior with approximately 22,000 hand-pounded cedar fish-scale shingles in cooperation with the National Register of Historic Places—the home was placed on the register in 1976.

The common rooms are sparingly decorated with antique sofas, simple wooden tables, and a baby grand piano. The sunny and large living room has a brick Syrian Arch Inglenook fireplace flanked by oak benches, a lattice-work arch, and a unique bull's-eye glass porthole window—perfect for a cool winter's night of cuddling. In the summer, guests can relax on the front spindle-work porch or take advantage of the walkways and bike paths along Minnehaha Creek, just one block away.

The guest rooms, all done in simple floral motifs, are somewhat generic but provide unique modern amenities. For example, the Grey Room has a large-screen TV/VCR in a separate porch-like sitting room. The blue-and-maroon third-floor suite is suited for groups or families, with a full bed in one room and two twin-size beds in an adjacent bedroom.

📠 *1 E. Elmwood Pl., Minneapolis, MN 55419, tel. 612/822–4558. 2 doubles share 1 bath, 1 suite. Air-conditioning, TV/VCR in rooms, refrigerator, laundry facilities. $55–$85; Continental breakfast. AE, MC, V. Smoking on front porch only, no pets, 2-night minimum weekends June–Aug.*

Evelo's Bed & Breakfast

Opening their inn in 1979 made David and Sheryl Evelo the Twin Cities bed-and-breakfast pioneers. They picked a convenient location and managed to keep the prices reasonable. "We try to be the affordable alternative," says David.

From the screened front porch with white wicker furniture, their 1897 neoclassical Victorian house looks fairly modest. Inside, it's a different story: The first-floor parlor and combined dining room/sunroom are full of distinguished ball-and-stick woodwork, walnut-and-oak parquet floors, a fireplace, lush greenery, and gorgeous art-nouveau glassware and lamps.

The three third-floor guest rooms, accessible by a second stairway, are under the eaves in the former servants' quarters. The cozy rooms have slanted ceilings, 1940s chenille bedspreads, and painted wood floors with rag rugs.

As testimony to the Evelo's comfortable atmosphere, many visitors are repeat or long-term guests.

📠 *2301 Bryant Ave. S, Minneapolis, MN 55405, tel. 612/374–9656. 3 double rooms share bath. Clock radio in rooms, refrigerator, coffeemaker, and phone on 3rd-floor landing, additional single bed in 2 rooms. $50; full breakfast. AE, D, DC, MC, V. Smoking on porch only, no pets.*

The Garden Gate Bed and Breakfast

Charming hosts Miles and Mary Conway are happy to socialize with their guests, but if you prefer solitude, it's easy to find in this unusual duplex Victorian house built in 1906. The Conways live in one half, while in the other the guests share their own dining room, first-floor half bath, and living room with television. Mary is a massage therapist, so you may want to make an appointment, rather than making yourself scarce.

Lots of white woodwork, refinished oak-and-maple floors, and an inviting front porch make the Garden Gate bright and comfortable. Upstairs, the vividly painted guest rooms are named after appropriate flowers: The Delphinium is a purplish blue; the Gladiola, a rich yellow; and the Rose, a deep pink. The Delphinium has floral bedspreads, twin beds, a table and chairs, and two large, south-facing windows. They've now added a third-floor suite done in light peach tones, which lends itself to a contemplative mood.

On a quiet block just south of St. Paul's historic district and busiest shopping area, the inn is quite convenient. A happy note for travelers from the East Coast: the *New York Times* is delivered daily.

📠 *925 Goodrich Ave., St. Paul, MN 55105, tel. 612/227–8430 or 800/967–2703. 3 double rooms and 1 suite share bath. Air-conditioning. $55–$75; Continental breakfast. No credit cards. Smoking on porch only.*

Harvest Restaurant and Inn

In busy downtown Stillwater, the Harvest Restaurant and Inn (once known as the Brunswick Inn) shouldn't be taken for a retreat from civilization—

rather it's the perfect spot from which to explore Stillwater's many notable antiques shops. About 150 years old—the oldest surviving frame structure in Stillwater—it is quite an antique itself. Mark Hanson, an experienced chef and restaurateur, and his wife, Lydia, opened this dual venture in 1995 after spending time in New York and the Virgin Islands. Mark runs the restaurant, and Lydia maintains the guest rooms.

Inside the simple 1848 Greek Revival, everything is geared toward romance and relaxation. Miss Amelia's Room, the Harvest's most popular accommodation, has a matching baroque mahogany bed frame and mantel from the 1880s. The sunken bathroom sits under pleasantly wallpapered dormered eaves. Miss Emma's Room, done in soothing pinks and sea greens, has a walnut fireplace and a double whirlpool.

The elegant downstairs area, open to both the public and to guests, consists of formal dining chambers where Mark serves a constantly rotating menu of his contemporary gourmet creations. A final grace note: the elegant sherry decanter left on the upstairs landing.

▦ *114 E. Chestnut St., Stillwater, MN 55082, tel. 612/430–8111. 3 double rooms with baths. Air-conditioning, double whirlpool, and fireplace in rooms. $129–$139; full breakfast. AE, D, MC, V. No smoking, no pets.*

James A. Mulvey Residence Inn

When avid pottery collectors Truett and Jill Lawson entered the Mulvey Inn and saw a magnificent Grueby tile fireplace in the living room, they knew they had to buy the beautiful little 1878 Italianate house. In 1905, owner and prosperous lumberman James A. Mulvey bought the fireplace (one of only two in Minnesota) from the

Grueby Tile Co. of Boston and then added the dining room's heavy oak beams and wainscoting and the gold-and-green tulip-design stained-glass windows bordering the front door. Indicative of the Italianate style, huge windows make the house light, airy, and seemingly larger than it is.

The Lawsons' pottery collection is spread throughout the house, and each guest room, named after a pottery style, includes a book describing the specific technique, while also maintaining a sense of Victorian elegance. The nicest guest room is the Rookwood Room, in gold, black, and maroon with Renaissance Revival furniture, inlaid oak-and-walnut floors, cranberry-glass lamps, and huge corner windows.

▦ *622 W. Churchill St., Stillwater, MN 55082, tel. 612/430–8008 or 800/820–8008. 5 double rooms with baths. Air-conditioning, fireplace in 3 rooms, whirlpool baths in selected rooms. $99–$159; full breakfast, afternoon refreshments, picnic lunches available. AE, D, MC, V. Smoking on porch only, no pets.*

Laurel Street Inn

Surrounded by a delicate white picket fence, the imposing Laurel Street Inn stands directly on a bluff overlooking the dramatic St. Croix River valley in Stillwater. Built in 1859 by Judge Murdock, it was later the home of Mildred Comfort, author of the many *Peter and Nancy* books. The current owners, Doug and Debbie Thorsen, were driving through town one day and were so impressed with the storybook image that they couldn't resist. Indeed, the blue-and-white Greek and Italianate home's best assets are its picturesque gardens and its sweeping view.

While the downstairs parlor is bright and comfortable, with a soothing stained-glass window, guests may wish to spend their time wandering the property, with its many flowery retreat areas. Stepping off the genteel wraparound porch will lead you to a gazebo, in which guests may be served breakfast. Following a downward path, guests will pass a natural waterfall, a lilac-lined walking path, daylilies, and a rose garden—each with a secluded reading bench.

The rooms mix antique Eastlake-style dressers with newer bed frames, and are all bright and well kept. The cream-and-rose St. Croix Suite, with a dried floral arrangement woven through the brass bed frame, is so named because it has the best view of the river. The warm Murdock Suite, originally Judge Murdock's library, contains the original family safe and lots of rich woodwork. All of the rooms have gas fireplaces, whirlpool baths, and fresh flowers from the gardens.

🏨 *210 E. Laurel St., Stillwater, MN 55082, tel. 612/351–0031 or 888/ 351–0031, fax 612/439–0903. 3 double rooms with baths. Air-conditioning, whirlpool baths and gas fireplaces in two rooms. $105–$125 Nov.–Apr., $155–$175 May–Oct.; full breakfast. AE, D, MC, V. Smoking on porch only, no pets.*

Lumber Baron's Hotel

No fewer than five local B&B owners combined their enterprising skills to restore Stillwater's original Lumber Exchange Building, circa 1890, into an elegant Victorian hotel overlooking the St. Croix River. Working closely with the Minnesota Historical Society and the National Trust, John Berglund, Chuck and Judy Dougherty, and Duane and Martha Hubbs reclaimed its grandeur by rediscovering such historical elements as the original tin ceilings and several large walk-in vaults. They added richly hued Victorian wallpapers, reproduction furniture, and plush carpeting, combining old-fashioned sensibilities with modern amenities, such as whirlpool baths.

The nicest rooms are those facing the river, which all have balconies. The Presidential suites, done in warm burgundies, offer queen-size mahogany canopy beds, parlors with Murphy beds, double whirlpools, and gas fireplaces. The Grand Baron suites, named after famous lumber barons, all have river views, as well as double whirlpools and gas fireplaces. Unless you enjoy an urban view, avoid the Dutchess' Chambers.

Breakfast is served in the formal downstairs restaurant. Guests can choose from a variety of traditional or health-conscious items—steak and eggs or whole wheat French toast, for example. In the evening, the restaurant serves a full dinner menu, and a lucky couple may dine inside one of the original vaults, each of which houses the hotel's red wines and a cozy table for two.

🏨 *101 Water St. S, Stillwater, MN 55082, tel. 612/439–6000, fax 612/ 430–9393. 16 double rooms with baths, 20 suites. Restaurant, pub, air-conditioning, TV, phone, double whirlpool bath, and gas fireplace in rooms, 5 conference rooms. $109–$184 weekdays; $139–$229 weekends; full breakfast. AE, D, DC, MC, V. Designated smoking rooms, no pets.*

Nicollet Island Inn

This 1893 limestone building, on a small island in the middle of the Mississippi River, was the J. R. Clark Company and later the Island Sash and Door Company. In the late 1980s, the building was gutted, leaving only maple floors and a few exposed-brick and limestone walls, and then converted into the Nicollet Island Inn.

The first floor is occupied by a restaurant where you can dine on regional cuisine at tables overlooking the river. There's also a pleasant, sunny bar with equally good views and a lounge with a fireplace.

Guest rooms, on the second and third floors, have Early American and country-style reproduction furniture. The rooms aren't large, but they are quite comfortable, and half have river views. The best rooms are the corner rooms 209 and 309, which overlook the river and the park, where free concerts are held on summer evenings.

🏨 *95 Merriam St., Minneapolis, MN 55401, tel. 612/331-1800, fax 612/ 331-6528. 24 double rooms with baths. Restaurant and bar, air-conditioning, cable TV, VCR, phone, hair dryers, mineral water, cookies, newspapers; tubs in 2 rooms, 3 meeting rooms, movies for rent, off-street parking. $115-$150; breakfast extra. AE, D, DC, MC, V. No smoking in some rooms, no pets.*

1900 Dupont

This B&B in the prosperous, tree-lined Kenwood/Lowry Hill neighborhood is the best-located B&B in Minneapolis. It's just blocks from downtown, the Guthrie Theater, Walker Art Center, and Lake of the Isles.

Location is only the beginning of what this 5,000-square-foot 1896 Colonial Revival house has to offer. The unusual library—you enter through leaded-glass doors on the landing between the first and second floors—is a wonderful mahogany-lined retreat of leather sofas, built-in bookcases, and a huge fireplace. In contrast to the masculine library is a lovely small solarium with a glass table and chairs. Owner Chris Viken's background is in museum curation, so there are well-kept antiques throughout.

Three of the guest quarters are corner rooms with bay windows. Joseph's

Room, the largest, has a mahogany bed, as well as an antique sleigh bed hidden in a window nook, which serves as a plush reading or nap spot. Leslie's Room, the nicest of the three, has a bay window, a queen-size bed, sunny exposure, and a private blue-and-white tiled bath. Margeret's room, the newest addition, combines antiques with contemporary art.

🏨 *1900 Dupont Ave. S, Minneapolis, MN 55403, tel. 612/374-1973. 4 double rooms with baths. Air-conditioning, TV available upon request. $85-$119; Continental breakfast. No credit cards. No smoking, no pets.*

The Rose Bed and Breakfast

The Rose Bed and Breakfast is a charming 1925 English Tudor brick house set on nearly 2 acres. Owners Carol Kindschi and Larry Greenberg's tastes are quite eclectic: There's a built-in buffet in the dining room, Oriental rugs, leather furniture, folkloric art from Central America, and—the final touch?—some very modern purple barrel chairs. Even more unexpected are the Welsh deacon's bench from the 19th century and the turn-of-the-century dental cabinet (complete with tools) in the living room.

Both suites overlook the University of Minnesota's golf course and the house's tennis court, as well as their newly planted prairie and woodland gardens. The third-floor Rosepointe Suite has the best views of the grounds and the most privacy. Its large, carpeted bedroom has a Scandinavian bed, a sitting area has a wicker chaise longue, a new black-and-white bathroom centers around a large, deep bathtub, and sliding glass doors lead to a private deck.

🏨 *2129 Larpenteur Ave. W, Falcon Heights, MN 55113, tel. 612/642-9417 or 800/966-2728, fax 612/647-0954. 2 suites. Air-conditioning, phone, TV,*

VCR, *and clock radio in suites, down comforter, bedtime snacks, and refrigerator in 3rd-floor suite, tennis court. $85; full breakfast. No credit cards. No smoking, no pets.*

Schumacher's New Prague Hotel

Schumacher's New Prague Hotel was originally the Broz Hotel, established in 1898 and designed by Cass Gilbert, the architect who also designed the Minnesota State Capitol and the Library of Congress. Although the exterior, which is listed in the National Register of Historic Places, was restored in 1974, the interior was later essentially gutted by owner John Schumacher and remodeled into an immaculate Bavarian-style inn. Now managed by John and his wife, Kathleen, the hotel is well run and eclectic in decor. The guest rooms, each with

an eiderdown German feather bed, are a comfortable, elegant, and colorful mixture of modern amenities, European antiques, and handmade Bavarian-style furniture.

John, a former chef for the Marriott Hotel Corporation, has brought his culinary talent to the hotel's well-respected Central European Restaurant. Especially popular are the home-baked goods, such as the *kolaches* (sweet rolls), as well as the roast duck and wild game entrées.

▦ *212 W. Main St., New Prague, MN 56071, tel. 612/758-2133, fax 612/758-2400. 11 double rooms with baths. Air-conditioning, whirlpool tub in selected rooms, gas fireplace in 7 rooms, restaurant, gift shop. $137–$167; breakfast extra. AE, D, MC, V. Smoking allowed in dining rooms, no pets.*

Mississippi River Valley and Bluff Country
Including Red Wing, Wabasha, and Lanesboro

The glaciers that steamrollered Minnesota eons ago somehow missed shearing off the high points in the southeastern part of the state. The result is a sawtooth collection of bluffs and valleys known as Bluff Country.

Bluff Country is farm country, but it's also heavily wooded with oaks and maples. Here you'll find soaring hills and plunging valleys marbled with gently flowing streams and top-notch bike and Nordic ski trails. Scattered about are drowsy little towns, some that bear few signs of modern times. One is the almost impossibly picturesque town of Lanesboro, nestled in the bluffs just east of the intersection of U.S. 16 and Route 52. This isolated community of 900 or so souls is so unspoiled that its entire downtown district has been placed on the National Register of Historic Places.

The Mississippi River is the headline act in this region, of course. There's no better way to view it than from U.S. 61 between Red Wing and Winona. This is a dramatic drive. The road unravels past towers of limestone that at times stretch 500 feet into the sky. According to legend, a despondent Native American maiden named We-No-Nah jumped to her death from these bluffs, giving Winona its name. Today, falcons and eagles can occasionally be spotted circling in the sky where We-No-Nah made her fatal plunge.

Once lumber and shipping centers, the river towns that populate the banks of the Mississippi now vacillate between maintaining their character and giving in totally to the tourist trade.

Popular as destinations for folks from Rochester and the Twin Cities, places like Wabasha, Frontenac, and Lake City are still largely uncrowded and pleasant. Unlike in Red Wing, which is particularly frenzied on autumn Saturdays, it's still possible to quietly enjoy river scenes in these communities.

Places to Go, Sights to See

Cannon Valley Trail (306 W. Mill St., Cannon Falls, tel. 507/263–3954). Bike, hike, or ski along the 19.7-mile asphalt and crushed-limestone Cannon Valley Trail, which follows the Cannon River from Cannon Falls to Red Wing along the Cannon Valley Line's abandoned rail bed. The trains ran from 1883 until 1976; bicyclists and skiers can be found there almost year-round now.

Frontenac State Park (29223 Cty. 28 Blvd., Lake City, tel. 612/345–3401), 10 miles southeast of Red Wing along the Mississippi River's Lake Pepin, comprises more than 1,700 acres, including 13.4 miles of hiking trails, 6 miles of cross-country skiing trails, rustic and semimodern campsites, and picnic grounds. It's also a premier site for watching the migration of birds, including warblers, bald and golden eagles, and peregrine falcons.

Northfield, home to both St. Olaf and Carleton colleges, is just 45 minutes south of the Twin Cities. On September 7, 1876, eight members of the infamous James-Younger band of outlaws rode into this community with the intent of robbing the First National Bank. The gang, thwarted midway through their crime by alarmed townspeople, didn't get a dime. Only Frank and Jesse James escaped. Northfield holds a "Defeat of Jesse James Celebration," reenacting the seven-minute bank raid and shoot-out, on the weekend after Labor Day. The bank is now the Northfield Historical Society Museum (408 Division St., Northfield, tel. 507/645–9268).

Red Wing. A historic limestone-bluffed river port and former grain-milling and -shipping town, Red Wing is just an hour south of the Twin Cities. Partake of three self-guided walking tours of the town's historic districts by picking up maps at the Red Wing Heritage Preservation Commission (City Hall, 315 W. 4th St., Red Wing, tel. 612/385–3622). On your tour check out what's playing at the recently restored T. B. Sheldon Performing Arts Theater (3rd St. at East Ave., tel. 612/385–3667 or 800/899–5759), which hosts everything from dramas to country-western concerts. Golfers will love the 27-hole course at the world-class Mississippi National Golf Links (409 Golf Links Dr., tel. 612/388–1874). Observe pottery being made at the Red Wing Stoneware Company (U.S. 61, 4 mi north of Red Wing, tel. 612/388–4610). The Goodhue County Historical Society (1166 Oak St., tel. 612/388–6024) remembers the area's history from its geological sculpting to its settlement to recent developments. Red Wing has many lovely and historic homes and buildings, and from May through October you can enjoy a narrated ride through these historic sections of town aboard Red Wing Trolley's *Spirit of Red Wing* (706 W. 4th St., tel. 612/388–5945).

Winona. The River City Carriage Company (601 Winona St., tel. 507/452–4221) offers horse-drawn carriage tours of this historic river town, as well as package rides that include a picnic, dinner, and lodging. History buffs will also enjoy the Julius C. Wilkie Steamboat Center (in Levee Park on Main St. at the river, tel. 507/454-1254), a full-scale replica of an old-time steamboat. The first deck contains a museum of the river's history, steamboat artifacts, and a video presentation prepared by Winona State University. The Polish Cultural Institute of Winona (102 Liberty St., tel. 507/454-3431) houses Kashubian artifacts, family heirlooms, religious articles, and folk art. Garvin Heights Park (straight south on Huff St. past U.S. 14 and U.S. 61) offers hiking trails, a scenic drive, and a 500-foot overlook, all with splendid views of the city, the Mississippi, and of Wisconsin on the opposite shore.

Restaurants

In Lanesboro there are two pricey places and an alternative noted for its traditional home-cooked meals. The **Victorian House** (709 Parkway Ave. S, Lanesboro, tel. 507/467-3457), a French restaurant in a house setting, offers lamb Provençal and filet mignon. **Mrs. B's** (101 Parkway Ave. S, Lanesboro, tel. 507/467-2154) serves multiple-course meals table d'hôte style, using such Minnesota products as wild rice and berries. The lower-priced **Chat and Chew Cafe** (701 Parkway Ave. S, Lanesboro, tel. 507/467-3444) stands out for home-baked rolls and homemade soups. The American-style dining is good at the St. James Hotel's **Port of Red Wing** (406 Main St., Red Wing, tel. 612/388-2846 or 800/252-1875). The newer **Staghead Coffeehouse** (219 Bush St., Red Wing, tel. 612/388-6581) offers gourmet fish and pastas in a casual bistro setting, as well as an extensive beer and wine list. In Wabasha stop in at the **Anderson House** (333 W. Main St., Wabasha, tel. 612/565-4524 or 800/862-9702), where the country-style cooking is hearty and the breads and pastries home-baked. Many people staying in Wabasha, Lake City, and even Winona cross Lake Pepin to Pepin, Wisconsin, to have dinner at the justifiably famous **Harbor View Cafe** (1st and Main Sts., Pepin, tel. 715/442-3893), to savor its superb breads, creative cookery, and equally creative wine list.

Tourist Information

Minnesota Office of Tourism, Southern Regional Office (Box 286, Mankato, MN 56002, tel. 507/389-2683); **Red Wing Area Chamber of Commerce** (420 Levee St., Red Wing, MN 55066, tel. 612/388-4719); **Winona Convention and Visitors Bureau** (67 Main St., Winona, MN 55987, tel. 507/452-2272); **Northfield Area Chamber of Commerce** (Box 198, Northfield, MN 55057, tel. 507/645-5604 or 800/658-2548).

JailHouse Inn

L aw-abiding citizens of the past
century hurried past this 1869
Italianate redbrick building, which
served as the Fillmore County Jail for
more than 100 years. After then sitting
empty for 15 years, the jail and the
adjacent sheriff's quarters and offices
were turned into a 13-room inn, after a
renovation so extensive it is almost
impossible to guess the structure's
original use. Almost. One room provides an unforgettable reminder: The
Cell Block Room still has its bars. Otherwise, it is much more comfortable
than any inmate could have dreamed.
Two queen-size beds with tufted bedspreads occupy separate cells, which
are fitted with rag rugs, a whirlpool
bath big enough for two, a sitting area,
and the original toilet and basin.

Rest assured you won't feel the least
bit incarcerated in the other bedrooms,
all with beautiful pine or oak floors and
many decorated with Eastlake furniture. The blue-and-rose Master Bedroom has a wood-burning fireplace,
large windows, and a huge, old 1,000-
pound china tub. The Oriental Room
has a purple-and-black marble fireplace and a large, comfortable bathroom with a claw-foot tub. The
pine-floored, maroon-and-rust Deten-
tion Room has access to the south-facing second-floor porch. The newest
room, once the drunk tank, has the
original oversize sheriff's tub. Even
some of the JailHouse's smaller
rooms—such as the bright yellow-and-
white Sun Room or the blue-and-white

Amish Room—are just as light and
clean as the larger rooms.

There are plenty of public spaces,
including the front parlor, which has a
pine floor, marble fireplace, and grandfather clock; the larger and brighter
oak-floored kitchen; and the first- and
second-floor porches. Breakfast is
served in a sunny, spacious basement
dining area.

Owners Jeanne and Marc Sather, former restaurant designers from San
Francisco, are accomplished cooks and
veteran hosts, happy to lend their
premises and their talents to special
events or even to make impromptu
trout dinners if you should find yourself lucky enough to catch one in the
nearby Root River.

🏨 *109 Houston NW (Box 422), Preston, MN 55965, tel. 507/765–2181, fax
507/765–2558. 11 double rooms with
baths, 1 2-bedroom suite. Air-
conditioning, fireplace in 4 rooms,
whirlpool bath in 3 rooms, breakfast
room and parlor, meeting room,
audio-visual equipment; near Root
River trailhead. $40–$115 weekdays,
$60–$149 weekends; Continental
breakfast weekdays, full breakfast
weekends, afternoon refreshments. D,
MC, V. No smoking, no pets.*

Mrs. B's Historic Lanesboro Inn

A cheery, four-story 1872 limestone structure on the Root River in downtown Lanesboro, this inn spent part of its 125-year history as a combination retail furniture company and funeral home. No vestige of its former use can be found today: Mrs. B's is bright, light, and bursting with the energy of the outdoorsy people who make up much of its clientele.

Lanesboro is a picturesque small town in the heart of the bluffs. The 45-mile asphalt recreation trail for hiking, biking, and cross-country skiing that follows the Root River runs right by Mrs. B's. You can rent bikes and canoes just down the street, or enjoy the view of the river from the two side decks or the backyard garden patio that faces it.

Inside, Mrs. B's is cozy if not historically significant. Before opening as an inn in 1984, it was essentially gutted—and rooms and baths added. The bathrooms are jarringly modern, but the guest rooms are much more creatively decorated, with most of the furniture (including sleigh and cupboard-style beds) locally made, some of it reflecting the Scandinavian heritage of the town's residents. The nicest rooms are the two back corner ones, which have river views. Also desirable are the three rooms with direct access to the inn's wooden side decks, furnished with large, comfortable wooden rocking chairs.

The inn's only common area is a rather small but comfortable lobby, equipped with a piano, warmed by a fireplace, and brightened by huge arched windows facing the street. In summer, guests can use the two-story side porch and the riverfront patio.

"Our goal is to make guests comfortable," says owner Bill Sermeus, who along with his wife, Mimi Abell, bought the inn in early 1991. "We don't have antiques, but we do have good beds, soft chairs, and good food."

Indeed, Mrs. B's is well known for its dinners, which are five-course table d'hôte affairs that take advantage of local products. Dinners are available by reservation only and include such specialties as wildflower salad, corn and wild-rice chowder, and wild-berry sorbet.

🏨 *101 Parkway Ave. (Box 411), Lanesboro, MN 55949, tel. 507/ 467–2154 or 800/657–4710. 10 double rooms with baths. Restaurant, air-conditioning, gas fireplace in 2 rooms. $50–$68 weekdays, $60–$95 weekends; full breakfast, afternoon tea on weekends. No credit cards. Smoking on porches only, no pets. Closed Dec. 24–26.*

Pratt-Taber Inn

If you're interested in antiques, there are few better choices in this region than the Pratt-Taber Inn. Owners Jim and Karen Kleinfeldt fell in love with this house, not only for its location in historic Red Wing away from the bustle of big city life, but also for its potential as a historically authentic backdrop for their extensive antiques collection. The sturdy, white-trimmed brick Italianate Victorian inn is named after A. W. Pratt, a banker who built the house for his family in 1876, and his son-in-law, Robert Taber, who bought it in 1905. Ninety years later, it has become the Kleinfeldts' home, passion, and profession. Along with their gracious hospitality, they offer some of the best B&B breakfasts around.

The house, which is listed in the National Register of Historic Places, was restored in 1984. Old photographs guided much of the exterior work, including the replacement of the porches; one of them is embellished with a detailed star pattern honoring the United States' Centennial in 1876, the year the inn was built. Inside there are parquet floors, butternut and walnut woodwork, glass chandeliers, feather-painted slate fireplaces, and in the dining room, a large bay window. Throughout the house you'll find early Renaissance Revival and country Victorian antique furniture that dates from the late 1700s to the late 1800s, including a 112-year-old Murphy bed housed in a Victorian buffet and a stereopticon with a rare and complete *Tour the World* collection.

Three of the four upstairs rooms are corner rooms, and all are large and filled with impressive antiques. Polly's Room is particularly nice, with its queen-size brass bed, soft blue-and-ecru decor, black marble fireplace, and inviting claw-foot tub. Mary Lu's Room has views of Barns Bluff, and Beatrice's Room has an 1860s burled walnut Victorian dresser topped with Limoges china items, lending an aura of a time gone by.

Breakfasts—specialties include eggs Benedict with asparagus on homemade sourdough bread or cinnamon-orange French toast—are served in the dining room, on the porches, or in the guest bedrooms, all of which contain tables for two (Jim and Karen will serve from their collection of 1870 Limoges china upon request).

Being a bit of a town booster, Jim is also glad to provide guests with information on local activities, especially the summer trolley tours, which stop right at the inn's front door.

🏠 *706 W. 4th St., Red Wing, MN 55066, tel. 612/388–5945. 2 double rooms with baths, 4 doubles share 2 baths. Air-conditioning, clock radio in rooms, fireplace in 1 room, storage for bicycles, pickup service at airport, dock, or train station. $89–$110; full breakfast, afternoon refreshments. No credit cards. No smoking, no pets.*

Thorwood Historic Inns

If you want a luxurious bed-and-breakfast visit, as so many of the repeat guests do, the Thorwood Historic Inns—the 1880 Queen Anne Rosewood and the 1880 Second Empire–style Thorwood—are for you.

Pam and Dick Thorsen, a down-to-earth and friendly couple, fell in love with the river town of Hastings, 20 miles south of St. Paul, and opened Thorwood in 1983. The 6,600-square-foot house was built by a local lumber baron, William Thompson, and his wife, Sara, as their family home. Then, in 1989, the Thorsens opened the 10,000-square-foot Rosewood, six blocks away.

Interestingly, both inns had been hospitals, and occasionally people born in the buildings come back as guests to celebrate their birthdays.

Thorwood and Rosewood are not cozy, family-style bed-and-breakfasts. Thorwood has retained more of its original rooms and fixtures and because the Thorsens live there, is the homier of the two inns. It has a bay window and a fireplace in its main parlor, an interesting square bay in the front parlor, and maple-and-oak floors throughout.

Rosewood has a grand piano, a large fireplace, large ornate public rooms, and several bay windows big enough to park a Volkswagen in. Dark-green-and-rose wallpapers and carpets and white-and-oak woodwork, along with the building's great size, make Rosewood's parlors almost overwhelmingly formal.

Remodeling has given fireplaces and whirlpool baths to both inns' guest rooms. The largest and most ornate is a 900-square-foot suite called Mississippi Under the Stars, which has five skylights, a fireplace, a teakwood double whirlpool tub under a skylight, a round shower, a copper soaking tub, and a queen-size bed.

Thorwood's most elaborate rooms are Sara's Suite, a lavender-and-white three-level arrangement, with a skylight over the bed, a double whirlpool tub, and the best view; and the Steeple Room, with a built-in whirlpool bath set right into the steeple and a glass-domed fireplace dividing the bath area from the bedroom. Any of the other third-floor rooms at either inn are also bound to both intrigue and spoil even the hardest-to-please of people.

The Thorsens have taken to offering breakfast either in the public rooms or in baskets at your door.

🏨 *315 Pine St., Hastings, MN 55033, tel. 612/437–3297 or 888/846–7966. 13 double rooms with baths, 2 suites. Air-conditioning, TV/VCRs available, fireplace in 9 rooms, whirlpool bath in 12 rooms, gift shop. $87–$217; full breakfast, afternoon refreshments, dinners available. AE, D, MC, V. No smoking, no pets.*

The Victorian Bed & Breakfast

Wonderful views of Lake Pepin from each guest room make Lake City's Victorian Bed & Breakfast special. The lake, which many people claim is the most beautiful spot on the Mississippi, also dominates the perspective from the large windows in the downstairs public rooms.

Owners Ione and Bernie Link—originally from Wichita, Kansas—traveled far to settle in Lake City. One look at the grand view from the porch, and they decided on the spot to buy the inn.

The building, although an 1896 Stick-style Victorian, has a refreshing simplicity inside. Butternut wood on the staircase banisters and elsewhere is carved, but not elaborately so; small and simple stained-glass windows in rose, amber, and blue are set atop larger plain-glass windows.

Decorated with antiques and modern sofas, the Victorian is eclectic and comfortable, but not overstuffed. The most interesting items are the oak pump organ, made in 1905, and the many delicate glass lamps, some of which are handcrafted by Bernie himself.

The Redbud Room is best, with sweeping lake views from the huge bay window, a king-size bed, a private bath with a wide-plank pine floor, an oversize footed tub, and a rare antique pillbox toilet. The chaise lounge provides an excellent opportunity for getting lost in a book.

The sunny Magnolia Room is a large corner room at the front of the house with wonderful lake views, a canopy bed topped with a feather mattress, and an antique claw-foot tub with brass fixtures. The Dogwood Room has carved oak furniture, a reading desk, and a unique stereopticon, but its bathroom is downstairs off the den.

Breakfast is served either in the sunny dining room, which also overlooks the lake, or in guest rooms. Wherever you partake your wake-up meal, you'll probably love Ione's baked apple pancakes, often made with just-picked apples from local orchards.

🏨 *620 S. High St., Lake City, MN 55041, tel. 612/345–2167. 3 double rooms with bath (1 nonadjoining). Air-conditioning, TV/VCR in den. ceiling fan, down comforters, and feather beds in rooms. $65–$85; full breakfast, afternoon refreshments. No credit cards. Smoking on porch only, no pets.*

The Anderson House

Minnesota's oldest operating hotel, the Anderson House was built in 1856, two years before Minnesota became a state, and was purchased in the early 1900s by the Anderson family. Except for 12 years in the 1960s and '70s, it's been run by Andersons and their heirs ever since.

Owner John Hall, who has been restoring the hotel in stages since 1976, has taken care to leave some of the things that give character to an old lodging. Thus, although the baths are modern, the floors slant, the halls are crooked, and the doors occasionally stick.

Guest rooms are furnished with a mixture of original pieces from the 1800s, reproductions, and locally handmade quilts designed specifically to match the wallpaper in each room.

The Anderson House is justly famous for two things: the 15 resident cats, which guests can "check out" for the night (complete with food and litter box), and the Pennsylvania Dutch–style food served in its first-floor restaurant, where all baking is done from scratch.

🏨 *333 W. Main St., Wabasha, MN 55981, tel. 612/565–4524, fax 612/ 565–4003 or 800/535–5467. 18 double rooms with baths, 6 suites. Restaurant, bar, air-conditioning, TV available upon request, whirlpool bath in 4 suites, 17 rooms have river views, banquet/conference room. $50–$125; breakfast extra. D, MC, V. Closed Mon.–Thurs. Nov. 2–Mar.*

The Archer House

This 1877 Second Empire–style hotel is nestled in Northfield—the small college town where in 1876 Jesse James and his gang met their defeat. Between the Jesse James convention and the constant college trade, the hotel is a busy establishment.

The hallways and guest rooms—heavy on dried flowers, crocheted bedspreads, and wallpaper—are mostly small and dark, for this was originally a modest tradesman's hotel. Hence, the smaller rooms seem right; the larger ones with whirlpool baths, however, seem a bit out of place.

The lobby is cluttered with bric-a-brac, but there's a nice restaurant on the riverfront level that's especially cozy on a winter's day. In summer, have dinner outdoors on a patio overlooking the river.

🏨 *212 Division St., Northfield, MN 55057, tel. 507/645–5661, fax 507/ 645–4295. 17 double rooms with baths, 19 suites with whirlpool baths. Restaurants, air-conditioning, cable TV and phone in rooms, complimentary champagne for rooms with whirlpool baths, ice and soft-drink machines, shops, 3 conference rooms. $45–$150; breakfast extra. AE, MC, V. No pets.*

Bridgewaters Bed and Breakfast

Bill and Carole Moore's B&B, just a block from tiny Wabasha's main street and the Mississippi River, is an ideal spot for those seeking a country-style inn in town. A wraparound porch outlines two sides of the slate-and-forest-green home, and the rest of the house is hardly less sunny. Four picture windows, accented with stained and leaded glass, light the common area's sitting room and formal and casual living rooms—neatly furnished with plenty of couches and chairs and such interesting items as a 1920s icebox turned beverage cabinet—and the dining room, which has oak paneling, a built-in buffet, and large oak table.

The five guest rooms, named after bridges on the Mississippi, are all on the second level. The largest is the Wabasha Bridge Room, which has floors of original yellow pine, a hand-carved walnut bed, walnut bureau with marble top, and antique wash pan and sink. Three other rooms share two baths, but are all sunny and tastefully furnished with unique antique dressers and down-filled quilts. The newest room, the Lafayette Bridge Suite, includes a two-sided gas fireplace, dormer ceilings, and a double whirlpool bath tucked under a west window.

🏠 *136 Bridge Ave., Wabasha, MN 55981, tel. 612/565–4208. 2 double rooms with baths, 3 doubles share 2 baths. Air-conditioning, stereo with CD player in common area. $68–$145; full breakfast on weekends, Continental breakfast on weekdays. MC, V. Smoking on porches only, no pets.*

The Candle Light Inn

This 1877 Victorian was built by Horace Rich, who once managed the Red Wing Stoneware Company. Now owned by Mary Jaeb (a former caterer) and her husband, Bud, the home retains its original grandeur.

Much of the woodwork, including the grand staircase, is of walnut, although oak, cherry, and butternut accent the cabinetry, parquet floors, and trim. There are six fireplaces, including a feather-painted one in the parlor and another in the cherry cabinet–lined library. Unusual rose, blue, and orange beveled stained-glass windows mark the entryway, and over 30 Quesale globes—the first lights installed with the advent of electricity—are still found throughout the house. Given all this, it's not surprising the inn is listed on the Minnesota Register of Historical Places.

The Butternut Suite, a spacious room with a gas fireplace, an exquisitely carved 1840s mahogany bed, and double whirlpool bath, is the best of the four second-level rooms. The Rose Garden Room, done in green, rose, and white, is also especially charming, with its sunny corner location, white woodwork, fireplace, whirlpool bath, and large bay window.

🏠 *818 W. 3rd St., Red Wing, MN 55066, tel. 612/388–8034. 4 double rooms with baths, 1 suite. Air-conditioning, fireplace in 2 rooms, whirlpool bath in 3 rooms. $85–$145; full breakfast, afternoon refreshments. MC, V. No smoking, no pets.*

Carriage House Bed & Breakfast

This 1870 carriage house is the largest remaining in a river city that once had many such buildings. The three-story structure, white with green shutters, lies behind a matching Italianate house, the home of bed-and-breakfast proprietors Deb and Don Salyards. Both houses are directly across the street from the Winona State University campus, where Don—also a local entrepreneur—works as an economics professor.

All four guest rooms are on the second floor of the carriage house. Two are expanded versions of the former stable boys' quarters, which retain their original windows and woodwork; the other two are somewhat larger, with high ceilings and windows. The best guest room is the Village Loft, which has a small table and chairs and a large bathroom with a skylight above the oversize claw-foot tub.

Guests can have tea and coffee on the first floor in a sunny, four-season porch. Breakfast is delivered to the porch at a time arranged by guests. Deb can direct guests to bike trails, golf courses, and other local activities.

🏠 *420 Main St., Winona, MN 55987, tel. 507/452–8256, fax 507/452–0939. 4 double rooms with baths. Air-conditioning, fireplace in 2 rooms, free bicycles, shuttle service from boat docks or train station. $70–$110; Con-*

tinental plus breakfast. *D, MC, V. No smoking, no pets.*

Carrolton Country Inn

Half the fun of staying at this 100-year-old farmhouse is getting to it. From Lanesboro follow an old oxcart trail for 3 miles, crossing the Root River and the historic Scanlon-Ford Bridge, as the trail winds along a narrow valley. At the end, you'll reach the Carrolton Country Inn, a nine-room farmhouse built by a Norwegian immigrant family in 1880. Owners Gloria and Charles Ruen opened it as a bed-and-breakfast in 1987 when they moved to a nearby farm (guests pick up the keys there).

The charm of the modest and rather inexpensively decorated house lies in its bucolic setting on 389 cow-dotted acres. In keeping with the rustic mood, guests prepare their own breakfast each morning, helping themselves from the well-stocked refrigerator.

The guest rooms are on the dark side, with a mix of antiques and modern furniture. The best one by far is the Carrolton Room, a large corner room facing north and east, with a fireplace, a small private balcony, and views of the beautiful farm and dramatic bluffs beyond.

🏠 *RR 2 (Box 139), Lanesboro, MN 55949, tel. 507/467-2257. 2 double rooms with baths, 2 doubles share bath. Air-conditioning, clock radio in rooms, phone in 2 rooms, piano, TV/VCR in parlor, picnic table. $60–$90; full breakfast. MC, V. No smoking, no pets.*

Historic Scanlan House

All of downtown Lanesboro is on the National Register of Historic Places. At the quiet end of the main street, the Scanlan House is an architectural gem, with its whimsically painted 1889

Queen Anne exterior and balconied, onion-dome turret. It's also just a few blocks from the Root River and the popular 45-mile-long bike-ski trail.

The public areas and bedrooms of the Scanlan House are true to the tradition of Victorian clutter. The rose-and-blue parlor with its three-windowed turret provides an attractive contrast to the adjoining, darker library, which has rich green wallpaper and antique lamps; the dining room contains a large table and classic oak buffet. The small porch outside provides a relaxing spot for two.

Most of the guest rooms are sunny, and several (including the Masquerade and Grandma Bell's rooms) are spacious corner rooms. The Masquerade Room also has the best view of the neighboring bluffs from its second-floor balcony.

🏠 *708 Parkway Ave. S, Lanesboro, MN 55949, tel. 507/467-2158 or 800/944-2158. 5 double rooms with baths. Air-conditioning, cable TV, chocolates, and minibottle of champagne in rooms, whirlpool bath in 3 rooms, bicycle and cross-country ski rentals, off-street parking. $65–$130; full breakfast, coffee and baked goods all day. AE, D, MC, V. Smoking on porch only, no pets.*

Hungry Point Inn

As you drive up the road to the Hungry Point Inn, you may feel you've been transported to the 18th century. The inn is part of an unusual 1960 development where all the houses' exteriors were made to look as if they had been built before 1820—in other words, before Minnesota was even settled. The atmosphere continues inside Merriam Carroll Last's inn, with its wide-plank pine floors, beamed ceilings, giant fireplace with copper kettle, and cast-iron candle chandelier. Rooms are furnished with quilts, rag rugs, and antique beds and chests, but most popular is a separate little house—an authentic 1870s log cabin restored to hold a kitchen, two bedrooms (with two beds in each), a small parlor with a Vermont casting fireplace, and a whirlpool tub. A hearty breakfast is delivered to the door in a basket.

Guests can roam the inn's secluded grounds, which also host chickens and Jacob sheep. Hiking trails cut through the wild prairie grasses and forests, and you can also ski, bike, or canoe in the Cannon River valley (boat rentals are available in nearby Welch).

🏠 *1 Old Deerfield Rd., Welch, MN 55089, tel. 612/437–3660 or 612/388–7857. 4 double rooms share 1½ baths, 1 2-bedroom log cabin with bath. Air-conditioning, fireplace in 2 rooms and cabin, whirlpool bath in cabin. $73–$135; full breakfast, afternoon herbal tea and cookies. MC, V. No smoking, no pets.*

Martin Oaks

Harkening to a time when afternoons were filled with artful conversation and fresh lemonade, Martin Oaks stands out not for opulence but for its gracious simplicity, quiet setting, and the great charm of its proprietors. Frank and Marie Gery's 1869 Victorian Italianate bed-and-breakfast is in tiny Dundas, near where Frank is a professor emeritus of economics at St. Olaf College. Marie works as a professional storyteller and is an accomplished cook. Lovely multiple-course breakfasts of fresh fruit, homemade breads, herbed French toast, or wild-rice pancakes are served in the dining room, on the screened porch near a flower bed frequented by hummingbirds, or on the reconstructed front porch, which has a gazebo-shaped corner section and a fine view of a recently installed flower-surrounded fountain.

Guest rooms overlook the trees and lovely gardens, and two rooms have the original wide-board pine floors. The largest, William's Room, has an extra single bed and a sitting area. Sara's Room, which may be the most attractive, has a hand-stenciled floral pattern along the tops of the walls. Marie changes the rooms' decor seasonally, with cozy handmade quilts and warm draperies in winter and white chenille spreads and airy sheer curtains in summer.

🏠 *107 1st St., Box 207, Dundas, MN 55019, tel. 507/645–4644. 2 double rooms and 1 single share 1½ baths. Air-conditioning, ceiling fan in 2 rooms, grand piano in living room. $55–$69; full breakfast, evening dessert. MC, V. No smoking, no pets.*

Quill & Quilt

Jim and Staci Smith had been looking far and wide for the ideal B&B, when they were fortunate enough to purchase this 1897 Colonial Revival home in serene Cannon Falls—just one short block from their old home! On a warm summer day, guests can relax on one of the house's several porches or wander down the street to Minnieska Park, where swans have been known to linger in a small pond. In the winter, the parlor's oak-and-marble fireplace and oak, cedar, and hemlock woodwork make it a cozy spot. Breakfast is either served in the sunny dining room, on a chosen porch, or is brought to guests' rooms, all of which have handmade quilts and curtains.

The Colvill Suite is probably the nicest room: It has a bedroom, a sitting room, a great airy bathroom with a double whirlpool bath, and a private deck overlooking the town baseball diamond as well as downtown Cannon Falls and when the leaves have fallen, the Cannon River. Avoid the Quilters' Room unless you don't mind a downstairs room right by the front door and a bath adjacent to the dining room.

🏨 *615 W. Hoffman St., Cannon Falls, MN 55009, tel. 507/263–5507 or 800/488–3849. 3 double rooms with baths (2 nonadjoining), 1 suite. Air-conditioning, coffeemaker and clock radio in rooms, whirlpool bath in suite, biking, hiking, cross-country skiing on nearby Cannon Valley Trail. $60–$130; full breakfast, evening dessert and coffee. MC, V. No smoking, no pets.*

Red Gables Inn

Douglas DeRoos, a lifetime military man, traveled with his wife, Mary, throughout Europe, staying in bed-and-breakfasts. The DeRooses decided to buy the already-operating 1865 Italianate Red Gables Inn as their "retirement project."

On a summer afternoon, the most pleasant place to sit at the Red Gables is on the screened porch, where Mary often serves hors d'oeuvres and wine at twilight. The home, built from trees found on the site, is unusual because it doesn't have hardwood floors, but instead painted fir floors, which Mary has overlaid with Oriental rugs.

The best room is the large, bright Annie Laurie, a white, rose, and blue corner guest room that faces east and south but stays cool even on the hottest summer days. Its spacious bathroom has a huge comfortable claw-foot tub (furnished with plenty of bubble bath), a pedestal sink, cheerful pink wainscoting, pink-and-yellow wallpaper, and a large west-facing window.

🏨 *403 N. High St., Lake City, MN 55041, tel. 612/345–2605. 5 double rooms with baths. Air-conditioning, ceiling fans in rooms, bicycles, antiques store. $85–$95; full breakfast, all-season picnic boxes, mystery evenings. D, MC, V. Smoking on porch only, no pets.*

St. James Hotel

In 1875, when the St. James Hotel was built by 11 local businessmen, Red Wing was a bustling river town and the largest wheat market in the world. Today what remains (besides the facade) are the black walnut–paneled library and the lobby with its grand staircase, tin ceiling, and 108-year-old Steinway. The guest rooms, about half of which have river views, have mostly reproduction Victorian furniture and modern baths, although there's generally one antique in every room and a handmade quilt on every bed. Stay in the hotel's original section; a newer wing built in 1979 has lower ceilings, narrower corridors, and generally less charm, although the large, horizontal bay windows do look over the Mississippi River.

The St. James is a hotel, restaurant, shopping area, and meeting complex of a size that belies its Main Street facade. If you're looking for a quiet spot, try the library on the main floor; in the afternoons stop in at Jimmy's, the elegant top-floor English-style pub.

🏨 *406 Main St., Red Wing, MN 55066, tel. 612/388–2846 or 800/252–1875 or 612/227–1800 (metro line), fax 612/388–5226. 60 double rooms with baths. 2 restaurants, 2 bars, air-conditioning, newspaper, phone, cable TV, and clock radio in rooms, whirlpool bath in 10 rooms, 11 meeting and banquet rooms, 11 shops, shuttle service from airport and dock. $80–$165; breakfast extra, complimentary champagne, coffee. AE, CB, D, DC, MC, V. No pets.*

Duluth and the North Shore

For many outdoorsy types, the Upper Great Lakes' most ruggedly handsome wilderness isn't in Michigan's Upper Peninsula or northern Wisconsin. It's to be found in this arrowhead-shaped section of northeastern Minnesota, squeezed between Lake Superior to the east and Canada to the north. Because of its size and distance from most large urban areas, the region is never really crowded—good news for those in dogged pursuit of solitude and pristine settings.

The most intimate way to explore the area is via the Superior Hiking Trail. The wilderness trail, which is still being developed, will offer nearly 250 miles of continuous hiking between Duluth and Canada when it is completed. You can now take day hikes or overnight backpacking trips on sections between Castle Danger and Little Marais and between Schroeder and Grand Marais.

If chance encounters with moose aren't your style, hit the asphalt on U.S. 61, which runs along the lakeshore from Duluth to the Canadian border, 183 miles away. This highway has consistently been named one of the country's top 10 scenic drives by travel magazines. Sometimes creeping to within yards of the clear, cold waters of Lake Superior, the road winds past waterfalls, streams, secluded harbors, rocky overlooks, ancient bridges, and in fall, brilliantly colored foliage. Alternate routes include well-groomed hiking trails and the North Shore Scenic Railroad, which offers three-hour round-trip excursions between downtown Duluth and the state's first iron port, Two Harbors.

The north shore was only spottily settled until the highway was built in the 1920s, and the towns between Duluth and Thunder Bay, Ontario, are still little more than flyspecks. Duluth, however, is the state's fourth-largest city. Along with its sister city Superior, Wisconsin, it remains a major seaport. More than 300 years old, Duluth has several museums and neighborhoods that call to mind the glory days of the late 19th

century, when the iron and steel industries made it a harbor
city of great wealth.

*Lake breezes have a moderating influence on temperatures
along the shoreline. Winters are surprisingly mild, while
summer temperatures rarely top 80. This accounts for the wild
beauty visitors enjoy year-round. Yellow marsh marigold,
hawkweed, and stands of purple-and-pink lupine share space
during the summer with wild strawberries, gooseberries, and
blueberries. In autumn the hardwood forests are ablaze with
red, gold, and orange, while in winter the pines poke holes in
the lumpy gray clouds, releasing snowflakes as fat and lazy as
feathers. Despite the growing number of Nordic ski trails,
tourists are rare this time of year. On a weekday in the middle
of January you can stop in the woods, break open a bag of trail
mix, and feel as if you have the entire world to yourself. It's a
bit of selfishness that's understood by anyone who has ever
been here.*

Places to Go, Sights to See

Canal Park Marine Museum (1st Ave. at the foot of Main St., Duluth, tel. 218/
727–2497). This free museum, adjoining Duluth's famous Aerial Lift Bridge and
Lighthouse, exhibits shipwreck relics, reconstructed ships' cabins, and other
artifacts relating to Lake Superior and its history.

Glensheen (3300 London Rd., Duluth, tel. 218/724–8864). The restored 39-room
Jacobean-style mansion of attorney, mining entrepreneur, and state legislator
Chester Congdon, Glensheen is furnished with period pieces and antiques, some
original furnishings. Seven and a half acres of lawns and formal gardens overlook
Lake Superior. For Minnesotans, the mansion holds dark allure as the site of the
1977 double murder of Chester's daughter, Elizabeth Congdon, and her nurse;
you won't hear much about the murder on the tour, however.

Gooseberry Falls State Park (17 mi north of Two Harbors on U.S. 61, tel.
218/834–3855, fax 218/834–3787). This 1,600-acre park 40 miles north of Duluth
has picnic tables and 12 miles of trails for hiking and cross-country skiing.
Interpretive programs include nature tours. The Gooseberry River enters the
park at a height of 240 feet, creating five waterfalls, two of which are 30 feet high.
Interesting igneous volcanic rock outcroppings are common in the second-growth
forest of birch, poplar, alder, and black spruce.

Grand Marais is a village of 1,300 at a natural harbor. It's a bustling little town,
and one of the jumping-off places for trips to the Superior National Forest and

Boundary Waters Canoe Area (U.S. 61, Grand Marais, tel. 218/387–1750). Many outdoors lovers consider this area the greatest canoe country in the world. The Gunflint Trail, a 57-mile paved, scenic roadway offering access to many hiking and cross-country ski trails and running northwest to Saganaga Lake on the Canadian border, begins in the forest.

Judge C. R. Magney State Park (15 mi north of Grand Marais on U.S. 61, tel. 218/387–2929). In this state park the waterfalls and turbulent rapids of the Brule River have carved unusual designs into the hardened lava. There are campgrounds, picnic areas, hiking trails, and fishing spots. It's directly across the highway from Naniboujou Lodge.

Kayak and Canoe Institute (University of Minnesota, Duluth, tel. 218/726–6258), part of University of Minnesota-Duluth Outdoors Program, offers weekend and day kayak trips as well as longer excursions. The package includes three days of instruction and kayaking along the north shore of Lake Superior, meals, and three nights of lodging at local resorts and bed-and-breakfasts.

Lutsen Mountains Resort (90 mi northeast of Duluth on U.S. 61, tel. 218/ 663–7281) is the area's largest downhill ski resort, with 50 runs and an average annual snowfall of 9½ feet. Mountain gondola and chairlift rides operate year-round and are especially popular during the fall foliage season. Lutsen Resort (tel. 218/663–7212 or 800/2–LUTSEN) offers lodging on the lake, while Lutsen Village Inn and Resort (tel. 218/663–7241 or 800/642–6036) offers lodging on the mountain. Area activities include horseback riding, cross-country skiing, tennis, stream fishing, hiking, and an 18-hole championship golf course, which stretches along the lake and the Poplar River.

Split Rock Lighthouse State Park (18 mi northwest of Two Harbors on U.S. 61, tel. 218/226–3065 or 218/226–6377, fax 218/226–6378). Perched on a cliff that juts 170 feet above the water, this 54-foot octagonal lighthouse was built in 1910 to help prevent fog-enshrouded iron-ore ships from wrecking on the rocky reefs. The lighthouse is no longer in use and is now open to tourists, as is the lighthouse keeper's home. An interpretive center is on the site. Also in the park are 12 miles of hiking trails, 8 miles of cross-country ski trails, and 6 miles of mountain-biking trails.

The **St. Louis County Heritage and Arts Center,** better known as the **Depot** (506 W. Michigan St., Duluth, tel. 218/727–8025), is in the restored 1892 Duluth Union Depot and houses a wide array of cultural organizations, as well as a historical society, a children's museum, a vintage railroad collection, and an art gallery.

Vista Fleet (610 Missabe Bldg., Duluth, tel. 218/722–6218) has narrated sightseeing boat tours of Duluth-Superior Harbor. Lunch, dinner, or moonlight cruises are offered from May through October.

Wolf Ridge Environmental Learning Center (230 Cranberry Rd., Finland, tel. 218/353–7414 or 800/523–2733, fax 218/353–7762). A few miles west of Little Marais, the center offers classes for adults, kids, and family groups on forest ecology, birds, nature photography, cross-country skiing, rock climbing, and more.

Restaurants

Duluth, a sizable city, has many fine restaurants. If you crave something spicy, go down to the tiny **Hacienda Del Sol** (319 E. Superior St., Duluth, tel. 218/722–7296), which has what some consider to be the best Mexican food in the state. All-American steak-and-seafood meals are offered at the **Pickwick Restaurant** (508 E. Superior St., Duluth, tel. 218/727–8901). Sandwiches and salads are offered at **Grandma's** (522 Lake Ave. S, Duluth, tel. 218/727–4192), a waterfront landmark.

Restaurants are harder to find as you make your way up the north shore so don't miss **Betty's Pies** (on U.S. 61, 4 mi north of Two Harbors, tel. 218/834–3367). If you get as far north as Grand Marais, try the **Birch Terrace** (W. 6th Ave. and Wisconsin St., Grand Marais, tel. 218/387–2215), a log cabin with a view of the lake and a menu of great steaks and fish. Right on the water is the smaller and more casual **Angry Trout Cafe** (U.S. 61, Grand Marais, tel. 218/387–1265), whose specialty is coal-grilled lake trout. Fourteen miles farther north along the lake, the **Naniboujou Lodge and Restaurant** (U.S. 61, 15 mi east of Grand Marais, tel. 218/387–2688) serves a Sunday brunch that is a favorite with the locals.

Tourist Information

Minnesota Office of Tourism's Northeastern Minnesota Regional Office (320 W. 2nd St., Suite 707, Duluth, MN 55802, tel. 888/UP–NORTH or 218/723–4692, fax 218/723–4689); **Duluth Convention and Visitors Bureau** (100 Lake Place Dr., Duluth, MN 55802, tel. 218/722–4011 or 800/438–5884, fax 218/722–1322); **Grand Marais Chamber of Commerce** (Box 1048, Grand Marais, MN 55604, tel. 218/387–2524 or 800/622–4014).

Bearskin Lodge

Dave Tuttle worked at Bearskin Lodge Resort when it was just an old lodge and several cabins 25 miles down the Gunflint Trail from Grand Marais and Lake Superior. Then in 1973, while still a senior in college, he bought it.

Today it remains low-key and woodsy, but a bit more ambitious. Since it's adjacent to the Boundary Waters Canoe area, you'll find hiking and cross-country ski trails; boat, ski, and mountain-bike rentals; and a naturalist program. There's even a masseuse. The new lodge, built in 1980, has four large town houses; there are also 11 new or spruced-up log or log-frame cabins. The multilevel town houses, though within a wing of the lodge, feel secluded, and each has a private deck. Some of the seven older cabins, built in the '20s, '30s, and '50s, have been remodeled to include room-brightening skylights above the beds. All are pleasant and have two or three bedrooms, woodstoves, and large, well-equipped kitchens. In addition, several have screened porches—critical during the buggy north-woods summers.

Rooms in both the town houses and the cabins are simple and comfortable, with chenille bedspreads and pine furniture. Each of the five two- or three-bedroom log cabins is charming, though cabins 9 and 10, built in 1990 of Engelmann spruce, are especially lovely. These cabins, although they're a bit far from the lake, have birch hardwood floors, braided rugs, renovated kitchens as well-outfitted as any home's, and big, screened porches. The new pinewood cabin is wheelchair accessible.

One of the resort's most popular spots is the Hot Tub Hus, which guests sign up for in advance for private use. Its walls, benches, and ceiling are of pine, and it has a large deck and separate men's and women's changing rooms and showers.

Originally a summer-only resort, Bearskin now draws kudos from winter-sports lovers for its ice rink and 55 miles of cross-country ski trails (1 mile of which is lighted). Lodge-to-lodge skiing packages are available.

🏠 *Box 275, Grand Marais, MN 55604, tel. 218/388–2292 or 800/ 338–4170, fax 218/388–4410. 11 2- to 3-bedroom cabins and 4 1- to 3-bedroom lodge town houses. No air-conditioning, woodstoves in cabins, kettle grill outside cabins; full meal service available in lodge dining room, wine and beer for sale, sauna, masseuse, spa house, baby-sitting, children's program, sand beach, boat and mountain-bike rental, 55 mi of hiking/cross-country ski trails, ski school, ski rental, ice-skating rink, broomball rink, naturalist program. $110–$231 with spring and late-fall specials; breakfast extra. D, MC, V. No smoking in public areas of lodge, no pets.*

The Ellery House

If it's a comfortable family place you're looking for, Jim and Joan Halquist's beautiful 1890 Queen Anne is the place to stay. The house is on a fairly busy street yet feels rather removed because of its ¾-acre lot, hilltop location, and backyard ravine with creek.

The large, sunny rooms, lighted by large picture windows that face in three directions, are decorated in a trim, moderate Victorian style. The large bay window in the living room has a lake view that's best in winter (shade trees partially obscure the view in summer). In the adjoining dining room, a collection of turn-of-the-century tables and cabinets surround the dark oak dining table.

Breakfast is served in the dining room or in three of the four guest rooms. All are delightful. The Ellery Suite, at the front of the house, has a small private balcony and a 1920s-style bathroom. The Sunporch, a three-room suite, is composed of a cozy, floral-wallpapered bedroom with a brass bed, a large bath with oversize claw-foot tub, and a sunny, plant-filled porch with a wood-burning stove and treetop views. The Thomas Wahl Room is particularly nice, with a tiny table for two tucked into a large lake-view bay window; it also has an 1890s gas fireplace in the corner, a double marble shower, maple floors, and a cabbage rose–motif hooked rug.

Joan, a violinist with the Duluth-Superior Symphony Orchestra, encourages duets on the parlor's baby grand piano. Jim, whose background is in hotels, makes a point of offering comfort and relaxation to tired and stressed-out guests. The popular lake walk is just 2½ blocks from the inn, and the Halquists, both active, outdoorsy folks, can also recommend their favorite bike and cross-country ski trails; they even have a storage shed for any equipment you may bring. In addition, with two small children themselves, the Halquists don't mind accommodating the families of others. Their congeniality make the Ellery House very homey indeed.

🏠 *28 S. 21st Ave. E, Duluth, MN 55812, tel. 218/724–7639 or 800/355–3794. 2 double rooms with baths, 2 suites. No air-conditioning, ceiling fans and fresh flowers in rooms, fireplace in 2 rooms, balcony in 1 room, off-street parking. $69–$98 winter, $85–$125 summer; full breakfast. AE, MC, V. Smoking on porches only, no pets.*

Finnish Heritage Homestead

About 1891, Finnish immigrant John Kangas nearly froze to death for lack of shelter in the wilds of northern Minnesota—the state's Mesabi Iron Range region. As a blizzard moved in, Kangas shot a moose and—so the legend goes—cut the animal open to crawl inside as protection against the elements. Having survived a night there, he decided this had to be the place the heavenly powers wanted him to build his family's home. Almost 100 years after John began building his Embarrass, Minnesota, homestead, the area remains pretty wild, but the accommodations have improved considerably—thanks to Kangas's hard work and Finnish craftsmanship. He built nearly half a dozen log structures, including a rare 2½-story log building that served as a Finnish *poikatalo*, or boardinghouse, for loggers, miners, and railroad workers. Today, some of these buildings survive and can be explored, along with the fields and woods of the 32-acre farm.

In 1991, Buzz Schultz and his wife, Elaine Braginton, left the sweltering heat of Arizona to be closer to their beloved Boundary Waters Canoe Area (just a half hour away from Embarrass). The new owners of the Kangas homestead learned Embarrass townfolk frequently advised visiting dignitaries to "go stay with Buzz and Elaine. They've got room." So it seemed natural to convert the multiple-dwelling grounds of the farm into what the Finnish immigrants called a *matka koit*—a house to stay in while on a journey. The B&B offers five cozy, though somewhat small, upstairs rooms laid out in simple, comfortable farm style, with comforters on the beds and a few Norman Rockwell porcelain plates, photos, and memorabilia as wall hangings. All rooms share a bath, but guests are provided with terry-cloth robes and in winter, warm footies. The bathroom is almost as large as a guest room: One wall offers a bookcase stocked with everything from Garrison Keiller to guides on log-house restoration, and there's even an ironing board.

Short jaunts around the "neighborhood" can lead to skiing resorts in the winter or nifty places for fishing, swimming, canoeing, golfing, or hiking during warm weather. In Embarrass itself (the name derives from the term French voyagers gave the region's difficult-to-navigate rivers), townsfolk have revived the Finnish immigrant heritage with a gift shop, a heritage park, and the Heritage Pioneer Homestead Tour that, needless to say, includes the Kangas farm.

🏠 *4776 Waisanen Rd., Embarrass, MN 55732, tel. 218/984–3318 or 800/863–6545. 5 double rooms with shared bath. No air-conditioning, TV/VCR in parlor, wood-fired sauna. $58.50–$87.50 with special block rates to rent entire upstairs; full breakfast, bag lunch available for hikers, dinners available for extended-stay guests. MC, V. Smoking in designated areas only, no pets.*

The Mansion Bed & Breakfast Inn

Though imposing from the front, this 1928 rubble-stone and half-timbered Tudor mansion is really oriented toward its backyard. And what a backyard it is: Five hundred feet of Lake Superior shore provides the house with incredible views from almost every room. Who can resist sitting on the ample lawn in summer or fall to watch the many ships go by?

Built for mining executive Harry C. Dudley and his wife, Marjorie Congdon Dudley, daughter of Duluth lumber baron Chester Congdon, the Mansion is an inviting combination of grandeur and comfort. The main floor has a sunny dining room with a terrazzo floor, a wood-paneled library with a large fireplace and antique books, a large gallery with four window seats and three sets of French doors leading to a lakefront stone terrace, and a huge living room that opens onto a screened porch, a favorite spot for guests.

Sunny, lined with bear and wolf skins and moose heads, guarded by a suit of armor, and fitted with a huge lakeview window seat, the third-floor Trophy Room is the inn's designated quiet room. Guests use it for reading and dreaming, and "fall asleep here all the time," says proprietor Sue Monson, who, along with her husband, Warren, bought the building in 1983. Warren is a busy physician, so Sue, who likes to cater to the guests, runs the Mansion herself with some help from her three grown children and a small part-time staff.

The bedrooms that belonged to members of the Dudley family, such as the Anniversary Suite and the Master Suite, are the largest, but the coziest are the former maids' quarters, now called the Peach and Beige rooms. The Master Suite can expand to an additional bedroom, while the carriage house offers one-, two-, or three-bedroom accommodations. Some of the bedrooms, all of which are carpeted and contain antiques and reproductions, do pale in comparison to the absolute splendor of the Mansion itself, but as one of the guests said, "I can't imagine anyone coming here and not being completely impressed and comfortable."

The 7-acre grounds are given over to lawns, gardens, and a forest of northern hardwoods, pine, and cedar; there's also a private beach, where guests often build bonfires on summer evenings.

🏠 *3600 London Rd., Duluth, MN 55804, tel. 218/724–0739. 6 double rooms with baths, 4 doubles share 2 baths, 1-bedroom carriage-house suite. No air-conditioning, large-screen TV and VCR in living room, kitchenette in carriage house, private beach, off-street parking. $105–$205, $165 for carriage house; full breakfast. MC, V. Smoking on screened porch only, no pets.*

The Olcott House

At the turn of the century, William Olcott, president of Oliver Mining and onetime employee of John D. Rockefeller, and his wife, Fannie, traveled around the country, sketchbook in hand to record their favorite houses. In 1904, their dreams and sketches came together to create an impressive Georgian Colonial mansion, the Olcott House. The white-columned mansion set on emerald green lawns was built with hospitality in mind—as visitors will note when they discover its small basement ballroom. Today, that tradition continues, since the Olcott is now a hostelry that fits comfortably into Duluth's East End, just four blocks from Lake Superior and minutes to Canal Park and downtown. Since 1994 the Olcott has been the cherished possession of Barb and Don Trueman, and they've appropriately furnished the 12,000 square feet of the house, plus a carriage house, for its new life as a B&B.

Their choices make the house lush but not cluttered. People who had lived, worked, or studied in the house during its incarnations as a family home and later as a school of music for the University of Minnesota-Duluth made contributions to the house collection, such as the photographs of the Olcott family that now grace several walls or the chapter about life in the house from an Olcott daughter's biography—charmingly copied for guests to peruse.

The Truemans revel in their historic dwelling and give interested guests a tour of the home on their first evening. The entryway is suitably elegant, with dentil work and a gracefully curved staircase. The music room, to the left of the entry, was built with coved corners for acoustic quality and now sports a baby grand piano. The side-by-side dining rooms, where breakfast is served, have tables set with all the crystal and china trimmings and matched-pattern mahogany sliding doors, wainscoting, and beams. Upstairs, the house has five suites and one double room, each with a special offering, such as the three-season porch and bay window with lake and harbor view from the Lake Superior Suite, or the charm of the blue-and-white Summer Suite with its inlaid-tile fireplace.

The separate carriage house has a small, equipped kitchen, a large living room with a fireplace, arched paladium windows, and a queen-size bed beneath an overhead fan, along with white wicker furniture. Families will be pleased to know the Olcott House's gracious welcome also embraces children from toddlers on up.

2316 E. 1st St., Duluth, MN 55812, tel. 218/728–1339 or 800/715–1339. 1 double room, 5 suites, and a carriage house. No air-conditioning, cable TV, telephone, and stereo in carriage house, TV in rooms on request, fireplaces in suites. $85–$155 June–Oct, $75–$145 Nov.–May; full breakfast. MC, V. Smoking on porch only, no pets, 2-night minimum weekends June–Oct.

Pincushion Mountain Bed & Breakfast

After spending four snowless winters in Flagstaff, Arizona, Scott Beattie, a longtime cross-country skier and instructor, moved to a place where snow was guaranteed. He and his wife, Mary, checked out locations around the country and came to a spot 3 miles up the Gunflint Trail from Grand Marais. They built the Pincushion Mountain Bed & Breakfast in 1986. The almost unreal quiet here is broken only by the occasional birdcall.

The modern pine building sits on the Sawtooth Mountain ridgeline, 1,000 feet above Lake Superior. The woodsy inn has fir beams, pine and aspen paneled walls, and country-style furnishings and knickknacks.

Downstairs is a living room equipped with a woodstove and a dining room where a hearty breakfast is served. There are spectacular views of Lake Superior and the surrounding pine, aspen, and birch forest. This is the true north woods; don't be surprised if you see a deer, a moose, or even a bear passing by.

The four guest rooms upstairs are somewhat small but comfortable. The largest and probably most desirable is the corner Pine Room, which has a fold-out love seat, a comfortably sized bath, and a majestic view of Lake Superior in the distance. The Birch and Aspen rooms have tiny but adequate built-in baths with showers only; the latter has no lake view. The Maple Room has a private bath across the hall.

Scott, a certified ski instructor, gives skiing lessons, rents and repairs skis, and grooms Pincushion's own 15½ miles of trails. Although Pincushion accommodates skiers in particular, its 44 acres are equally attractive in summer and fall, when its ski trails are used for hiking. Because the inn's trails adjoin the 200-mile Superior Hiking Trail, Pincushion takes part in the north-shore lodge-to-lodge hiking program and in ski programs.

220 Gunflint Trail, Grand Marais, MN 55604-9701, tel. 218/387–1276 or 800/542–1226. 4 double rooms with baths. No air-conditioning, fan and clock radio in rooms, sauna, mountain bikes and cross-country skis for rent, 15½ mi of cross-country skiing and hiking trails, 1 mi of kerosene-lighted trails on winter Sat. nights, cross-country ski instruction, trail bag lunches available. $80–$100 with late spring specials; full breakfast, afternoon refreshments. MC, V. No smoking, no pets, 2-night minimum winter, late summer, and fall weekends, closed Apr.

The Stone Hearth Inn Bed & Breakfast

In 1989, when Charlie Michels came to Little Marais, he wanted to buy some land on Lake Superior. Two years later he had a five-bedroom, 70-year-old inn, and a wife, Susan, who'd been one of his first guests.

The Stone Hearth Inn was the original homestead of the Benjamin Fenstad family. Benjamin built a log cabin on the site in 1893 and in 1924, built the home that Charlie owns today. An accomplished Twin Cities carpenter and contractor, Charlie did most of the renovation work himself. He made 10 rooms into six, stripped the narrow-plank maple floors, added beams and molding downstairs, and collected stones from the shores of Lake Superior to use in the construction of the large living-room fireplace.

Just 80 feet from the lake, the house has a wonderful long porch furnished with Adirondack chairs, perfect for relaxing in these serene surroundings. French doors open onto it from both the simple dining room, whose large handmade pine table sits in the center, and from the living room, where soft chairs and sofas flank the giant hearth and guests take turns playing the piano.

In all five guest rooms, you can fall asleep to the comforting sounds of the lake, but you'll get the best views from Rooms 2, 3, and 4. Room 2, a corner room in blue and white with a four-poster canopy bed, has a lake view even from its pink-and-white ceramic-tile bathroom.

An old boathouse just 30 feet from the lake was renovated in 1992 and rebuilt as a two-unit cottage. One unit is a suite with a bedroom, bathroom, living room with sofa bed, and kitchenette. Both are upstairs and have gas fireplaces, whirlpool baths, and especially dramatic views from their picture windows. On the drawing board are two more double units with whirlpool baths and gas fireplaces, to be constructed in the carriage house.

Blueberry–wild rice pancakes, Austrian apple pancakes, lake trout sausage, and vanilla poached pears are perfect examples of Susan and Charlie's innovative cooking. On most clear nights, there is a bonfire down by the lake, with s'mores provided by the Micheleses and if you're lucky, northern lights provided by Mother Nature.

🏠 *1118 Hwy. 61 E, Little Marais, MN 55614, tel. 218/226–3020, fax 218/226–3466. 5 double rooms with baths, 1 suite with kitchenette. No air-conditioning, gas fireplace, coffeemaker, and whirlpool bath in 1 room and suite, kitchenette in suite, trail lunches available, bonfire, lodge-to-lodge hiking program. $79–$130; full breakfast in inn, Continental breakfast in boathouse double room, fully equipped kitchen in boathouse suite. AE, D, MC, V. No smoking, no pets.*

Fitger's Inn

Only the stone walls in a few of the guest rooms and the lovely lead-glass skylight and 19th-century iron registration cage in the high-ceiling lobby reveal the origins of this inn on Lake Superior, near downtown Duluth: In the 1850s, it was a brewery. Now extensively renovated, it is listed on the National Register of Historic Places.

Although the guest rooms are furnished with reproduction antiques, they seem more like upscale hotel rooms than those of a historic inn. But all are spacious and have big beds, desks, wing chairs, and modern baths. Thirty-seven rooms have lake views, and binoculars for boat- and bird-watching are provided. A new set of suites offers balconies, whirlpool baths, and double Jacuzzis, as well as terry-cloth robes and a box of locally made chocolates.

Fitger's is centrally located, convenient for exploring the town. There is a restaurant on site—a popular neighborhood spot—which overlooks Duluth's Lake Walk, well trod by visitors for its Aerial Lift Bridge and Canal Park sights. In summer, outdoor concerts are held nearby.

▥ *600 E. Superior St., Duluth, MN 55802, tel. 218/722–8826 or 800/726–2982 or 888/FITGERS. 42 double rooms with baths, 18 suites. Air-conditioning, phone, cable TV, and clock radio in rooms, room service, conference facilities, including 160-seat theater, off-street and free valet parking, adjoining shopping and restaurant complex. $92–$115, suites $150–$250; breakfast extra. AE, D, DC, MC, V. No unattended pets.*

The Inn at Palisade Bed & Breakfast

This little five-unit motel, built in 1955 and now a unique B&B, lies in one of the prettiest coves on Lake Superior's north shore. Owners Mary and Bob Barnett were driving in the area in 1986 when the property caught their eye; it was in good shape, and the location was a winner.

The four main-level units have private entrances onto the parking lot and 1950s-style pink ceramic-tile showers. They are all comfortably and neatly furnished, with small bay windows overlooking Lake Superior and the inn's crescent-shaped beach. The common room has a fireplace, a large picture window facing the lake, and an adjoining dining room where breakfast is served. On the building's lower level is one large guest room that contains a queen-size bed, a sitting area with a fold-out sofa, a table and chairs, a kitchenette, a fireplace, and two large picture windows. Also on this floor are a flagstone patio with a campfire circle and stairs leading down to the beach. Adjoining the inn's property on the northeast side is Tettegouche State Park, with hiking paths and waterfalls—one end of the state's new "water trail," on the shore of Lake Superior, which runs from Gooseberry Falls State Park to Tettegouche.

▥ *384 U.S. 61, Silver Bay, MN 55614, tel. 218/226–3505, fax 218/226–4648. 4 double rooms with baths, 1 suite with kitchen. No air-conditioning, TV, clock radio, kitchen, and fireplace in 1 room, campfire. $80–$105; full breakfast, afternoon snack, coffee available all day. D, MC, V. No smoking, no pets, closed mid-Oct.–Memorial Day.*

Lindgren's Bed & Breakfast

This log house is now a B&B run by Shirley Lindgren, who is a go-getter and then some. "My home is your home," she says—and a rather unique home it is, where the refined and the frontier mix below 18-foot beamed ceilings of knotty cedar. Just about every known denizen of the vast forests of the north shore—from black bear, moose, and wolf to deer, owl, and beaver—reside in stuffed form (bagged, no less, by Shirley) in the living-dining area, which also has a fireplace, tall windows overlooking Lake Superior, and plenty of comfortable chairs and sofas. A large, handmade cherry cabinet holds delicate crystal and fine china; across the room, a baby grand piano awaits a tune.

Except for a double whirlpool bath in Bobby's Room, the two front bedrooms are identical, down to the king-size bed placed under huge windows overlooking the lake. The large, rec room–style basement has a fireplace, glass doors with lake access, and enough bunks and sofa beds to accommodate a party of up to a dozen people.

🏠 *County Road 35, Box 56, Lutsen, MN 55612-0056, tel. 218/663-7450. 3 double rooms with baths, basement room with bunks and sofa beds. No air-conditioning, TV in rooms, phones in 2 rooms, whirlpool bath in 1 room, fireplace in 1 room, Finnish sauna, bonfire pit, horseshoe pit, volleyball area, lodge-to-lodge ski and hiking program. $85–$125; full breakfast, trail lunch available. MC, V. No smoking, no pets.*

Mathew S. Burrows 1890 Inn

Having driven through the Duluth area many times, Alan and Kathy Fink decided to give up their life in the busy city of Chicago to run a bed-and-breakfast in the Northland. Not wanting to start from scratch, they purchased the 1890 Inn, housed in an imaginative red-and-green Queen Anne with an unusual gazebo-style front porch.

The public rooms—a music room with a player piano and a parlor with a carved mahogany fireplace—are Victorian minus the usual Victorian clutter.

But the house's standout feature is its white oak-paneled dining room, which has a carved, built-in white oak mirrored buffet; a maple, walnut, oak, mahogany, and birch parquet floor; and what is undoubtedly the most magnificent blue-and-gold stained-glass window ever seen outside a church.

The best guest room is the new Ballroom Suite, which offers two bedrooms separated by a large, sparely furnished private sitting room with a daybed. The Lakeview Suite downstairs has a lace-draped four-poster canopy bed and twin French doors joining the bedroom to a private sitting room with corner windows and beautiful views.

🏠 *1632 E. 1st St., Duluth, MN 55812, tel. 218/724-4991 or 800/789-1890. 2 double rooms with baths, 3 suites. No air-conditioning, alarm clock, radio/tape player, fireplace and unique full-body marble shower in 1 suite; off-street parking. $95–$118; full breakfast. AE, D, DC, MC, V. No smoking, no pets, 2-night minimum summer weekends, closed Dec. 24–25.*

Naniboujou Lodge

Conceived in the 1920s as the cornerstone of an exclusive sportsmen's club, the Naniboujou Lodge, 15 miles northeast of Grand Marais, never grew beyond the hotel and its restaurant— but what a hotel and restaurant they are.

The lodge's focal point is the Great Hall, which has a huge 200-ton native rock fireplace. This room, now used for dining, is emblazoned with Cree motifs. The guest rooms are small but pleasant, remodeled and furnished with pine furniture and modern baths. Owners Tim and Nancy Ramey have kept the prices reasonable.

There is an abundance of recreational opportunities, but the lodge, which is on the National Register of Historic

Places, is definitely a place to sit back in the Adirondack chairs and enjoy the views of Lake Superior.

▦ *U.S. 61 (Box 505), Grand Marais, MN 55604, tel. and fax 218/387-2688. 24 double rooms with baths. Restaurant, no air-conditioning, fireplace in 5 rooms, lake view from 12 rooms, basketball and volleyball courts. $50–$90; breakfast extra, afternoon tea. D, MC, V. No smoking, no alcohol in restaurant, no pets, closed Oct. 20–May 17 except for a Christmas-week special and weekend packages Dec.–mid-Mar.*

The Superior Overlook B&B

Perched on a hill overlooking Lake Superior, 2 miles north of Grand Marais, this bed-and-breakfast truly lives up to its name.

Jack and Viola Kerber built their house in 1985 when they retired here from California. A few years later they converted the first floor to a three-bedroom B&B. It's a good spot for those who prefer to minimize their interaction with innkeepers, since there's a separate entrance, deck, living room with woodstove, and a kitchenette with toaster oven, microwave, coffeemaker, and beverage-stocked fridge.

It's quite a modern house—the living-room walls are light-blue cinder block, and the ceiling is acoustic tile—but then the real view is outside. The living room and the two guest rooms have wonderful views. The Deck Room can be arranged with twin beds or a king-size one; the Lake Suite has a queen-size bed, pink walls, a floral spread, a double whirlpool bath, and a separate entrance leading down a lake path.

▦ *U.S. 61, Milepost 112 (Box 963) Grand Marais, MN 55604-0963, tel. 218/387-1571 or 800/858-7622. 1 double with nonadjoining bath, 1 suite. No air-conditioning, TV, VCR, phone, and wood-burning stove in living room, kitchenette in suite, sauna. $95–$130; full breakfast. AE, D, MC, V. No smoking, no pets.*

The Northwest and the Cuyana Iron Range
Including Brainerd and Detroit Lakes

When Twin Cities residents talk about "going up north," they usually mean to Arrowhead, along the Lake Superior shore from Duluth to the Gunflint Trail. But to people in the more rural western parts of the state, "up north" means the northwest and the Cuyana Iron Range, around Alexandria, Detroit Lakes, Brainerd, and Walker.

Studded with lakes and state forests and threaded through with hiking trails and streams teeming with fish, the region is ideal for outdoorsy vacations. Here you'll find crystal-clear Lake Itasca, source of the Mississippi River, surrounded by the virgin-pine forest of Itasca State Park. Leech Lake, much lovelier than its name implies, sits within the Chippewa National Forest; the town of Walker, on Leech Lake's southwestern corner, is a fishing favorite. Mille Lacs Lake, just east of Brainerd, is another popular body of water, and the towns of Detroit Lakes and Alexandria, to the west, have long attracted tourists for their proximity to a number of small, beautiful lakes. Farther north, in a much more rugged and thinly settled part of Minnesota, Lake of the Woods stretches its many fingers up into neighboring Ontario and Manitoba. Fishing aficionados consider this lake among the best sporting destinations in the state, especially valued for its stock of large, battling muskies.

Besides such watery diversions as swimming, sailing, and fishing, there are plenty of other opportunities to enjoy the outdoors in these parts. The Heartland Trail, a blacktop bicycle path created from an old rail bed, runs 27 miles from Walker to Park Rapids. The North Country National Scenic Trail, 68 miles long, winds through the Chippewa National Forest between Walker and Romer. Among the many rivers designated as canoe trails are the Crow Wing River, Red Lake

River, Pine River, and the Mississippi River, from Lake Itasca down to Anoka, just north of Minneapolis.

Tying into the region's logging past, several towns (notably Brainerd and Bemidji) are touted as "Paul Bunyan's Hometown." An even more exotic bit of history is represented in Alexandria: A stone there with a rune on it is said to be evidence Viking explorers visited here in the 14th century.

Although Alexandria and Detroit Lakes have long been tourist oriented, the region was traditionally supported by logging and taconite mining. (The Cuyana is one of three iron ranges in the United States; the Mesabi and Vermilion ranges to the east are more familiar to Minnesotans.) Once the old-growth trees were felled and the mines were worked out, the region fell on hard economic times, but is now making a modest comeback, thanks in large part to tourism.

Accommodations tend to be smaller and not as fancy as those in Arrowhead or the St. Croix Valley, but consequently, prices are lower.

Places to Go, Sights to See

Bunyan House Information Center (300 Bemidji Ave. [Rte. 197], Bemidji, tel. 218/751–3540). A so-called collection of the mythical lumberjack's tools and memorabilia is the main attraction here; there's also the requisite giant statues of Paul and his blue ox, Babe. Open Memorial Day–Labor Day, daily; weekdays the rest of the year.

Deer Town (U.S. 71, 1 mi north of Park Rapids, tel. 218/732–1943). Deer, goats, geese, and sheep roam around this re-created pioneer village, which also has a small museum and playground. Open May 12–Labor Day, daily.

Itasca State Park (Hwy. 200 and U.S. 71, about 35 mi southwest of Bemidji, tel. 218/266–2114). Minnesota's oldest state park is still one of its best—a 32,000-acre sanctuary of pine forest known for its excellent bird-watching (at least one pair of loons stays on the lake each summer), hiking, biking, and cross-country ski trails. Canoe, boat, pontoon, and bike rentals are available. Lake Itasca contains the headwaters of the Mississippi River. Up here, you can cross the river by walking on a few smooth stepping-stones; farther down, it is a gentle, honey-colored stream, nothing like the muddy colossus it later becomes. Also highly recommended is

Zippel Bay State Park (Lake of the Woods, Williams, tel. 218/783–6252), which gives you a taste of wild northern Minnesota.

Lumbertown USA (U.S. 77, 15 mi northwest of Brainerd, tel. 218/829–8872). More than 25 replicas and restorations of 19th-century buildings re-create a logging town of the 1870s, complete with a maple-sugar plant, a general store, an ice-cream parlor, a pioneer home, a wax museum, an old-fashioned train, and a riverboat. Open daily Memorial Day–Labor Day.

Oliver H. Kelley Historic Farm (U.S. 10, 2½ mi southeast of Elk River, tel. 612/441–6896). A living museum of 19th-century agricultural practices, this farm on the banks of the Mississippi River has guides, in period costume, out with their horses and oxen demonstrating farm chores of the day. The original owner, Oliver Kelley, founded the Patrons of Husbandry, also known as the Grange, a farmers' fraternal organization that grew to have significant political influence in the 1870s. Open daily May–October.

Paul Bunyan Amusement Center (Junction of Rtes. 210 and 371, 2 mi west of Brainerd, tel. 218/829–6342). Offering the standard assortment of children's rides, minigolf, go-carts, and performing animals, this small park has one outstanding feature: a 26-foot animated statue of Paul Bunyan (with a 15-foot Babe, the blue ox, behind him) that spins tall tales to youngsters. Open daily, Memorial Day–Labor Day.

Sinclair Lewis Interpretive Center and Museum (Junction of I–94 and U.S. 71, Sauk Centre, tel. 320/352–5201). There was no love lost between Sinclair Lewis and his hometown, Sauk Centre, when the Nobel laureate-to-be depicted the town as "Gopher Prairie" in his novel *Main Street*. More than 70 years later, Sauk Centre folks have embraced their most famous native son, renaming a street after him. This museum is full of interesting artifacts related to Lewis and his hometown, which is a fairly typical Minnesota small town—neither gorgeous nor plain, but pleasant and practical. Here the **Sinclair Lewis Boyhood Home** (612 Sinclair Lewis Ave.) displays family memorabilia and 1900s furnishings.

Summerhill Farm (U.S. 71, 7 mi north of Park Rapids, tel. 218/732–3865). Several buildings of an old farmstead have been converted into this collection of gift shops selling artwork and gifts. There's also a restaurant on the premises.

Restaurants

The area's restaurants, such as Bemidji's **Union Station** (Union Sq., 1st St. and Beltrami Ave., tel. 218/751–9261), serve a lot of steak, seafood, and prime rib. If you're looking for something different, head for the **Brauhaus** (U.S. 34, Akeley, tel. 218/652–2478), a little German place in the middle of the county, or **Companeros** (U.S. 226, Dorset, tel. 218/732–7624), a big, colorful Mexican spot in a very small town.

Tourist Information

Bemidji Chamber of Commerce (300 Bemidji Ave., Bemidji, MN 56601, tel. 218/751–3541); **Brainerd Lakes Area Chamber of Commerce** (110 N. 6th St., Brainerd, MN 56401, tel. 218/829–2838); **Detroit Lakes Regional Chamber of Commerce** (700 Washington Ave., Detroit Lakes, MN 56501, tel. 218/847–9202 or 800/542–3992); **Fergus Falls Chamber of Commerce** (202 S. Court St., Fergus Falls, MN 56537, tel. 218/736–6951); **Minnesota Office of Tourism, Northcentral/West Regional Office** (422 James St., Brainerd, MN 56401, tel. 218/828–2334); **Sauk Centre Area Chamber of Commerce** (1220 S. Main St., Sauk Centre, MN 56378, tel. 320/352–5201).

Elm St. Inn

In the prairie town of Crookston, Minnesota, historic buildings are not a rarity: Thirty-five buildings in its business district alone are listed in the National Register of Historic Places. The architect of several of those buildings also designed this charming Arts & Crafts–era house in 1910. From lawyer to doctor to banker, the house served as a presentable, livable home for the town's professional families until it fell to the Crookston School Board, which had plans to demolish it. John and Sheryl Winters, both involved in a local law firm, saved it from that fate in 1976. By 1992, their children had left home, and the Winterses decided it was time to open their home to guests rather than ramble around in the suddenly all-too-ample space.

Downstairs, the small Grandmother's Room has a hunter green iron bed from the family's heirlooms as well as a maple antique vanity dresser with an hourglass-shaped mirror. Upstairs, the maple-floored rooms "blossom." The Prairie Rose Room's sponge-painted walls are done in dusty rose and peach. A white wrought-iron bed with eyelet comforter and ruffles is accented with a hand-painted pillow, while a restored oak rocker cradles a teddy bear. The Morning Glory Room, done in pink-and-blue floral patterns, has a hand-made "quilter's quilt" on the high queen-size bed (a wooden step is stowed below the bed for those needing a boost).

The passionate purples of the Lilac Room have become a favorite with guests, according to the Winterses. Pinks and purples dominate just about everything—even the hangars are purple. A hand-tied quilt covers the Pennsylvania cherry-wood antique bed. The private bath next door is another reason so many guests lay claim to this room. Its delicate floral patterns of faded greens and peaches, a stained-glass window of greens and lavenders, and an assortment of bubble baths and an oversize claw-foot tub (big enough for two) make long soaks a luxurious temptation. For more aquatic relaxation, you can opt for a pass to the township's enclosed pool, just across the lawn from the inn.

Breakfast is served—charmingly by candlelight—on stylish china in the dining room, and guests benefit from John's upbringing in the family bakery. Wild rice–buttermilk pancakes with sunflower seeds top the favored fare. A music room, and a library room with a TV, a well-stocked bookcase, and a couch, and the airy upstairs screened porch with white wicker furnishings and a beguiling assortment of wind-chimes—all conspire to make the inn a hard place to leave.

🏨 *422 Elm St., Crookston, tel. 218/281–2343 or 800/568–4467, fax 218/281–1756. 4 double rooms with baths. Air-conditioning in some rooms, TV/VCR in living room, alarm clocks in rooms. $55–$65; full breakfast. AE, D, MC, V. No smoking indoors, no pets.*

Hallett House

As you drive out of Crosby and approach the grand front lawn of Hallett House, you may feel you've stepped back in time. A driveway that curves beneath oaks and jack pines brings you to the front door of a pale Georgian Revival house with green trim and a small arched portico. Inside, painted Georgian paneling suggests grandeur, but the lush green wool carpeting somehow shrinks the large rooms to livable size. Sun streams through the windows of a porch that's been made into a wicker-furnished guest room. The library, with a fireplace and built-in bookshelves, has the air of a corner in an old-fashioned men's club.

Upstairs, past yellow-and-blue 1950s-era wallpaper with Early American scenes, the guest rooms give off that same feeling of luxury. The big, carpeted rooms, which have solid, often antique furniture and bay windows with venetian blinds, encourage the fantasy that you're staying in the home of some long-lost rich uncle. Here is the room of "the lady of the house," with its mirror-lined dressing area and vanity—you can almost smell the Chanel No. 5 and hear the faint tinkling of silver bracelets. Here is the master bedroom, with a baronial bed facing the bay window, or the maid's quarters, with her rather small bed and her own sitting room (and an up-to-date TV set). Down the hall, the eldest son's room seems to have been kept as it must have been before he left for college, all hardwood floors and a big oak bedstead.

In truth, the house was built in the early '20s by E. W. Hallett, a construction and real-estate magnate who was once one of the richest men in the county. Hallett was a fiscally conservative man—he didn't lose his shirt in the stock market crash—and his house, though large, is not ostentatious. He died in 1983 (at the age of 101!), and six years later a local couple, Kathy and Wes Pernula, bought the well-preserved home and turned it into a bed-and-breakfast. They've had the sense to leave well-enough alone, adding only a few frills and figurines, most of them downstairs, so the delicious feeling of quiet privilege still prevails.

Hwy. 210 (Box 247), Crosby, MN 56441, tel. 218/546–5433. 5 double rooms with baths. Air-conditioning units available and ceiling fans in all rooms, cable TV in 2 bedrooms and in library. $55–$75; full breakfast. AE, MC, V. No smoking, no pets.

Hospital Bay B&B

You'd think the name of this hostelry would be named after the neighboring bay; in fact, it's the other way around—the bay in Warroad, Minnesota, got its moniker from this turn-of-the-century house, which spent a spell as the region's hospital. Its heyday was during the Midwest's logging and commercial-fishing boom from the 1920s through the 1940s. Today, however, the area still boasts one of the lowest unemployment rates in the Midwest, with the nearby Marvins Windows and Polaris factories employing all comers in this sparsely populated region.

The house was built in 1906 by local merchant Carl Carlquist for his family and at one time featured a magnificent turret (now removed). Happily, the picturesque horseshoe arches remain over the outside windows. The original interior of the house has been altered several times, particularly when the structure was a hospital ward. It's current owners, Harvey and Mary Corneliusen, purchased this onetime sanctuary of healing in 1985, when ill health forced them to leave their nearby farm and settle down to a less rigorous way of life. Together, they've made it airy and bright, with white walls and white lace curtains as a tranquilizing backdrop. Two special spots invite guests to relax and mellow out: a charming paisley-print love seat and matching armchair in the living room, and the sitting room—a comfy cocoon with brick fireplace and built-in bookcases. Many eyes remain focused on the views out the windows: Warroad is on the state's Wildflower Route and offers some of the best bird-watching around, with several migration routes traversing directly around the site.

Just off the sitting room is the Parkside Room, done in pale rose-colored floral wallpaper, with a four-poster Broyhill bed covered simply with a white spread. Here you'll find one of the many porcelain lamps scattered through the house—in this case, a lovely blue-and-pink number that complements the room's palette. An antique accent is a turn-of-the-century oak washstand with an inset of birds'-eye maple. Upstairs beyond the dining room is Lisa's Room, named after the Corneliusens' daughter, who actually designed the room—which has a river view—from its compelling dark pink hue to its wallpaper border of an undersea motif. The white wrought-iron bed is a pleasing touch to this homey chamber. Next door, the room's small private bath has an enclosed claw-foot tub.

All in all, this is a pleasant and relaxing B&B—its ambience all the more welcome for this is as far north as a B&B gets in rugged Minnesota.

🏨 *620 Lake St. NE, Warroad, MN 56763, tel. 218/386–2627 or 800/568–6028. 3 double rooms with private baths. Air-conditioning in all but 1 room, TV/VCR in living room, fireplace in sitting room, free docking on river for guests with boats. $45–$60; full breakfast. MC, V. No smoking, no pets.*

Oakhurst Inn

It was perhaps the most prestigious house in the prosperous town of Princeton at one time, but when David and Suzie Spain bought Oakhurst in 1989, it was a cluttered near ruin. It took two years of hard work to return the house to something close to its days of glory. Unlike the original owner, banker John Skahen, the Spains aren't made of money, so Oakhurst today feels more like a family home than a ostentatious mansion. Still, much of the grandeur remains.

Built in 1906, the three-story house is one of those Victorians that borrowed from many styles, hence the Queen Anne wraparound porch and the magnificent Romanesque fireplace in the front parlor. The front door opens onto a grand vestibule, with ceilings nearly 10 feet high, oak floors and woodwork, and a long bench built into one wall. To the right are the front and back parlors (the Spains have added oak wainscoting to the back parlor and turned it into a library); to the left is the dining room, complete with plate rail. The Spains hope to make the decor more consistent with one period: At present, an Eastlake chair, a mission rocker, and a reupholstered camelback couch sit incongruously near one another. An air of homey middle-class nostalgia is perpetuated by Norman Rockwell plates, small stuffed bears, and braided area rugs.

Upstairs, the tasteful, comfortable guest rooms do better at creating a period look. The John J. Skahen Room, for instance, features a velvet fainting couch and a pencil-post four-poster queen-size bed covered with reproduction quilted lace. The smaller Sterling Room has a bathroom with such 1906-type features as a pedestal sink, a claw-foot tub, and wainscoting. The sunny Lucy Room has a white iron bed with lace coverlet and lace curtains at the windows, making for a pleasant mixture of frill and simplicity.

The Spains and their children live on the third floor of this big house, and perhaps their presence has something to do with the down-to-earth family atmosphere of the place. Guests are welcome to visit Suzie in the kitchen, where they may be offered a chocolate-chip cookie or two while she talks of the horrors of renovation. While the remodeling was no doubt hard to live through, the result is a cozy success.

 212 S. 8th Ave., Princeton, MN 55371, tel. 612/389–3553 or 800/ 443–2258. 3 double rooms with baths. Air-conditioning, TV/VCR in library. $70–$85; full breakfast on weekends, Continental on weekdays, evening refreshments. MC, V. No smoking, no pets.

Park Street Inn

This little jewel box sits on a little street in a little town you'd miss if you drove too fast. Nevis, once a prosperous logging town, now makes a bid for tourism with the nearby Heartland Bike Trail and Lake Belle Taine. The Park Street Inn represents this newer Nevis, although it is also rooted in the town's history.

Built in 1912 by Justin Halvorson, a well-to-do banker and local land developer, the house is more of a bungalow than a mansion, but it was done up in style—or more accurately, all kinds of styles, for Halvorson apparently was no purist. The compact oak stairway and banister were constructed out of state and brought to town by train. Other Midwestern craftsmen contributed a beveled-glass fan window and exquisite entry arches of carved oak in a French Empire style, with acanthus-topped fluted columns and flower-basket bas-reliefs. In contrast, an oak mantel sports the clean, simple lines of mission-style design.

Halvorson lost his money in the Depression and moved to California. Given that Nevis, too, was declining, it's surprising so many of the original treasures in the house remained. Irene and Len Hall bought the place in 1996 after it had already been a B&B for several years. Many of the house furnishings are original, but the Halls added their own personal touches to the rooms so tactfully that returning guests felt sure several new pieces had been there all along.

In the living room and dining area, subdued wallpaper and matching valances complement lace-curtained windows. The Halls decided to make a major statement in the living room; they adorned it with a bubbling fountain, and dominating one corner is a striking backlit stained-glass window whose original home was a Methodist church.

The upstairs is a bit less restrained, but still interesting. The largest guest room, which has a wicker-furnished sleeping porch facing Lake Belle Taine, also features a built-in cupboard bed whose oak arch came from a Lutheran church altar—a nice ecumenical touch given the stained-glass window below, Len likes to note. Each room has its own wallpaper pattern and quilt—a handmade double wedding-ring quilt in one bedroom, a bright star pattern in another. The Halls also restocked the numerous built-in bookshelves (with both new and antique vintage editions) and added many more, making the house a sort of BBB—Bed, Book, and Breakfast.

🏨 *Rte. 1 (Box 254), Nevis, MN 56467, tel. 218/652–4500 or 800/797–1778. 3 double rooms with baths, 1 suite. No air-conditioning, TV in sitting room. $55–$90; full breakfast, evening refreshments. MC, V. Smoking in designated area only, pets and small children by arrangement.*

Peters' Sunset Beach

One look inside the main lodge's dining room gives you the flavor of this classic lakeside resort: knotty-pine paneling, fish trophies, paintings of scenes from a Hiawatha-like Native American legend, light fixtures done up like painted drums, and a broad porch overlooking Lake Minnewaska.

The lodge, a gorgeous example of Craftsman-style design, is one of the resort's three buildings on the National Register of Historic Places. The place has changed a bit since train conductor Henry Peters jumped off the Soo Line in Glenwood and opened his summer hotel in 1915. It has grown from a small hostelry to a resort, complete with its own 18-hole golf course, accommodating up to 175 guests in a variety of up-to-date rooms, cottages, and luxury town houses. But it's still run by the Peters family, and they have restored the historic 1923 Annex to its old-fashioned appearance—making it, in the words of Henry's grandson Bill Peters, "our country inn."

From the outside, the Annex looks a lot like the main lodge, almost like a wing that detached itself and settled several steps away.

The Peterses have installed antique bedsteads, tables, and dressers, many of them from the turn of the century, to fit in with the refinished original woodwork. Quilts, made by a local artisan, grace each bed; the wallpaper is quietly floral. The whole building has an agreeable, unpretentious air about it, although there are some discordant touches left over from the Annex's pre-restoration interim years.

Still, the Annex has a certain charm, and there are other compensations: The restaurant serves some of the best food in the area. The nearby town of Glenwood is pretty, the resort's grounds are gracious, and Lake Minnewaska itself is lovely. You can certainly see why Henry Peters made this the end of his line.

2500 S. Lakeshore Dr., Glenwood, MN 56334, tel. 320/634–4501 or 800/ 356–8654 in MN. 20 double rooms (12 in Court Bldg., 8 in Annex) with baths; 3 suites in Main Lodge, 10 town houses sleep 4–9 people; 2 1-bedroom cottages, 5 2-bedroom cottages, 3 3-bedroom cottages, 1 4-bedroom cottage; 1 7-bedroom housekeeping cottage. Restaurant, snack bar, air-conditioning, cable TV in all units, meeting room, beach, boat rentals, tennis, golf, racquetball. $65–$95, $250 for town houses and cottages; full breakfast and dinner. MC, V. No pets, 2- to 4-night minimum, closed Oct.–Apr.

Spicer Castle

I f you somehow missed the opportunity to live in an old country mansion circa 1913, here's your chance. This imposing house, now on the National Register of Historic Places, was built in 1895 by farm developer John Spicer, one of the founders of Minnesota's branch of the Democratic Party. According to current owner Allen Latham, Spicer's grandson, the last renovations on the house were done in 1913, shortly after it was wired for electricity, and the building hasn't been changed since. Set on the wooded shores of Green Lake, the Tudor-style half-timbered house was originally called Medayto Cottage, but in the 1930s fishermen on the lake started referring to it as "the Castle," perhaps because of its crenellated tower. Though it's otherwise not particularly castlelike, the name stuck.

However beautiful its exterior, it's the interior that makes the Castle distinctive. The furnishings, rugs, china, and Craftsman-style lamps and clocks are all antiques and have been in place since the 1913 redecoration. Walking across the gleaming maple floors, through the living and dining rooms, the well-stocked library, and the grand porch overlooking the lake, you get the sense you are not just viewing the past, but actually participating in it.

The first floor, with dark furniture and burlap wall coverings (a typical period Craftsman touch), might seem dark, but it's not oppressive—rather, it encourages quiet reflection and talk. In winter, it becomes downright cozy, as the fireplaces throw their flickering light on the ceiling beams.

Upstairs, it's almost like a different house. White beaded paneling and large windows give the place the bright air of a Nantucket summer cottage. Some renovation has been done up here, primarily in the bathrooms, but Allen and his wife, Marti, have kept to the period, with pedestal sinks and claw-foot tubs (some in the rooms themselves). The bedsteads and dressers are in various styles, but all belonged to the Lathams' forebears. Two equally well-preserved cottages offer more privacy.

Breakfast is served in the dining room in cool months, on the lakeside porch in summer. There are no TVs, telephones, or air-conditioning. This is pure 1913—they won't be missed.

▥ *11600 Indian Beach Rd. (Box 307), Spicer, MN 56288, tel. 320/796–5870 or 800/821–6675. 8 double rooms with baths, 2 cottages. No air-conditioning, ceiling fans in selected rooms, whirlpool bath in 1 bedroom and 1 cottage. $60–$130; full breakfast, afternoon tea. AE, D, MC, V. No smoking, no pets, closed weekdays Sept.–Apr.*

Carrington House

Save for its antebellum roof railing, the simple facade of Carrington House gives the deceptive impression that the rest of the house is similarly plain. It's the back that's really inviting—a long, enclosed porch with tall windows faces Lake Carlos, awnings shade the windows, and stairs lead down to a waterside deck.

Built in 1911, this is a typical lakeshore "cottage" of its era. Throughout the house, hardwood floors, high ceilings, and textured-plaster walls contribute to a calm, light-filled setting. The enormous living room, with its big fireplace and wicker furniture, mingles antiques and modern items.

Redecorated by owners Janet and Bruce Berg, the guest rooms each have a unique flavor, ranging from simple country to ornate. One unifying motif comes from the different stenciled patterns found on the walls of each room. In back is a cottage with pink furnishings and a whirlpool tub. Though some rooms are a little too frilly, the overall feeling is of a comfortable summerhouse made for easy relaxation.

🏠 *4974 Interlochen Dr., Alexandria, MN 56308, tel. 320/846-7400 or 800/806-3899. 4 double rooms with baths, 1 cottage. Air-conditioning, cable TV on porch, ceiling fans in commons area, whirlpool bath in cottage and 1 room. $85-$130; full breakfast. No credit cards. No smoking, pets by prior consent.*

Heartland Trail Inn

The village of Dorset—population 38—was once the smallest town in the world to have its own bank. The bank has since closed, and in 1970 so did its three-room, two-story schoolhouse. Still, the town comes alive at night, thanks to four popular restaurants, and it also attracts cyclists on the Heartland Trail, which runs between Walker and Park Rapids. Its former schoolhouse now serves as the town's B&B—charmingly filled with American flags, Americana trinkets, and some of the cutest B&B touches around.

Surrounded on three sides by fields and woods, the plain clapboard structure with its neat red roof still has a spare, wind-whipped look. The original three schoolrooms have been cleaned up and broken into six bright guest rooms, with their grade school–based names—Geography, Art, Astronomy, Reading, etc.—posted on miniature slate boards. Refinished maple floors are cool and spotless, the walls freshly painted, and the sliding glass doors factory fresh. Each room opens onto a deck. The old cloak room has been enlarged and turned into a common room. Stroll down the hallways and take in the old-fashioned school desks, maps, and chalkboards. Even the stairways still show the wear and tear of generations of young feet.

🏠 *Rte. 3 (Box 39), Park Rapids, MN 56470, tel. 218/732-5305. 6 double rooms share 3 baths. Air-conditioning, ceiling fans in selected rooms. $45-$60; full breakfast. MC, V. No smoking, no pets.*

Log House on Spirit Lake and Homestead

Bad weather put Lyle and Yvonne Tweten into the B&B business. After retiring to northern Minnesota, they bought 115 acres on Spirit Lake, built a house, and settled in. Then in 1984 a tornado in McIntosh, Minnesota, hit Lyle's boyhood home, a by-then decrepit white clapboard farmhouse that had been in the family since 1889. Several boards were ripped off, revealing a surprise underneath: The house was made of square-hewn poplar logs. The Twetens moved the structure to their land, setting it on a hill a few steps from the lake, and restored it as a B&B.

Inside the three-story house are the original whitewashed walls, reproduction fir floorboards, and period furnishings. The upstairs bedroom has a dark ceiling beam and old-fashioned rag rugs on the wide-plank floors. The lower-level bedroom is more modern, but its private deck and porch are built from old silo wood. Small touches, like the "nest and breakfast" bird feeder on the porch and the tea, coffee, and bottled beverages in the kitchen, make the old house homey.

In 1993, the Twetens opened up the neighboring, turn-of-the-century Homestead. Daughter Susanne takes care of the Hometead's rooms and suites, bringing breakfast on a tea cart sometime after the early morning beverage, newspaper, and fruit kabob. Christina's Room upstairs offers a separate, connected room for sitting or enjoying the whirlpool bath, while Augusta's Room, done in floral patterns of black, white, and deep red, has a fireplace as well.

The top floor has now been converted into the Fredholm Suite, accented with modern imported Swedish furniture. The simple, clean lines of the furniture echo the bedroom's multiple-angled roof, dotted with six skylights, two of which bracket the queen-size wooden bed. To one side of the bed is a whirlpool bath and shower with a small European-style water closet, and on the other side is a large sitting area offering a wall-size window looking onto the lake. The pickled birch floors and the refreshingly cool white-and-blue palette of the room make it even brighter. A small refrigerator sits next to the two-sided fireplace. Just outside the bedroom, a library-style table from Sweden resides beside another lake-view window; here, breakfast is served in private comfort. Outside, cold weather often transforms the land-scape into a winter wonderland; the owners happily supply guests with snowshoes for hiking the surrounding area.

🏨 *Ottertail Rte. 4 (Box 130), Vergas, MN 56587, tel. 218/342–2318 or 800/ 342–2318. 5 double rooms with baths. Air-conditioning, terry-cloth robes and fresh flowers, fireplace and whirlpool bath in 3 rooms. $85–$135; full breakfast, welcome tray. D, MC, V. No smoking, no pets.*

Nims' Bakketopp Hus

Bakketopp Hus is Norwegian for Hilltop House, and it's an appropriate name—the hillside views of rural Long Lake are perhaps the strongest asset of this large house, which Dennis and Judy Nims turned into a bed-and-breakfast after their children were grown. Judy is of Norwegian ancestry, hence the inn's name. While there are some antique items here, most notably the huge buffet that dominates the living room, the overall decor befits a house built in 1975. It's essentially a suburban split-level built larger than usual and with some rustic touches added—particularly sweet is the small Norwegian bathtub for babies, crafted from a single piece of hardwood.

The mauve-and-blue Master Suite, popular with newlyweds, offers an oversize whirlpool hot tub and a view of and direct access to the front garden. Another guest room, which opens onto a lake-view patio, has peach country French decor, with a draped canopy bed and a love seat.

Downstairs, a game room with pool table and player piano is available for guests, as is a large outdoor deck upstairs, which faces the lake.

🏨 *R.R. 2 (Box 187A), Fergus Falls, MN 56537, tel. 218/739–2915 or 800/ 739–2915. 3 double rooms with baths. Air-conditioning, cable TV available* *on request, phone in rooms, oversize whirlpool bath in 1 room. $65–$95; full breakfast, evening refreshments. D, MC, V. No smoking, pets by prior consent.*

Prairie View Estate

Thank goodness for Norwegian bachelor farmers who throw nothing away. When sisters Phyllis Haugrud, Carol Moses, and Janet Malakowsky inherited the 800-acre family farm from their unmarried uncle in 1990, his will forbade them to sell it. Inside this Craftsmanesque beige stucco house, they found loads of old family furniture and decided to turn the home into a B&B.

Exposed rafters and dark wood furnishings—some more than 100 years old—create a portrait not only of old Minnesota farm life, but also of Old Norway. The three guest rooms have solid, well-made antiques—not fancy pieces, but often beautiful.

Some restoration has yet to be completed, but it's easy to ignore the remaining details when you sit enjoying breakfast on the lovely long, enclosed porch with hardwood floors. At Prairie View Estate, the past—and homey hospitality—is alive and well. Children are particularly welcome here.

Rte. 2 (Box 443), Pelican Rapids, MN 56572, tel. 218/863–4321 or 800/298–8058. 1 double room with bath, 2 doubles share bath. Air-conditioning, TV in parlor. $50–$65; full breakfast, evening refreshments. D, MC, V. No smoking, no pets.

Stonehouse Bed and Breakfast

Stonemason Craig Nagel and his wife, Claire, built Stonehouse in 1988 on wooded acreage that's just a short walk from Lund Lake, a marsh with nesting birds. The low-angled house is somewhat stark and ordinary from the out-side, but the Nagels have emphasized a sense of nature. The exterior walls are made of cedar and stone that Craig prepared; the pine interior walls and floors came from trees right on the property. Craig also split the stones for the fireplace. Claire added decorations and crafted the stained glass that appears here and there throughout the house.

There's a double bed in the bedroom and a queen-size bed in the living area, so up to four people can stay here at a time. Though comfortable, furnishings may remind some visitors of a good-quality motel—track lighting, nubby wall-to-wall carpeting, and modern TV and kitchen appliances. One may wish the Stonehouse were more eccentric and charming, like the Nagel's own house nearby, where breakfast is usually served. (Breakfast will be served at the cottage upon request.) Still, this homemade (and well-made) cottage has the right location, nestled in a grove of pine trees, and its screened porch and stone-walled terrace are pleasant.

HCR 2 (Box 9), Pequot Lakes, MN 56472, tel. 218/568–4255. 1 cottage with double bed and queen-size bed. No air-conditioning, TV/VCR, kitchen. $80–$125; full breakfast. MC, V. No pets.

Walden Woods

It's not nearly as austere as Thoreau's famous cabin in Massachusetts, but Walden Woods has the same back-to-basics spirit. Seventeen years ago, Richard Manly, a Minnesota-trained forester who had worked many years for the Audubon Society in New York City, built his own log cabin near Mud Lake, a wooded pond about 17 miles east of Brainerd.

Though of recent vintage, Walden Woods doesn't look raw or artificially rustic. The quietly tasteful antique furnishings, in an eclectic mix of styles, work well inside these Norwegian pine walls. A porch faces the pond and the surrounding woods. Up the split-log staircase is a well-stocked library. The guest rooms all have hardwood floors, antique bedsteads, and subdued floral curtains, and Anne Manly, a straw weaver and basket maker, has accented them with her work.

The worthier elements of civilization are provided—bathrooms are up-to-date, though with older-style fixtures. There are many beautiful clocks here, but the Manlys don't bother to wind them. As for TV and air-conditioning, who needs them when you can listen to the loons serenade at dusk on "Walden Pond"?

▥ *16070 Rte. 18 SE, Deerwood, MN 56444, tel. 320/692-4379. 4 double rooms share 2 baths. No air-conditioning. $55–$75; full breakfast. AE, MC, V. No smoking, no pets.*

Whistle Stop Inn

This must be the only B&B in the world with a caboose outfitted with a whirlpool bath. Named for its proximity to a set of railroad tracks, this 1903 Queen Anne Victorian opened as a B&B in 1992. Owners Jann and Roger Lee had always dreamed of opening a bed-and-breakfast, and while vacationing in Roger's hometown of New York Mills, they spotted the perfect house. They bought it and opened for business six months later. Originally

owned by August Nylan, a Finnish newspaperman, the house's exterior is standard Victorian, but the Lees have added a whimsical touch inside while maintaining the original elegance.

Filled with railroad memorabilia and nostalgia—miniature trains, a red 1947 Coca-Cola machine, and even a mannequin dressed in authentic railroad gear—the parlor is almost a museum. The rest of the house is more classically decorated, with period antiques and photos of the Nylan family. Upstairs, the blue-and-rose Northern Pacific Room has a delicate but sizable antique armoire and a claw-foot tub. The sunny Great Northern Suite has the original pine-and-fir woodwork and built-in glass shelves. A remarkably appointed house in every way—guests can even enjoy a working sauna—the Whistle Stop recently added a real caboose, quaintly outfitted, complete with whirlpool bath and queen-size Murphy bed for guests who want an extra bit of privacy.

▥ *Rte. 1 (Box 85), New York Mills, MN 56567, tel. 218/385-2223 or 800/328-6315. 2 double rooms with baths, 1 suite, 1 caboose with whirlpool bath. No air-conditioning, cable TV in suite and 1 bedroom, ceiling fans in suite, sauna. $39–$69; full breakfast, evening refreshments upon request. AE, D, MC, V. Smoking on porch only, no pets.*

The Southwestern Prairie

Southwestern Minnesota, along with St. Louis and Texas, once served as a gateway to the American West. The West that begins here is the northern prairie, a vast sea of grass that sustained herds of buffalo. This expanse was also the home of one of the greatest of all Native American nations, the Dakota—otherwise known as the Sioux, although that's actually an insulting term that roughly means "snake." The Dakota considered the region near the South Dakota border sacred, and they quarried its soft red stone to make peace pipes (hence the town named Pipestone). They believed that their tribe originated here, and that the color of the stone came from the blood of their ancestors.

The white people who settled here were predominantly German and Scandinavian immigrants, who brought with them cherished relics of their homelands—the German influence in New Ulm, for example, is still very strong. For all the prairie's beauty, what the newer settlers valued even more was its rich soil. Families like the Ingallses, whose daughter Laura grew up to immortalize her Walnut Grove home in such books as The Little House on the Prairie, *were called sodbusters because they had to plow up dense mats of roots in order to plant their corn. It took a lot of pioneer grit, but once the land was plowed, it yielded good crops.*

On the prairie, the pleasures of life are generally on a small-town scale. Many towns proudly celebrate their heritage with summer events such as Pipestone's Civil War Festival and Walnut Grove's yearly Little House pageant. Their small county historical museums provide fodder for an hour's low-key browsing, nothing more. St. Peter, a trim college town in the bucolic Minnesota River valley, was originally planned as Minnesota's capital (until St. Paul's wheeler-dealers stole that plum for themselves), and it still has the original wide streets, along which many gracious homes proudly stand. Other county seats, such as Blue Earth and Pipestone, are equally prosperous and charming, with typically handsome country courthouses (often constructed from the same local quartzite that you can occasionally see cropping out, even in the farm fields). The southwestern prairie's lesser communities, although pleasant, are practical rather than beautiful; many communities lost a good deal of their historic charm during the 1960s, when the main streets were modernized.

When it comes to outdoor activities, the offerings are quietly unspectacular. There's fishing and swimming in many fine small lakes here, especially around New Ulm and Mankato, but don't expect the pine-ringed sky blue waters of the North. The prairie terrain makes for pleasant, if unchallenging, cycling; a 68-mile loop has been mapped around the Pipestone countryside.

The mid-19th-century white settlers called the land "plains" because it is relatively flat and treeless. The prairie, however, is anything but plain: It is one of the richest and most subtly beautiful ecosystems on earth. These days, farming has made untouched prairie as hard to find as the great herds of buffalo that once grazed here, but there are untilled patches to be found. Good places to start are in several of the state parks: Blue Mound State Park (near Luverne) has some attractive grasslands as well as a small buffalo herd; you'll also find grasslands in the Kilen Woods, near Lakefield. Make your base camp in a town, then go out and explore the world of the Dakota. Like many things of subtle beauty, the prairie is better appreciated the more you learn about it.

Places to Go, Sights to See

August Schell Brewery (Schell Park, 18th St. S, off Rte. 15, Box 128, New Ulm, tel. 507/354–5528). One of the prettiest little breweries in the United States, Schell's is set on the founder's estate, where there is also a mansion and a deer park. It's not only the source of some fine beer (its Pils and Weiss beers have won national awards), it's also rich in regional history, for beer has been brewed here for more than 125 years. Schell's survived the Dakota conflict of 1862, local historians claim, because the Schell family maintained good relations with the local Dakota. Tours (including beer tastings) are available.

End-O-Line Railroad Park & Museum (440 N. Mill St., Currie, tel. 507/ 763–3708 [summer only]). After viewing the extensive exhibition of vintage railroad equipment and train memorabilia, you can ride the manually operated turntable that once turned the heavy steam-engined locomotives in the grand old days of railroading.

Jeffers Petroglyphs (Jeffers Mountain; 4 mi north on Hwy. 30, 3 mi north on Hwy. 71 and 3 mi east). Examine millennia-old Native American figures etched on red quartzite rock; an interpretive center helps visitors learn more about these fascinating carvings of human figures, weapons, and animals.

Katherine Ordway Prairie (Near Sunburg, 7 mi southwest of Brooten, tel. 612/331–0750). Managed by the Minnesota Chapter of the Nature Conservancy, the Ordway Prairie comprises 582 acres of sharply rolling hills with numerous moist lowlands. It was once cultivated and has not yet been completely retaken by prairie plants, but it is still one of the best places in the state to see what Minnesota looked like before the coming of what the Dakota called the *wasicu* (white man).

Laura Ingalls Wilder Museum (330 8th St., Walnut Grove, tel. 507/859–2358). Exhibits depict the life of the *Little House on the Prairie* author and her family, as well as the early history of the tiny town of Walnut Grove. Memorabilia include Laura's hand-stitched quilt, family photos, and a bench from the Congregational church attended by the Ingalls family. The museum is generally open daily from May through October, with visits by appointment during the rest of the year, but it's best to call ahead.

Lower Sioux Agency (Box 125, Morton, tel. 507/697–6321). The Interpretive Center at this Mdewakanton Dakota community, set in the Minnesota River valley south of Willmar, is key to understanding Dakota life and culture. Also on the grounds are Tipi Maka Duta, the Lower Sioux pottery shop, and St. Cornelia's Episcopal Church (listed on the National Register of Historic Sites). A powwow open to the public is held the second weekend in June.

New Ulm Glockenspiel (Schonlau Park Plaza, 4th and Minnesota Sts., New Ulm). New Ulm, settled by German immigrants in 1854, was nearly destroyed in the Dakota Conflict of 1862. Animated figures in this 45-foot-high musical clock tower depict the town's history daily at noon, 3, and 5, while the 37 bells in the carillon ring on the hour.

Pipestone Historic District (Stop by Pipestone County Museum, 113 Hiawatha Ave. S, tel. 507/825–2563). Guided tours (on request) or self-guided tours (outlined in a free brochure) explore the historic center of the town of Pipestone, where 20 buildings are listed on the National Register of Historic Places. Nearly all were built before the turn of the century; local quartzite was used to render the then-fashionable heavy Romanesque style, which is full of quirky details.

Pipestone National Monument (1 mi north of Pipestone, then ½ mi west, tel. 507/825–5464). These quarries were legendary throughout Native American lands for their soft red stone, prized for making the sacred calumets (peace pipes) used by the Dakota and other tribes. Native craftspeople still quarry and make pipes here. The 283-acre monument also features an Indian Culture Center and walking trail.

Sod House on the Prairie (Rte. 2, Sanborn, tel. 507/723–5138). This authentic reconstruction of two pioneer sod houses—a poor man's dugout and a richer man's "soddy"—is open as a small museum of early settlers' life; it is also available for overnight guests as a bed-and-breakfast (*see below*).

Restaurants

Minnesota's special restaurants are nearly all in the eastern part of the state, but the **Calumet Inn** (104 W. Main St., Pipestone, tel. 507/825–5871) has a restaurant that's highly regarded for its creative touch with beef and pork. In New Ulm, the **Glockenspiel Haus** (400 N. Minnesota St., tel. 507/354–5593) serves good German food and the locally brewed Schell's beer. Off the beaten path but well worth the trip, **Kinbrae Supper Club & Meat Market,** in Kinbrae (tel. 507/ 468–2404), is noted for its special meat dishes and other delicacies. Renowned for its steaks, seafood, and spaghetti, **Michael's Restaurant,** in Worthington (130 S. Spring Ave., tel. 507/376–3187), attracts diners from miles around. Though it's not the colorful joint it once was, the **Magnolia Steak House** (U.S. 75 exit off I–90, Luverne, tel. 507/283–9161) still has custom-aged beef, and its onion rings are legendary.

Tourist Information

Mankato Chamber and Convention Bureau (112 Riverfront Dr., Mankato, MN 56001, tel. 507/345–4519); **Minnesota Office of Tourism, Southern Regional Office** (Box 286, Mankato, MN 56001, tel. 507/389–2683); **New Ulm Chamber of Commerce** (1 N. Minnesota St., New Ulm, MN 56073, tel. 507/354–4217); **Pipestone Chamber of Commerce** (Box 8, Pipestone, MN 56164, tel. 507/ 825–3316); **Travel Southwest Minnesota** (Box 64, Jackson, MN 56143, tel. 507/532–4484); **Worthington Area Chamber of Commerce/Conventions & Visitors Bureau** (1121 3rd Ave., Worthington, MN 56187, tel. 507/372–2919).

Park Row Bed and Breakfast

Like many of the older large houses in rural Minnesota, Ann Burckhardt's bed-and-breakfast, a few blocks from St. Peter's Main Street, is two houses fused together. The larger of the two, a Carpenter Gothic, was built in 1874 with wooden gingerbread trim on its porch railings and eaves. In 1903, the house was purchased by a probate court judge, who added what was tantamount to another building, a Queen Anne–style wing with an apron porch and a turreted circular staircase. After the judge's death in the 1930s, his home suffered the fate of many such big houses: It was turned into a duplex. A local professor bought it in 1971, returning it to its eclectic late-Victorian grace.

It's this combination of styles that Ann, who bought the house in 1989, has maintained in her decor. The interior is as eclectic as the exterior, but its Victorian look is homey, not dark and heavy as this style sometimes is. The downstairs is light and spacious. In the dining room, where a huge bay window draws in daylight from three directions, late-Victorian antiques blend with modern reproductions. Small-scale furnishings, bright stained-glass windows, and lace curtains reinforce the sense of sunshine and fresh air.

Each of the four guest rooms is furnished with period antiques and has its own country theme. But Ann is not heavy-handed about it and is simply out to create a *feeling* of England (or France or Germany). There's a Norwegian-style painted floor in the Scandinavian Room. In other rooms, bright colors and fabrics project the same decorative frilliness as the exterior gingerbread. It never gets cutesy, however.

"I want my guests to feel as if they're stepping back into 1910," Burckhardt says. Granted, it's a somewhat modernized 1910—there's wall-to-wall carpeting, done in a Victorian pattern—but the shower you take will be in a claw-foot tub with its original oak rim, and there will be no TV in your bedroom.

Expect an exceptional breakfast. The indefatigable Burckhardt commutes 66 miles to Minneapolis three days a week to work as a food journalist, so food is a passion with her. She gets to try out new, and usually delicious, recipes on her guests. And since she is a writer, reading is another passion: Books and magazines, mostly of local and regional interest, are displayed throughout the house. Pleasures here are quiet ones, but never unrewarding.

🏠 *525 W. Park Row, St. Peter, MN 56082, tel. 507/931–2495. 4 double rooms share 2 baths. Air-conditioning, cable TV in living room. $58–$68 weekdays, $63–$73 weekends; full breakfast. AE, D, MC, V. No smoking, no pets, closed Jan.*

Sod House on the Prairie

When Stan McCone was growing up, older relatives told him tales of his forebears—sodbusting white settlers of the Great Plains, just like those that Willa Cather and Laura Ingalls Wilder wrote about. Since few trees sprouted on the grasslands, pioneers literally built their houses out of the earth. These sod houses, made of blocks of cut turf, were held together by the dense root systems of the prairie grass.

McCone dreamed of re-creating this lost type of architecture. After working for several years as a cattle buyer, he got a chance to make his dream come true when he learned one of his neighbors in rural Sanborn had a patch of virgin prairie on his land. Soon Stan set to work, with the same kind of grit and sweat as his pioneer ancestors, cutting massive blocks of sod (he describes the sound as "the ripping of a giant canvas"). The result is two buildings set amid acres of (reseeded) prairie grass: a rudimentary "poor man's dugout" and a larger "rich man's soddy," both open to the public as a museum. For those who want a full dose of pioneer experience, the larger is a snug, rustic bed-and-breakfast. Just recently, the McCones renovated an authentic 19th-century log cabin, which guests delight in touring.

The house's furnishings—antique bedsteads and buffets, kitchen and farm implements hanging on the walls and beams—are practical and sturdily beautiful. The only piece that could be considered at all fancy is the leather fainting couch that doubles as a bed, across which is spread a heavy, shaggy buffalo-hide blanket.

Authenticity is the key word here. There are no wires or pipes running through the soddy's turf walls—heating comes from a potbellied stove, air-conditioning from open windows, light from oil lamps. The bathroom is a two-seat outhouse steps away; to wash, guests must pour water from a jug into the 100-year-old pitcher and bowl.

Virginia and Stan McCone provide a simple, hearty country breakfast incorporating high-quality meats, which is Stan's other line of business. If you want to cook your other meals, throw some logs into the mighty Monarch stove. One family spent a prairie Christmas here, cooking up a feast on the Monarch, with the soddy so snug the kids padded about in shorts. Though few of us today would want to live day to day with the rigors of pioneer life, we can still savor a sample of it, thanks to the McCones. Needless to say, Laura Ingalls Wilder fans welcome!

🏠 *Rte. 2 (Box 75), Sanborn, MN 56083, tel. 507/723–5138. 1 house with 2 double beds and outhouse. No air-conditioning, wood-burning stove. $75–$125; full breakfast. No credit cards. Pets by prior consent.*

Fering's Guest House

Charles and Phyllis Fering freely admit that Blue Earth, while attractive, isn't a tourist hot spot, despite its attractive courthouse, many antiques shops, and lovely woods. The same can be said of this large, frame Victorian house, built in 1889, where the Ferings have lived for more than 20 years. Rather than a renovated showplace, it looks like the ideal small-town home, all porch and tall windows with a lush, shady yard. Original oak woodwork exists alongside more recent birch paneling and country-style wallpaper; family knickknacks are scattered about. When the Ferings opened their bed-and-breakfast in 1990, after most of their kids had grown and gone, they expected to attract folks who were just looking for a good night's lodging.

Still, the Ferings' guests often send them Christmas cards, bottles of wine, invitations to visit. Why? "We're like family," says Charles. They're affable, open-minded, and flexible—for example, although they usually serve only Continental breakfasts, once when guests were stranded by a sudden snowstorm, they whipped up three square meals a day until the snow cleared. That's small-town America for you.

⊞ *708 N. Main St., Blue Earth, MN 56013, tel. 507/526–5054. 1 double room with bath, 2 doubles share bath. Air-conditioning, cable TV in rooms. $36–$45; Continental breakfast. No credit cards. No smoking, no pets.*

Prairie House on Round Lake

In 1879, Chicago commodity trader Owen Roche built this grand American Bracket–style house, nicknamed "Roche's Roost" and surrounded by a 2,500-acre estate on Round Lake. It's smaller than it used to be, having been truncated to save money during the Depression (in an odd twist, the bottom floor rather than the top was removed); the estate has shrunk to 44 acres, but it still remains a good place to escape urban stress.

Now owned by horse breeders Ralph and Virginia Schenck, the house is set amid horse barns and wildlife preserves. Inside, there are some antiques (claw-foot tubs, some fine old tables) and beamed ceilings, but the wall-to-wall carpets, modern bathroom fixtures, and other furnishings suggest the interior of a suburban home more than a country inn. Fresh flowers from the Schencks' greenhouse and the whinnying of their American paint horses help remind you of your rural surroundings. Canada geese, white pelicans, and other waterfowl thrive in peace here. Except for outdoor recreation, there isn't much to do here—but that's enough.

⊞ *R.R. 1 (Box 105), Round Lake, MN 56167, tel. 507/945–8934. 1 double room with bath, 1 double with half-bath, 2 doubles share bath. Air-conditioning, lakeside beach, tennis court. $55; full breakfast. No credit cards. No smoking, pets by prior consent.*

Wisconsin

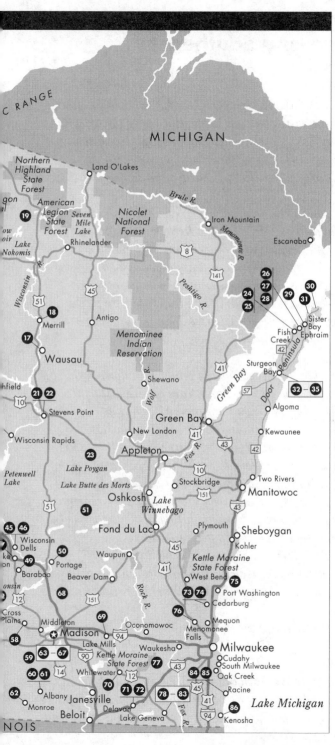

Milwaukee and Southeast Wisconsin

With a population of about 640,000, Milwaukee is Wisconsin's largest city and the nation's 24th largest; it covers nearly 96 square miles and has more than 15 suburbs. Metropolitan greater Milwaukee includes a four-county area with a population of nearly 1.4 million.

Nonetheless, a genial atmosphere prevails. Milwaukee seems not so much like a big city as a large collection of neighborhoods with respect for small-town values. Streets are clean, homes are tidy, parks and green spaces are boundless. Modern steel-and-glass high-rises occupy much of the downtown area, but the city's early heritage persists in the restored and well-kept 19th-century buildings that share the city skyline.

That heritage is diverse. Most Native Americans were gone by the mid-1840s, but a few Potawatomi huts could still be found as late as 1854 in what is now downtown Milwaukee. The city's population in 1845 was about 10,000, more than half of German descent. Many more Germans arrived in the 1850s, along with Italians, Poles, Scandinavians, Serbs, and Irish. By the second half of the 19th century, Milwaukee's German population was so large the city was often called the German Athens. Only the Polish and Irish populations came close in numbers, and English was rarely heard in some neighborhoods. The German influence is still found throughout the city—in its architecture, its language, and especially its food, with a legacy of Old World restaurants.

Today the city claims more than 50 ethnic groups and celebrates its "melting pot" origins with all kinds of ethnic and cultural festivals, along with the annual state fair. Milwaukee has become known as the "city of festivals," stemming from the nationally known Summerfest, which kicks off each summer's activities on a Lake Michigan lakefront park. Another annual highlight is the Great Circus Parade, a July spectacle that features scores of antique circus wagons from the famed Circus World Museum in Baraboo. More than a million people line the streets to watch it.

Besides the spectacular festivals, Milwaukeeans are proud of their 137 parks, the Brewers baseball team, the lakefront, the zoo, and the horticultural domes in Mitchell Park. The art and natural-history museums are quite good. The Milwaukee Symphony plays at the Performing Arts Center, and there are top-notch opera, ballet, and repertory companies.

Since Milwaukee is one of a handful of Midwest cities with a skywalk system, visitors staying in large downtown hotels can walk to restaurants, shops, theaters, and sporting events without having to step outdoors. The Riverspan section of this system is the only skywalk in the nation built over a navigable waterway, the Milwaukee River.

Milwaukeeans will readily admit their city doesn't dazzle like Houston or charm like San Francisco. But they don't mind. At the same time, the city lacks the hard edge of a Detroit or a Chicago, and they don't mind that, either.

Places to Go, Sights to See

Cedarburg. Restored to achieve the look of the 1840s, when German immigrants first harnessed the nearby creek to power their new mills, the entire downtown area of Cedarburg has been listed on the National Register of Historic Places. One of those mills now houses the Stone Mill Winery (tel. 414/377–8020), which offers tours, and the adjoining Cedar Creek Settlement, a restored village jammed with restaurants, art galleries, and shops. The Ozaukee Art Center (tel. 414/377–8230), in a former brewery, displays the work of regional artists. Wisconsin's oldest covered bridge spans Cedar Creek just 3 miles from town.

Lake Geneva. Ringing the lakeshore are the country homes of the 19th-century wealthy, who could afford pastoral retreats. Today's activities center around the water. There are seven public beaches, and boating is quite popular. A 26-mile-long footpath circles the lake, and there are 10 public golf courses and 10 hiking trails nearby, some of which are used for skiing in winter. Old World Wisconsin (north on Rte. 67, tel. 414/594–2116), a 50-building settlement comprising historic farmsteads and a village, is a short drive away.

Milwaukee. Beer made this city famous, but there's more to it than breweries, bratwurst, and ballparks. Its true life and backbone are found in its pockets of German, Polish, Serbian, African-American, Irish, and other ethnic communities. Numerous festivals, parades, and restaurants celebrate the city's diversity. It has always had a lively arts scene; its reputation as a center of publishing and graphic design is growing. The Performing Arts Center (929 N. Water St., tel. 414/273–7206) boasts a symphony orchestra, as well as ballet, opera, and theater companies. The Broadway Theater Center (158 N. Broadway, tel. 414/291–7800) houses theater and light opera companies. The Milwaukee Repertory Theater, (108 E. Wells St., tel. 414/224–1761), a major regional company, is housed in a new theater complex. Housed in an Eero Saarinen–designed lakefront building, the Milwaukee Art Museum (750 N. Lincoln Memorial Dr., tel. 414/224–3220) exhibits an impressive array of 19th- and 20th-century American and European art. The Milwaukee Public Museum (800 W. Wells St., tel. 414/278–2700) contains the fourth-largest collection of natural-history exhibits in the United States.

Racine. This city's best-known attraction, the S. C. Johnson Wax Building (1525 Howe St., tel. 414/631–2154), was designed by Frank Lloyd Wright and built in the 1930s, but it still looks like an office tower of the future. Free tours are given Tuesday to Friday; reservations are required.

Restaurants

One of the brightest stars in Wisconsin's culinary flag is **Sanford's** (1547 N. Jackson, Milwaukee, tel. 414/276–9608), an upscale storefront restaurant serving Franco-Californian creations. But ethnic fare is Milwaukee's specialty, and the proof is there for the eating at longtime favorites like **Karl Ratsch's Old World** (320 E. Mason St., tel. 414/276–2720), which serves German food, and **Old Town** (522 W. Lincoln, tel. 414/672–0206), where Serbian dishes are offered. **Buca** (1233 N. Van Buren, tel. 404/224–8672) serves great Italian food family style in a restaurant that even features a shrine to Frank Sinatra. In Cedarburg, **Victor's** (W62 N247 Washington Ave., tel. 414/375–1777), which serves Continental fare, is gaining a reputation as one of the Midwest's finest restaurants. **St. Moritz** (327 Wrigley Dr., tel. 414/248–6680), a Queen Anne summer cottage (read: mansion) on the shores of Lake Geneva, is proud of its house salad, its garlicky rack of lamb, and other dishes featuring Wisconsin veal and salmon.

Tourist Information

Cedarburg Visitor Information Center (City Hall, W63N645 Washington Ave., Cedarburg, WI 53012, tel. 414/377–9620, or 800/CDR–BURG); **Greater Milwaukee Convention & Visitors Bureau** (510 W. Kilbourne Ave., Milwaukee, WI 53203, tel. 414/273–7222 or 800/554–1448); **Lake Geneva Area Chamber of Commerce** (201 Wrigley Dr., Lake Geneva, WI 53147, tel. 414/248–4416).

Allyn Mansion Inn

When Alexander Allyn, along with Milwaukee architect E. Townsend Mix, built this palatial mansion in 1885, his motto may well have been "If you've got it, flaunt it—and do it in good taste." Current owners Joe Johnson and Ron Markwell followed that dictum when restoring Allyn's home, which had spent decades as a furniture store and then a nursing home. The house, listed on the National Register of Historic Places, is considered Wisconsin's best-preserved example of the Queen Anne–Eastlake style.

The duo filled the mansion's 23 rooms with American antiques that, along with six original gasoliers, French walnut woodwork, parquet floors, and 10 Italian marble fireplaces—four topped with grand Eastlake mirrors—create the very picture of late-19th-century elegance. The high, coved ceilings in each of the three parlors have been repainted with floral scrollwork, as in Allyn's day, following the designs uncovered during restoration. The front room glitters with gold French wallpaper, and green velvet portieres dangle from walnut rings over the doorway. Shutters on the tall windows shield from sunlight the room's stately grandfather clock, Victorian tufted-silk sofa, and matching chairs, and a cribbage board made from a walrus tusk stands ready on the marble coffee table. In another parlor is an 1890 Steinway grand piano, originally from a convent (and now the focus of the inn's musicales). The dining room displays English china from Chicago's

1893 Columbian Exposition. In the library, floor-to-ceiling bookshelves accommodate a collection of books about the Windy City.

The Empire Room is furnished completely in that period's antiques and dazzles guests with an 1830 tester bed with a slipper sofa at its foot, a mirror, fireplace clock, game table, curvy settee, and marble-topped table. In the Mary Elizabeth Room, guests can relax on the chaise lounge before bedding down on the 9½-foot-tall full-tester. To retain the historical integrity of the mansion, new bathrooms have been added in a separate wing.

Enormous trees and colorful flower beds surround the house, and the grand porte cochere, a replica, will have you looking for carriages to drive up and complete the picture.

🏠 *511 E. Walworth Ave., Delavan, WI 53115, tel. 414/728–9090. 8 double rooms share 7 baths. Air-conditioning. $90–$100, $60 single weekdays; full breakfast, evening refreshments. MC, V. No smoking, no pets.*

The Hitching Post

There really is a stone hitching post next to this inn. The original was used to tether the horse belonging to Dr. William Hoyt, a distinguished doctor who began the home for his family in 1869. Dr. Post died in 1870, and the house was completed by his wife, Nancy, who took over her husband's practice, although she had no medical training, and kept the household together until her son George completed medical school and took over both the practice and the home. The Colonial Revival home, now owned by Holly Smith, sits on a large, shaded, 1-acre suburban lot at the edge of Menomonee Falls, a half hour from downtown Milwaukee. Holly has landscaped the yard with lilac bushes, a wildflower garden, and 2,000 daylilies. Every spring, she adds to the garden color with hundreds of annuals.

The bright and airy living room, painted white and accented with floral stenciling, contains a number of Smith family antiques, including a mirror over the fireplace, which belonged to Holly's great-grandfather, and a large table clock. There are more antiques in the family room, where a comfortable sofa and easy chairs surround the fireplace. "In the winter, guests always find their way in here because it's so warm and embracing when we light a fire," Holly says.

Upstairs are two guest rooms. Dr. William's Room is furnished with an antique cedar chest, an antique rocker, and a king-size canopy bed with a cab-bage-rose pattern in pinks and greens on both the canopy and comforter. Dr. George's Room is decorated with blue-and-yellow sponge-painted designs and is furnished with a maple double bed that belonged to Holly's grandfather; the quilt covering the bed was sewn by Holly's grandmother. Just down the hall from the guest rooms, Holly keeps a guest library of hundreds of best-sellers, mysteries, and classics. Both guest rooms share the 1930s bathroom, which still contains a 6-foot tub, ideal for a long, relaxing soak, as well as the original sink, now topped by an antique mirror.

Holly serves her breakfast of home-made pastries and muffins, eggs, fresh fruit, juice, and gourmet coffee either in the dining room, with its cabinet displaying Smith family china and silver, outdoors on the deck overlooking the wildflower garden, or in the guest rooms.

🏨 *N88 W16954 Main St., Menomonee Falls, WI 53051, tel. 414/255-1496, fax 414/255-4552. 2 double rooms share bath. Air-conditioning, free newspaper, robes in rooms, pool, nearby bike trail, tennis courts. $60–$75; full breakfast, evening refreshments. MC, V. No smoking indoors, no pets.*

The Inn at Old Twelve Hundred

When Stephanie Bresette and her husband Ellie bought this magnificent Victorian home in 1990, they almost felt like they were the original owners. Built in 1890 by a wealthy local widower, it was purchased in 1920 by a Chicago bachelor. In 1945, it was acquired by a childless couple, who then sold it to the Bresettes. Because it had only a few owners—none of whom wanted to "modernize" it—the 6,000-square-foot home retains many original light fixtures, its original oak woodwork, lead and stained glass, and such period fixtures as pocket doors and quaint fireplaces.

Happily, Stephanie had an extensive antique collection, which fit perfectly into the home. The parlor and living room are now furnished in shades of Victorian plum, rose, and cranberry, with velvet-upholstered wing chairs and matching sofa. Two of the home's many Oriental rugs cover the floors. The dining room, where Stephanie serves breakfast on cool days, has oak paneling and a beamed ceiling and is furnished with two antique oak sideboards and a china cabinet that houses Stephanie's collection of Waterford crystal and antique cut glass.

Upstairs, the original master suite has a private porch and is furnished with a king-size brass-and-iron bed. The sitting area has two comfy wing chairs facing a fireplace. Another suite has a four-season enclosed porch, complete with fireplace. That suite is furnished in a light and informal 1920s cottage style.

Stephanie and Ellie completely refurbished the third floor, which was unfinished when they purchased the home. They removed 6 tons of original plaster and created two luxury suites. While decked out with whirlpool baths, the rooms retain the character of the house because the Bresettes reused original woodwork and custom-ordered new woodwork to match the old. The two suites have cable TV and VCRs as well as fireplaces; one also has its own treetop-level porch.

The Inn's annex, just 50 feet from the main house, includes two suites and a double room. One suite has a whirlpool bath as well as an oversize shower with two showerheads. It is furnished with an antique walnut bed and matching dresser. The second suite has Oriental rugs and antique oak furniture. All three rooms in the annex have a refrigerator, microwave, and coffeemaker.

🏠 *806 W. Grand Ave., Port Washington, WI 53074, tel. 414/268–1200. 1 double room with bath, 6 suites. Air-conditioning, cable TV and VCR in suites, fireplace in rooms, whirlpool bath in 4 rooms, bathrobes, refrigerator for guests. $95–$175; full breakfast. AE, MC, V. No smoking, no pets.*

The Manor House

When auto executive James Wilson became vice president of the Nash Motor Company, headquartered in Kenosha, he built this grand estate. Wilson's stately 1924 French Renaissance Revival mansion, its brick-and-stone walls covered with ivy and topped by a slate roof, is designed in the style of the great English manor houses. In the city's Lakeshore Historic District, surrounded by other opulent homes and just across the road from Lake Michigan, the Manor is listed in the National Register of Historic Places. Encircled by landscaped grounds with towering trees and a wonderful formal English garden that includes some 40 species of carefully tended ornamental trees and shrubs, a sunken pool with a fountain, and a gazebo and arbor, the house could easily be the setting for a *Masterpiece Theater* presentation.

Guests enter the grand hall, with its ornate oak paneling, slate floor, and thick rugs. A wide central stairway leads to the upstairs rooms. To the left down a wide hallway is the living room, which occupies one end of the first floor. A fireplace and a grand piano are the center of attention here. The library is paneled in mahogany and contains a fireplace with marble and mahogany facing. The more informally decorated sunroom provides a view of the formal gardens. The grand dining room, with oak paneling, also has a fireplace. When guests eat there, they sit at a massive table under the room's elaborate crystal chandelier.

Upstairs, the mansion's third-floor ballroom has been converted to a luxury suite that retains the original dark oak beams and coffered ceiling. A private balcony affords a view of Lake Michigan. Four large rooms and one suite on the second floor—three with lake views and all with private baths—are mainly furnished in Queen Anne antiques and reproductions. The lovely Rose Room, with a view of the garden, has a brass-and-iron bed and a huge walk-in dressing room.

Lest guests feel the Manor really is a stuffy English country house, owner Laurie Novak-Simmons puts everyone at ease with snacks in the kitchen, piano playing in the living room, and friendly conversation everywhere. She serves breakfast in the guest rooms, the garden, or in the dining room.

🏨 *6536 3rd Ave., Kenosha, WI 53143, tel. 414/658–0014. 4 double rooms with baths, 2 suites. Air-conditioning, phone and cable TV in rooms; whirlpool bath and fireplace in 2 suites, honor bar in library, snacks and ice in kitchen, bike trails, access to tennis courts, fishing wharf, marina. $100–$199; full breakfast. AE, MC, V. Smoking only in sitting room on lower level, inquire about pets.*

The Mansards on-the-Lake

This Second Empire–style house, built in 1867, sports a green mansard roof and neat rows of dormers. The structure has been occupied by a string of colorful people: Its first owners were an inventor and his wife, a suffragist who worked as an editor; they were followed by a family of musicians and a circus acrobat whose wife, also a circus performer, did trick horseback riding. Today's owner is a retired Russian-language teacher who inherited the house and many of its furnishings from her mother.

The second and third floors and the rear wing are now self-contained suites, each with a living room, a bedroom, a bathroom, and a kitchen. The high-ceilinged Polonaise Suite, on the second floor, is decorated with theatrical posters from Eastern Europe collected by the innkeeper during study tours. Its kitchen has a full-size refrigerator, stove, and microwave oven and is stocked with the makings for breakfast, including cheeses and the locally famous pretzel-shaped pastry known as Danish Kringle. The dining area, though small, has a view of Lake Michigan and contains a lively display of Polish circus posters, cut paper, and framed embroidery. Still other theatrical posters, these for European productions of *Romeo and Juliet* and *The Student Prince*, hang in the bedroom. An old-fashioned metal ice-cream parlor table and chairs sit beside the room's sunny bay windows. The crocheted bedspread was made by the innkeeper's mother, who sat in the very same wooden rocker you can relax in today. French doors open to a balcony with a lake view. The bathroom is "bigger than an airplane's," says the host—though not by much; it contains a tub and shower.

The third-floor Garret Suite has a Bohemian artist-in-residence ambience. Low dormer windows punctuate the sloped walls, and the living room is full of books and magazines. The white reproduction French provincial–style furnishings do little to enhance the room's charm—the living room's sectional sofa does even less. But a 1950s-style chrome dinette gives the kitchen lots of character, and its terrific view of the lake doesn't hurt, either. Here, too, the refrigerator is stocked with breakfast fixings. The Seascapes Suite, in the rear, has the best lake view and the best furnishings—a bright contemporary sofa and colonial reproduction bedroom set. The fourth suite is a two-room efficiency.

This inn is a good bet for guests who will be in town for longish stays. The backyard leads straight to Lake Michigan, and Racine's historic district is a stroll away.

🏠 *827 Lake Ave., Racine, WI 53403, tel. 414/632–1135. 4 suites. Air-conditioning, cable TV in suites. $55–$85; breakfast fixings stocked in kitchens; MC, V. No smoking, no pets.*

Stagecoach Inn

After careful restoration by historian Brook Brown and his wife, Liz, this compact Greek Revival limestone inn once again welcomes travelers, as it did when stagecoaches stopped in Cedarburg on their journey between Milwaukee and Green Bay in 1853, when the house was built. Restoring the corner pub was the Browns' first project. They uncovered the tin ceiling, set up a long, well-used wooden bar where the original had stood, refinished the rough plank floors, brought in some handsome tavern tables, and—in a place of honor behind the bar, next to the vintage silver cash register and grandmother clock—installed the original pub's wooden signpost depicting a fleet of white steeds. This is where the inn's guests gather for breakfast every morning and where, in the evenings, they congregate for draughts of Sprecher, a local root beer.

A prize wallflower bench from an old-time dance hall sits in the front-hall corridor, at the bottom of the steep, narrow cherry-wood staircase that leads to the guest rooms on the second and third floors. The rooms' sunny nooks and low dormers host a collection of rustic furniture, much of it 100-year-old pine. Braided rugs and Oriental carpets warm the rough pine floors.

One suite has an exposed limestone wall, an antique oak dresser, and a whirlpool bath. Another, one of three that overlook Cedarburg's beautifully preserved old main street, has a hand-stenciled frieze on the walls and a cherry-wood country Victorian bed, wardrobe, and dresser. The walls of the third-floor rooms are also stenciled, and the furniture is antique pine; two rooms have whirlpool baths, and another has two sleigh beds and is brightened by a skylight. The only guest room on the ground floor is a suite. In it are an 1860 four-poster bed, a sturdy immigrant chest that still looks capable of transporting all your worldly possessions, and a well-worn Oriental carpet.

The 1847 frame house across the street now houses three of the Stagecoach's whirlpool suites, all furnished with antiques. Guests return to the main building in the morning to join other guests for a breakfast of freshly ground coffee, juice, cereals, croissants, and homemade muffins.

🏨 *W61 N. 520 Washington Ave., Cedarburg, WI 53012, tel. 414/375–0208 or 888/375–0208. 6 double rooms with baths, 6 suites. Air-conditioning, cable TV in most rooms, fireplace in 2 suites, whirlpool bath in suites, pub, chocolate shop. $65–$130; Continental breakfast, afternoon refreshments. AE, D, DC, MC, V. No smoking, no pets.*

Washington House Inn

This cream-colored brick Victorian building, built on Cedarburg's main street in 1886, is actually the second hostelry to stand on this site; the first was established in 1846. Jim Pape, who restored Cedarburg's Stone Hill Winery (and spearheaded the town's historic-preservation movement), took on the task of returning the Washington House to its former glory. The building had been used as offices and apartments since the 1920s, and nearly the only thing that hadn't been modernized or covered up was the lobby's parquet floor. After removing decades' worth of "improvements," Jim and his wife, Sandy, decided to leave many of the building's broad supporting beams and rough limestone walls exposed and set about filling guest rooms with regional period antiques.

Guest rooms are named after pillars of 19th-century Cedarburg society. The Frederich Hilgen Room, dressed in Bradbury & Bradbury wallpaper popular in the late 1800s, has a half-canopy bed draped in burgundy paisley print, a vintage marble-topped walnut table, and two reproduction wing chairs flanking the tall, narrow, shuttered windows. The bathroom is done in 1-inch-square white tiles and contains a marble sink and an antique dresser.

Dr. Friedrich Luening's Room is genteelly rustic, with its tall South Carolina pencil-post bed and its plank floor strewn with rag rugs. Patchwork quilts decorate the walls, and a fire-engine-red circular iron stairway from the old Pabst Brewery leads to the loft sitting area under the exposed-beam ceiling. Plants adorn the spalike adjoining room, and there's a modern fireplace and a decidedly 20th-century double whirlpool bath.

Windows in the dining room, on the ground floor, overlook Washington Avenue, the town's main thoroughfare. But even when the comings and goings abate, there's plenty to look at inside, with the pressed-tin ceiling, the farm tables, and the rustic Victorian chairs. On your way in or out, glance at the original hotel register on display in the spacious lobby.

The nearby Schroeder House, an 1880s stone home now converted to an inn annex, houses five rooms. Ask for the Gertrude Schroeder Room, which has a private entrance and sitting room.

🏨 *W62 N573 Washington Ave., Cedarburg, WI 53012, tel. 414/375-3550 or 800/554-4717. 34 double rooms with baths. Air-conditioning, phone, cable TV, and HBO in 29 rooms, whirlpool bath in 31 rooms, gas fireplace in 14 rooms, social hour with locally made wine and cheese, elevator, sauna. $59–$179; Continental breakfast. AE, D, DC, MC, V. No pets.*

American Country Farm

Hams once hung from the ceiling beams of this snug fieldstone cottage, built in 1844 as a smokehouse for a country estate. Today, guests can toast their feet in front of the building's original broad fireplace. The cottage, its original stone walls whitewashed on the interior, consists of a single room—with a tiny kitchen and bathroom—and is comfortably furnished with a king-size bed with white coverlet, a plump wing chair, and a sofa. Murky oil paintings of farm scenes adorn the 2-foot-thick walls, and a large wreath hangs over the fireplace.

Outside the cottage's two Dutch doors is a private patio facing a wooded wildflower preserve. Also on the 2-acre property are a grape arbor, a kitchen garden, and the original white stone barn and farmhouse, sheltered by tall pines. Every morning, innkeeper and antiques dealer Donna Steffen arrives laden with hot baked goods for breakfast.

🏠 *12112 N. Wauwatosa Rd., Mequon, WI 53092, tel. 414/242–0194. 1 double room with bath. Air-conditioning, TV, kitchen, fireplace. $75 midweek, $95 weekends; Continental breakfast. MC, V. No pets.*

College Avenue Bed & Breakfast

In the late 19th and early 20th centuries, Racine's wealthy citizens built elaborate homes along Lake Michigan just south of downtown. This century-old Queen Anne stands out among its elaborate neighbors, partly because of its beautiful design and partly because it's pink. Gail Julius bought the house in the mid-1980s and has lovingly restored and furnished it with the help of 1890s photographs of the home and its original furnishings. Especially noteworthy is the interior woodwork—paneling, beamed ceilings, moldings, and the amazing parquet floors that were created using a different Victorian pattern in each room.

The dining room contains a built-in sideboard with lead-glass doors. A trio of magnificent stained-glass windows illuminates the landing on the ornate hardwood stairway. Upstairs, the largest room has an ornately carved Victorian bed and matching marble-top dresser. A small table and chairs occupy the large bay created by the house's turret. Another room includes the home's original bathroom, which is wainscoted floor to ceiling—and the ceiling is wainscoted as well.

In warm weather, Gail and her guests congregate for lemonade and conversation on the wraparound porch, which is furnished with comfortable wicker furniture. In the afternoons, guests like to take in the neighborhood with a spin in the inn's own Model A Ford.

🏠 *1520 College Ave., Racine, WI 53403, tel. 414/637–7870. 3 double rooms with baths. Air-conditioning in rooms, phone, TV, VCR with video library, and stocked refrigerator shared by guest rooms. $80–$95; full breakfast weekdays, Continental on weekends. D, MC, V. No smoking, no pets.*

Eagle Centre House

Riene and Dean Herriges were so intrigued with an 1846 Greek Revival–style stagecoach inn in a nearby town that they decided to create a replica. Dean, a master carpenter, spent a year directing the construction that cloned a twin but with the most modern amenities down to central heating and air-conditioning. After all, they were building the house to serve as a B&B.

While the conveniences are modern, the inn is decorated entirely with period furnishings. Riene picked out a fetching Whitman's Sampler of antiques from the 1830s to the 1880s. Most notable are the two melodeans—a forerunner of the pump organ—which grace the parlor and dining room. On winter nights, wood-burning stoves in the parlor and tap provide a comforting ambience. In the dining room, guests enjoy a hearty breakfast of fresh fruit, pastries, and quiche or French toast, all under the gaze of a cheerful portrait of Abe Lincoln. Upstairs, one guest room has a burled walnut bedstead; another has an Eastlake bedroom set. One room even has an antique rope bed—not to worry, there's another bed in that room. Outside, walking trails on 20 acres of woodland and restored prairie beckon.

🏨 *W370 S9590 Hwy. 67, Eagle, WI 53119, tel. 414/363–4700. 5 double rooms with baths. Air-conditioning, radio in rooms, double whirlpool bath in 2 rooms. $95–$145; full breakfast, evening refreshments, AE, MC, V. No smoking, no pets.*

Elizabethan Inn

As they say in real estate: location, location, location. Set on a long shady lot on the shore of Lake Geneva—two blocks from downtown, an hour's drive from Chicago, and 45 minutes from Milwaukee—this inn has it in spades. A gabled, 1903 Queen Anne clapboard with a square turret, a sunporch, and a deck, the inn looks—inside and out—like the archetype of Grandma's house. The ivory-toned living room holds just a few of the inn's collection of English antiques and reproductions.

The largest of the guest rooms in the main house faces the lake and takes up the entire front upstairs. It's popular because of its spaciousness and lake view, its four-poster bed, and its tufted floral settee. Four of the inn's rooms are in the Kimberly House—originally a coach house and converted to a resi-

dence at the turn of the century, now featuring a country-style decor. A breakfast of omelets, quiche, corned beef hash, or waffles is served at a long trestle table in front of a fireplace in the Kimberly House or on the sunporch in the main house.

🏨 *463 Wrigley Dr., Lake Geneva, WI 53147, tel. 414/248–9131. 10 double rooms with baths. Air-conditioning, TV in living room and available in all rooms, fireplace in 1 room, whirlpool bath in 4 rooms, private pier. $85–$155; full breakfast. MC, V. No smoking, no pets, 2-night minimum weekends and holidays.*

Lakeside Manor Inn

When wealthy Chicagoans wanted to build summer retreats at the turn of the century, many of them came to Lake Delavan, and no less than five summerhouses were built along its shore by Frank Lloyd Wright in the late 1890s and early 1900s. Near these noted abodes, set on the south shore, is this Victorian "summer cottage"—built in 1893 by businessman John Eldredge. At the time, it was one of the first summer homes on the newly fashionable lake.

The five rooms and one suite are decorated in a comfortable combination of modern and Victorian styles. One room has forest green walls and sparkling white woodwork and is furnished with white wicker and a brass and white-painted iron bed. A large downstairs suite has a sitting area and kitchenette, as well as a spectacular lake view. Perfect for families is a two-bedroom cottage, with a sleeping porch that practically touches the lake.

Breakfast is served in the dining room or on the veranda in warm weather. Guests find at least three kinds of homemade pastries, plus either omelets made to order, frittatas, eggs Benedict, or apple pancakes.

🏠 *1809 S. Shore Dr., Delavan, WI 53115, tel. 414/728-5354. 4 double rooms with baths, 2 doubles share bath; 1 suite, 1 2-bedroom cottage. Air-conditioning, cable TV/VCR in each room, fireplace in suite and living room, private pier and beach. $89-$149, cottage $189 for up to 6 people; full breakfast weekends, Continental breakfast weekdays, afternoon refreshments. MC, V. No smoking, no pets.*

Lawrence House

Although this house, built in 1885, is one of the oldest in town, its owner and innkeeper, Larry Joseph, has opted for creature comforts over strict historical re-creation. Enjoy the luxurious double whirlpool baths in each room's sun-filled, oversize bathroom, loaded with towels and toiletries. Reached through French doors, these are a bit of heaven for those who love to soak and dawdle in the tub. Room decor ranges from the hunter-green-and-burgundy tones of the walls, fabrics, and canopy bed of one first-floor room to the softer peach-and-blue scheme and floral print wallpaper and fabrics in another. All the rooms have big-screen TVs and VCRs concealed in reproduction Victorian armoires.

Guests gather in the upstairs sitting room or around the living room's fireplace. Joseph's seven-course breakfast often features such dishes as eggs Benedict, soufflés, or waffles and is served either in the dining room, the enclosed wraparound sunporch overlooking the lake, or the screened-in porch.

🏠 *403 S. Lake Shore Dr., Lake Geneva, WI 53147, tel. 414/248-4684 or 800/530-2262. 5 double rooms with baths. Air-conditioning, cable TV, whirlpool baths, video library. $120-$175; full breakfast, afternoon refreshments. AE, D, DC, MC, V. No pets, 2-night minimum weekends in summer.*

Lazy Cloud Lodge

First-time guests who see the Lazy Cloud as they enter the driveway are sure they've come to the wrong place. The modest building in front of them doesn't look like it could possibly contain nine luxury rooms—but it does. A wealthy Chicago family built the home in the early 1920s as a polo lodge. The long, narrow building is turned sideways on the lot; the main facade faced the neighboring polo fields. Today, innkeepers Carol and Keith Tiffany have used that positioning to their advantage: Eight of the nine rooms have private entrances, and most face the garden field. The inn, set on almost 3 acres on a quiet country road, is only a few minutes from the attractions of Lake Geneva.

Each room is decorated differently, though all include a fireplace and whirlpool bath. Several have rustic/country decor with wood paneling and stone fireplaces, while others have a more frilly decor, with canopy beds and flowered quilts. The Continental breakfast—with Carol's homemade pecan sticky buns as the centerpiece—is offered in the lodge dining room or can be served in the guest's room.

🏠 *N2025 N. Lake Shore Dr., Fontana, WI 53125, tel. 414/275-3322. 9 double rooms with baths. Air-conditioning, fireplace, and whirlpool bath in rooms. $125-$195; Continental breakfast. AE, MC, V. No smoking, no pets.*

Pederson Victorian Bed & Breakfast

When Kristi Cowles bought this picture-perfect 116-year-old Victorian house in 1990, she wanted to create an environmentally friendly B&B, so guests may see sheets and towels drying in the breeze in the backyard. The house, in the tiny hamlet of Springfield, only 3 miles north of bustling

Lake Geneva, is surrounded by a white picket fence and shaded by stately maple and walnut trees. Guests are invited to enjoy the porch swing and a pair of wicker rockers or the hammocks strung between two trees. Inside, the parlor and sunroom have old-fashioned floral-print carpets and are furnished with Victorian antiques and overstuffed chairs and sofas. The downstairs room, the Jennie Williams, has its own bath and turn-of-the-century furniture accented with wicker pieces. The three rooms upstairs are furnished with antique beds and dressers; they share a spacious bathroom with an antique claw-foot tub.

Kristi's prizewinning feta veggie quiche is a favorite on the extensive vegetarian breakfast menu; traditionalists can still choose from such dishes as raspberry buttermilk pancakes with Wisconsin maple syrup or homemade fruit muffins.

🏠 *1782 Hwy. 120 North, Lake Geneva, WI 53147, tel. 414/248–9110. 1 double room with bath, 3 doubles share bath. Air-conditioning, ceiling fans, hammocks and porch swing. $70–$80, $45 single weekdays Nov.–Apr.; full breakfast. MC, V. No smoking, no pets.*

Roses

This American four-square home, just a few blocks from downtown Lake Geneva, is easy to pick out as the Roses B&B—it's painted, you guessed it, a beautiful dusty rose with a trim of pale green.

Innkeeper Kym Davidson, who named the B&B in honor of her grandmother, has decorated the 1925 house with a wonderfully homey and eclectic collection of furnishings; an art-deco screen in the living room sits only a few feet from several lovely late-19th-century tables and sideboards. Somehow, it works. The four rooms all have large, sunny windows, and one has a balcony.

Two adjoining rooms are available for couples traveling together.

Kym's guests enjoy a full country breakfast, served, depending on the weather, in the dining room, on the wraparound enclosed porch, or on the outside deck overlooking her well-tended garden. Afternoon tea and sherry are served in front of the living room fireplace in winter and on the porch in warm weather.

🏠 *429 S. Lake Shore Dr., Lake Geneva, WI 53147, tel. 414/248–4344 or 888/ROSEBNB. 4 double rooms with baths. Air-conditioning, cable TV. $65–$95 Nov.–Apr., $85–$120 May–Oct; full country breakfast, afternoon tea and sherry. Smoking on 1st floor only, no pets.*

The Water's Edge

At the end of a dead-end street on the shore of Lake Como, this rambling structure is famous among local residents because its garage once served as the secret vault and money-counting room of a 1920s mobster connected with Chicago's legendary gangsters. On one side is the main house, built in the mid-1800s; on the other is a small abode originally constructed to house workers who harvested ice from the lake during winters. For several decades, the house stood empty, in great disrepair and supposedly haunted. What a difference new owners can make!

With some reluctance, a local realtor showed the house in 1985 to Sven Ramklint and Newell Friedman, who both had been looking to escape Chicago for the peace and quiet of the Lake Geneva area. Happily, the two interior designers were able to forget about the "before" and envisioned a beautiful new "after." They spent the next 10 years renovating the former warren of tiny rooms and garbled floor plan, decorating it with a mind to please discerning B&B guests.

Today, the Water's Edge welcomes travelers to its five guest rooms and two two-bedroom apartments. As you enter the spacious living room, your eye is drawn to the 25-foot picture window with its grand view of Lake Como, only a few feet away. In winter, guests gather here to enjoy the Cinerama-style view and the wood-burning stove.

The entire house is eclectically furnished by Sven and Newell with a wonderfully comfortable combination of antique, country, and contemporary pieces. One room has a wrought-iron canopy bed, another a brass bed. The big plus: Three of the rooms and both apartments have lake views.

Breakfast is served in either the dining room—on the actual table those mobsters once counted money—or on the open lakeside deck in warm weather. With more than 400 feet of lake shoreline, guests have plenty of space to walk off Newell's delicious spinach quiche, freshly baked cinnamon rolls, apple brown Betty, or French toast.

▦ *W4232 West End Rd., Lake Geneva, WI 53147, tel. 414/245–9845. 4 double rooms with baths, 1 suite, 2 2-bedroom apartments. Air-conditioning, cable TV, fireplace in 2 rooms, whirlpool bath in 1 room, private pier. $105–$140 (plus $10 per person in apartments); full breakfast. AE, MC, V. No smoking, no pets, 2-night minimum holidays.*

Madison and Environs

*Scenic Madison, with a population of 200,000, is a thriving
center for business, government, education, and recreation.
The ethnic and cultural diversity of the University of
Wisconsin–Madison campus and the charged political
atmosphere created by Madison's role as state capital add to
the city's appeal.*

*Madison lies on the edge of Wisconsin's "driftless area"—a
region bypassed by Ice Age glaciers some 10,000 years ago.
Marked by deep, narrow valleys and steep, wooded hills, this
area covers most of southwestern Wisconsin. The city has been
known since settlement times as Four Lakes, with lakes
Mendota, Monona, Wingra, and Waubesa lying within or just
outside the city limits.*

*The city center is on an eight-block-wide isthmus between
Lakes Mendota and Monona, with a skyline dominated (by
law) by the 285-foot dome of the state capitol. The city, filled
with green spaces and conservation areas, includes more than
30 municipal parks. In addition, three state parks are within a
20-minute drive of downtown Madison. The university
campus, stretching for more than a mile along the Lake
Mendota shore, is considered one of the nation's most
beautiful, and it has been a backdrop for a number of feature
films. Interesting nooks and crannies make the campus a
perfect spot for a stroll. At the western edge of the campus sits
the First Unitarian Society Meeting House, one of Frank
Lloyd Wright's finest designs. Madison's wide variety of
architectural styles, dating from the mid-19th century to the
present, include a handful of private homes designed by
Wright, a native son of Wisconsin.*

*Madison has a cultural scene usually found only in cities two
or three times its size. There are several major cultural
venues, including the University of Wisconsin's Elvehjem
Museum of Art, the Madison Art Center, and the State
Historical Society Museum. The Madison Civic Center offers*

an extensive program of music, theater, and entertainment, including touring concerts and Broadway shows, and is home to the Madison Symphony and the Madison Repertory Theater. Downtown Madison hosts more than 100 annual events, including the Wisconsin Chamber Orchestra's outdoor summer concerts on Capitol Square and the annual Art Fair on the Square, which attracts thousands of browsers for art, entertainment, and food. In addition, the university's theatrical, musical, and film offerings add spice and variety to the cultural scene.

Madisonians are a sports-minded lot. University of Wisconsin's football, basketball, and hockey events draw large crowds. Badger football games are, in essence, afternoon-long parties where the Rose Bowl–winning team attracts more than 70,000 red-clad fans to Camp Randall Stadium. Softball is a summer passion; city leagues have some 400 organized teams. Boating, sailing, canoeing, and bicycling are also tremendously popular. In addition, over 100 miles of cross-country ski trails in the city and county offer a wide variety of terrain for winter athletes.

For the most part, Madison is free of suburban sprawl, with green spaces and farms between the city and outlying communities such as Cross Plains and Belleville. Middleton and Monona are separate entities, but only city-limits signs insulate them from Madison. East and south of Madison, the land smooths out into rolling hills and farm fields where herds of black and white cattle graze. To the east, Lake Mills is convenient to either Madison or Milwaukee. Aztalan, near Lake Mills, was a Native American village, where the Middle Mississippian culture existed from 1075 to 1175. It is now a state park.

Places to Go, Sights to See

Blue Mound. West of Madison, Blue Mound State Park (tel. 608/437–5711) has hiking trails, picnic areas, a swimming pool, a large campground, and viewing towers offering glorious vistas.

Elvehjem Museum of Art (800 University Ave., tel. 608/263–2246). The university's museum is one of the state's best, with a permanent collection of paintings, sculpture, and decorative arts dating from 2300 BC to the present.

Farmers' Market. Held on Capitol Square each Saturday from May through October, this extensive farmers' market has several hundred vendors offering baked goods, flowers, and fresh produce.

Henry Villas Zoo (702 S. Randall Ave., tel. 608/266–4732). The zoo exhibits nearly 200 species of animals and has a children's zoo (open Memorial Day through Labor Day), where youngsters can pet and feed animals. The zoo is in Vilas Park, which has a swimming beach, tennis courts, and shady picnic areas.

State Street. A lively pedestrian mall runs between the capitol and the college, where coffeehouses, ethnic cafés, and shops vie for the attention of passersby.

University Arboretum (1207 Seminole Hwy., tel. 608/263–7888). Away from downtown, the arboretum has more than 1,200 acres of natural plant and animal communities, such as prairie and forest landscapes, and horticultural collections of Upper Midwest specimens. The large lilacs and apple-tree gardens are spectacular in spring. The miles of hiking, biking, and cross-country ski trails are popular with locals.

University of Wisconsin. The college opened in 1849 with 20 students. Today, with an enrollment of 42,000, it occupies a 1,000-acre campus on the shores of Lake Mendota. Guided walking tours of the campus may be arranged at the visitor information center in the Memorial Union (800 Langdon St., tel. 608/262–2511).

Wisconsin State Capitol (tel. 608/266–0382). The city center, on an eight-block-wide isthmus, is anchored at one end by the state capitol. Free tours of this magnificent Roman Renaissance structure take you through the Rotunda, the Supreme Court Room, the Senate and Assembly chambers, and the Governor's Conference Room.

Bicycling

The 23-mile **Sugar River State Trail** (tel. 608/527–2334 for information and fees) runs from New Glarus to Brodhead, crossing the Sugar River and its tributaries 14 times. The **Military Ridge State Trail** (tel. 608/935–2315 for information and fees) traces the path of the Old Military Ridge Trail of the mid-1800s for 39.6 miles between Verona and Dodgeville.

Canoeing

Canoeists can explore all four Madison lakes. **Lake Wingra,** where no motorboats are allowed, is a favorite. The **Yahara River** runs from Lake Mendota into Lake Monona, then south to Lake Waubesa and Lake Kegonsa. From there, it continues south through farmland and the town of Stoughton, joining the **Rock River** at a point just below Fulton, some 25 miles from Madison. The Rock River meanders through more countryside and the towns of Janesville and Beloit before entering Illinois and eventually running into the Mississippi. The current of both rivers is slow; some dams will require portaging, and in low water additional portages may be necessary. Access is available at the lakes and towns the rivers run through, as well as spots where roads cross over them.

Fishing

Northern pike, walleye, smallmouth and largemouth bass, bullheads, catfish, and a variety of panfish are found in southern Wisconsin's plentiful waters. Rainbow, brown, and brook trout are stocked in specially designated streams. Local bait-and-tackle shops or resorts can tell you where to look for fish or can recommend a professional guide.

Restaurants

Madison's Farmers' Market provides many of the ingredients for the dishes at **L'Etoile** (25 N. Pinckney St., tel. 608/251–0500), where regional food with a French flair is served in the shadow of the capitol. **Deb & Lola's** (227 State St., tel. 608/255–0820) is popular for its Southwest-inspired entrées, its terrific salads, and an array of rich desserts. **Quivey's Grove** (6261 Nesbitt Rd., tel. 608/273–4900) dishes out sturdy Midwest cuisine in an 1855 farmhouse.

Tourist Information

Greater Madison Convention & Visitors Bureau (615 E. Washington Ave., Madison, WI 53703–2952, tel. 608/255–2537 or 800/373–6376).

Arbor House

This handsome Greek Revival building began life in the 1830s as a one-room pioneer home. That original structure, the oldest residence in Madison, is preserved as the living room of the Arbor House. In 1854, an inn was attached to the front of the small house, which became a stagecoach stop on the route from Madison to the west. The building began to deteriorate after the stagecoach gave way to the railroad, but was saved in the 1940s when an art professor at the nearby University of Wisconsin purchased the historic structure and restored it, adding a rear wing that contained his studio.

The home has been a B&B since 1986, and today, thanks to careful restoration, the entire building retains its pioneer feel, with original pine-and-oak floors, stone fireplaces, and narrow hallways. But innkeepers Cathie and John Imes are not only preserving a venerable building. They're also developing an environmentally friendly B&B, with organic cotton sheets and towels, wool carpets and rugs, organic soaps and bath products, and water- and energy-saving plumbing and lighting—all while providing a quiet, luxurious retreat in the city.

The front rooms of the building, which served as the tavern in the 1850s, are now luxurious quarters called the Tap Room. Brass fixtures, a fish tank, and an old porthole window create a nautical theme, while a wet bar reminds guests of the room's original purpose. The antique brass bed in the Cozy Rose Room is made up with floral-patterned linens; one of the original stone fireplaces and a double whirlpool bath add to the relaxing, romantic mood. A view of the wooded yard and two skylights in the vaulted ceiling betray the origins of the top-floor suite called the Studio. Once the professor's atelier, it's now dominated by a brass bed with a lively Southwestern-design quilt; there's a separate dressing room, and another skylight crowns the cedar-paneled whirlpool room.

The adjoining annex features a two-story great room with beamed ceiling of massive Douglas fir timbers salvaged from a Sears building in Chicago. The annex's three rooms are furnished in comfortable style; one has a pine sleigh bed and plaid linens, another a four-poster bed with wildflower-patterned linens.

Breakfast is served either on an enclosed pine-paneled porch that overlooks the flower garden or in the Annex great room.

3402 Monroe St., Madison, WI 53711, tel. 608/238–2981, fax 608/238–1175. 7 double rooms with baths, 1 suite. Air-conditioning, TV in 6 rooms, radio in rooms, refrigerator in 2 rooms, whirlpool bath in 5 rooms, cotton robes for guests, phone, TV, fax, and computer available in common room, croquet, badminton, bird-watching, bike path across street. $84–$180; Continental breakfast weekdays, full breakfast weekends, evening refreshments. AE, MC, V. No smoking, no pets.

Collins House

This sturdy brick Prairie-style house, built for a lumber magnate in 1911, was divided into apartments, then used as an office building, and then abandoned. But it was on a prime corner lot in Madison's historic district, next to a small city park and overlooking Lake Mendota. So in 1985, Barb and Mike Pratzel bought it and dismantled its "modernizations," revealing ceilings with oak and mahogany beams, decorative leadglass windows, and the clean geometric lines of Prairie design. Then they polished the rare red-maple floors, filled the house with a collection of vintage mission and Arts and Crafts furnishings that complement the exquisite woodwork, and opened it as a bed-and-breakfast.

In the living room, a hassock and armchairs are grouped in front of a fireplace bordered in large, unglazed, moss green tiles, which are surrounded by a massive mahogany frame and mantel. The ceiling has beams, and an oak-leaf frieze is stenciled on the cream-colored walls; moldings are dark mahogany. Twin lead glass–fronted bookcases mark the entry to the library, whose frieze is in the Arts and Crafts style; inside, a plump upholstered armchair and sturdy rockers ring a well-worn Persian rug. Outside the library are three lakefront sunporches. Breakfast is served on one of the porches, where guests can watch the sailboats and crew teams, and, in winter, ice skaters and ice fishermen. Barb and Mike, who also own a gourmet catering firm, often serve Swedish oatmeal pancakes in the morning.

The light and airy guest rooms upstairs have handmade quilts, soothing color schemes, and striking mission and Arts & Crafts furniture. The largest room affords views in two directions, over Lake Mendota and the capitol building's dome. A tea cart filled with begonias and an immense oak breakfront and matching secretary give the room, which stretches the entire width of the house, a turn-of-the-century feel. Another suite, created by removing a wall between two small bedrooms, has its own balcony facing Lake Mendota.

The Collins House is only a short walk from the capitol, the university, State Street shops, a park on Lake Mendota, and Lake Monona.

▦ *704 E. Gorham St., Madison, WI 53703, tel. 608/255–4230. 2 double rooms with baths, 3 suites. No air-conditioning, TV in 1 room, TV and VCR in common room, phone in rooms, double whirlpool bath in 2 suites, whirlpool tub in 1 room, video film library. $85–$140; full breakfast. D, MC, V. No smoking, inquire about pets.*

Fargo Mansion Inn

The Wells Fargo Company was doing rather well in 1890, so when E. J. Fargo bought himself this grand house, he made it even grander. To the already stately Queen Anne building, Fargo added a gabled third floor, the cupola atop the showpiece octagonal turret, and an elaborate, gabled porte cochere. Over the years, however, the house fell into disrepair and sat empty and condemned until it caught the eye of a developer who drove past it after making a wrong turn; Barry Luce decided then and there to buy it. He completely renovated it, and the house became an inn, furnished with antiques from the town's Opera Mall Antiques Center, which the developer and his partner, Tom Bolks, also operate.

The sunny, spacious living room, a popular spot for weddings, is a Victorian confection full of sculpted moldings and other architectural furbelows. The focal point is the fireplace of laurel wreath–patterned tiles framed by an ornately carved wood mantelpiece; the shelves above are crammed with figurines and antique clocks. The music room holds a huge Federal dining table, two matching side tables, and two movable cabinets. The everyday dining room, wainscoted in oak, is no less elaborate, from its mirrored Victorian buffet and sideboard to the Corinthian columns that frame the doorway to the adjoining solarium. The small library contains a Victorian pump organ, a sled filled with antique

dolls and teddy bears, and a vintage toy ironing board.

Of the guest rooms upstairs, the Master Suite is the most popular because of its private balcony and its size— large enough to dwarf a bed with an 8-foot-tall headboard and to accommodate a teardrop chandelier and the plump velvet sofa by the white marble fireplace. A "secret" doorway, disguised as a bookcase, opens to reveal one of the inn's signature modern marble bathrooms; this one also has a whirlpool tub. The other rooms, of varying sizes, are decorated in late-Victorian style and filled with antiques.

On the house's double lot, lovely gardens of shrubbery and banks of daffodils have replaced the bear pit in which Mr. Fargo staged battles between bruins for the entertainment of his guests.

🏨 *Mailing address: 211 N. Main St., Lake Mills, WI 53551, tel. 414/648–3654; inn address: 406 Mulberry St., Lake Mills. 8 double rooms with baths. Air-conditioning, TV in living room, Jacuzzi in 5 rooms, conference facilities. $79–$160; full breakfast. MC, V. No smoking, no pets.*

Mansion Hill Inn

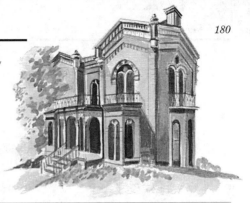

onsidered by Madisonites to be the height of opulence when it was built in 1858, this ornately carved sandstone Romanesque Revival mansion still upstages its neighbors in the historic district. Swagged with double tiers of delicate wrought-iron balconies, it would be more at home in New Orleans. Inside, a spiral staircase anchored by an immense, intricately carved newel post rises four stories from the jewel-box foyer to a turreted belvedere with sweeping views of the city. The tawny marble floor, flamboyant floral arrangements, elaborate gilt moldings, friezes, rich detailing, and three hand-carved Italian marble fireplaces create the atmosphere of a small European hotel and set the tone for the entire inn.

The small front parlor is arranged with conversational groupings of rococo revival–style furniture: settees upholstered in rose damask, side chairs with velvet ottomans. Guests can warm up at the elegant marble fireplace or sashay over to the Emerson square grand piano for a musical interlude. The carved walnut dining table, original to the mansion, holds plates and pitchers of refreshments and newspapers from near and far to which guests are welcome to help themselves.

Each of the guest rooms is individually and lavishly decorated, and most are embellished with ornate cornices and ceiling medallions and elegant, modern marble baths. In nine of the rooms, French doors open onto pleasant terraces. The Lillie Langtry Room has a white marble fireplace, a veranda, wallpaper hand-painted in neo-Grecian patterns, Renaissance Revival furniture, and a bed draped in lace. The room known as the Turkish Nook recalls the 1890s craze for Orientalia: The wallpaper depicts a stylized lotus blossom design, and the bed, whose spread is a Near East–style tapestry, sits under a lacy sultan's tent. Velvet pouf ottomans complete the look. Rooms on the lower levels are smaller and not as elaborately decorated, but have their own patios.

You can have breakfast delivered to your room on a silver tray, along with your choice of morning newspaper, or arrange to partake in the parlor.

🏨 *424 N. Pinckney St., Madison, WI 53703, tel. 800/798–9070, fax 608/ 255–2217. 11 double rooms with baths. Air-conditioning, phone, TV, and stereo in rooms, fireplace in 4 rooms, 6 rooms with sitting areas, 9 rooms with terrace, whirlpool bath in 8 rooms; private wine cellar, teleconference facilities; 24-hr valet service and valet parking, access to health club. $100–$270 single, $20 additional person; Continental breakfast. AE, MC, V. No smoking, no pets.*

Cameo Rose

Dawn and Gary Bahr wanted to open a B&B, and they also wanted to stay in the country. They were granted both wishes, as guests will discover. The couple built a new Victorian-inspired home and chose an idyllic site—120 acres adjoining the farm on which Gary grew up, 12 miles south of Madison. Guests can hike or ski on 4 miles of mowed trails that wind through the hills and woods behind the house. Also popular is a wraparound front porch furnished with wicker easy chairs and a porch swing, where guests come to read and relax.

The guests' living room is furnished in shades of blue and rose, with two overstuffed sofas and a large fireplace. Dawn serves her homemade breakfast on floral-pattern antique china in the adjoining dining room. The spacious lower-level suite can sleep four. The ground-floor Battenburg Lace Room includes a king-size brass bed and a double whirlpool bath. Upstairs, one room has a king-size bed with a floral print comforter and matching throw pillows. Another has a brass-and-iron bed and wicker rocker. The third has white eyelet lace draped above the bed and on the window shades.

🏠 *1090 Severson Rd., Belleville, WI 53508, tel. 608/424–6340. 4 double rooms with baths, 1 suite. Air-conditioning, TV and VCR in 2 rooms, fireplace in living room, ceiling fans, whirlpool bath in 1 room, hiking and cross-country ski trails. $79–$139; full breakfast, afternoon refreshments. MC, V. No smoking, no pets.*

Canterbury Inn

When Trudy Barash bought a dilapidated 1924 brick building in downtown Madison, she planned to fulfill her dream of opening a bookstore and coffeehouse. In 1991, after an award-winning renovation, Canterbury Booksellers Coffeehouse opened, offering authors' readings and musical performances in the café. Trudy's successful new venture didn't take up all the space in the building, however, so she commissioned six unique rooms and a large parlor for a second-floor B&B.

As the name suggests, the Canterbury Inn derives its inspiration from Chaucer's stories. Guests are greeted by a mural of medieval Canterbury, and murals also enliven each bedroom, all named after a pilgrim in the *Canterbury Tales*. (Don't worry—there's a cheat sheet for those who wouldn't know the Miller from the Wife of Bath.) Otherwise, the spacious rooms are far from medieval. Done in muted jewel tones, each offers a queen- or king-size bed, overstuffed wing chairs and sofas, a refrigerator, a TV, and a CD player. Breakfast is unique, as befitting the style of this B&B: It's offered in the bookstore/coffeehouse.

🏠 *315 W. Gorham St., Madison, WI 53703, tel. 608/258–8899 or 800/838–3850. 2 double rooms with baths, 4 suites. Air-conditioning, phone, TV, CD player, robes, and refrigerator in rooms, whirlpool bath in suites, VCR available, gift certificate for bookstore. $80–$300; Continental breakfast, evening refreshments. AE, MC, V.*

Jamieson House

Local merchant Hugh Jamieson was really prospering in the late 1870s, so in 1878 he decided not only to keep up with the Joneses, but to outdo them. Not content with commissioning an opulent brick home for himself—to reflect his new standing in the community—he then ordered the construction of a home even more opulent, if that were possible, to accommodate his son and heir. Today, they are a single B&B, thanks to innkeeper Heidi Hutchison, who has added (and renovated) a turn-of-the-century schoolhouse to the site and come up with a hostelry with a 19th-century feel and 20th-century amenities. The site encompasses a lovely 2-acre wooded and landscaped park on the edge of a small town 30 miles north of Madison.

All three buildings are furnished in late-19th-century antiques or reproductions. The Main House contains three guest rooms as well as the inn's common areas—two parlors, a formal dining room, and the conservatory. Upstairs, the Main Room is furnished with a brass bed with a crown canopy, an Italian painted armoire, and an 1876 marble-top dresser—the finishing touch is a settee upholstered in gold velvet, which occupies the bay window. Step in the bathroom, however, and you'll skip a century: A nifty double whirlpool bath awaits. Down the hall, cozy Lucy's Room has a brass bed and a brass daybed, a wicker settee, and a sunken tub in the bathroom. The Maid's Room actually incorporates the *Upstairs/Downstairs* back steps leading to the kitchen. This room is furnished much better than the Jamieson's maid ever dreamed—a king-size brass bed with half-canopy, a set of dark green wicker chaise longues and settee, and another double whirlpool bath. The son's residence, now called the Guest House, includes the Master Suite, with a magnificent antique bed of burled walnut and oak.

Nearby, the School House includes two suites, both with a fireplace, a TV, and a VCR. Heidi serves a full breakfast in the formal dining room of the Main House, with its wonderfully ornate gothic Victorian dining set, or in the bright and airy conservatory. She's famous for her asparagus quiche, her homemade muffins and croissants, and her baked apple pancakes. After breakfast or later in the day or evening, guests gather in one of the two parlors of the Main House to watch TV and—keeping in step with the Victorian grace of Jamieson House—enjoy afternoon tea and conversation.

🏨 *407 N. Franklin St., Poynette, WI 53955, tel. 608/635–2277 or 608/635–4100. 11 double rooms with baths. Air-conditioning, TV and VCR in 2 rooms and in common area, fireplace in 2 rooms, double whirlpool bath in 5 rooms. $70–$140; full breakfast. AE, D, MC, V. No smoking, inquire about pets.*

Past and Present Inn

First came the gift shop, carrying quaint collectibles and dried floral wreaths made on the premises. Next, tired of watching shoppers go elsewhere for lunch, owner Joyce Niesen opened a dining room that soon became legendary for its bacon-lettuce-tomato soup and cheesecakes. Then, three guest suites were added to this contemporary, Colonial-style house to accommodate people hiking the nearby Ice Age Trail and anglers who wanted to fish for trout in adjacent Black Earth Creek. The two-bedroom suite, reached by an outside staircase, has private decks at each end, a mix of old and new furnishings, and a kitchen. The other two suites, on the ground floor, face Black Earth Creek and are done in a country Victorian style with rattan furnishings, antique tables and chairs, and floral-patterned wallpaper. Each has a refrigerator and a double whirlpool bath.

Guests may order breakfast from the restaurant menu, which features omelets and other egg dishes, Belgian waffles, and specialty pancakes.

🏨 *2034 Main St., Cross Plains, WI 53528, tel. 608/798–4441. 1 2-bedroom suite, 2 1-bedroom suites. Restaurant, air-conditioning, phone and TV in each suite, whirlpool bath in 1-bedroom suites, gift shop. $75–$150; full breakfast (in restaurant). MC, V. No smoking, no pets.*

University Heights Bed and Breakfast

Local pharmacist Clement Bobb and his wife, Bertha, built this imposing brick four-square-style home on Madison's up-and-coming west side in 1923. Now this stately home, on a large lot shaded by century-old oaks, is a B&B, conveniently situated in one of Madison's most historic and architecturally interesting neighborhoods, an easy walk from the University of Wisconsin campus.

Betty and Bill Smoler, the home's third owners, bought it to fulfill their dream of opening a B&B. Inside, the living room boasts a large brick fireplace and original woodwork. Oak cabinets with beveled-glass doors and an ornate oak arch separate the living and dining areas. Upstairs, the Regent Room is a suite furnished with an Arts & Crafts–style queen-size bed and 19th-century wardrobe. The Chancellor Room has an iron bedstead and an antique American wardrobe and table. The Provost Room boasts a 19th-century bed and matching desk.

Betty serves breakfast on the sunny, all-season porch or in the more formal dining room. Guests are welcome to enjoy the shaded brick patio at the rear of the house.

🏠 *1812 Van Hise Ave., Madison, WI 53705, tel. 608/233–3340. 2 double rooms with baths, 1 suite. Air-conditioning, TV in common area, whirlpool bath in suite. $65–$125; full breakfast. AE, D, MC, V.*

Victoria-on-Main

This high-style Queen Anne house, on a corner adjacent to the university campus, was built by Whitewater's mayor in 1895, and the pediments, pillared porch, and octagonal, cone-topped turret signal the residence of a prominent citizen.

Inside, all the rooms are decorated in Laura Ashley wallpaper and fabrics and filled with antiques and bric-a-brac. Each guest room features a different Wisconsin hardwood. The Bird's Eye Maple Room contrasts blue and white chintz against the golden-toned wood; lead-glass windows add a touch of elegance. In the Cherry Room, a 6-foot-tall cherry headboard stands out against the airy, floral-print wallpaper. The most striking feature of the Red Oak Room is a fireplace of blue fleur de lis–patterned tiles, with a metal grate emblazoned with cavorting Grecian nymphs.

Breakfast, served in the bright and sunny kitchen, may include caramel-baked French toast, quiche, baked eggs, or the inn's special puffed apple dish.

🏠 *622 W. Main St., Whitewater, WI 53190, tel. 414/473–8400. 1 double room with bath, 2 doubles share bath. Air-conditioning, TV in sitting room, kitchen available for guests' use. $48–$75; full breakfast. MC, V. No smoking, no pets.*

Wisconsin River Valley
Including Wausau, Baraboo, and
Spring Green

Running north to south, the Wisconsin River wiggles through
the center of the state before suddenly veering west to join the
Mississippi. At times there is a distinct herd mentality here,
from the Holsteins munching on the grassy banks to the
armada of out-of-state vans and mobile homes making their
way down U.S. 51 (which parallels the river) to Wisconsin
Dells and other tourist meccas.

There's a sharp contrast between the original Winnebagos—the
Native American tribe that just three centuries ago silently
canoed the river's course—and their four-wheeled namesakes,
especially during the summer crush. That's when small towns
up and down the river host a stream of history pageants, arts
festivals, crafts fairs, band concerts, fireworks displays,
athletic competitions, and other weekend happenings.

The state's most-targeted town, Wisconsin Dells, is the spot
where the Wisconsin River twists its way through walls of
castellated sandstone. Originally called Kilbourn, the town
officially changed its name in 1931 in an unabashed attempt
to draw more visitors to the picturesque region, which had
garnered national renown through the stereoscopic
photographs of H. H. Bennett. It may have succeeded too well.
Outside of a museum dedicated to early photography in the
H. H. Bennett Studio and an exciting 15-mile boat ride
through the gorge, the overall experience has, to some, become
homogenized. It doesn't help that the roads leading in and out
of the dells are lined with hundreds of "family fun" venues
and neon-laced motels that wink at passersby like so many
painted ladies.

These pressures have not yet reached Baraboo, the original
winter quarters of several circuses, including those owned by

*the five Ringling brothers, themselves Baraboo natives. This
pleasant community, which took its name from an early
French trader, Baribault, is home to the Circus World
Museum and other big-top-related attractions. When you're
tired of circuses, take in the International Crane Foundation.
This fascinating center for the study and preservation of
endangered cranes is 5 miles north of town, off U.S. 12.*

*Spring Green is internationally renowned as the home of
architect Frank Lloyd Wright. Thousands of visitors annually
tour the buildings of Taliesin, his home and school on the
Wisconsin River, just south of town. Every summer, American
Players Theater offers first-class professional productions of
Shakespeare and other classics in repertory in an open-air
theater. There's also excellent canoeing on the Wisconsin River
and bicycling on local back roads. Farther south on Route 23
from Spring Green is the House on the Rock, Wisconsin's
single most-popular tourist attraction. This surreal museum
of kitsch is one of those places you have to see to believe—it
houses everything from the world's largest carousel to a
gigantic whale and sea monster diorama to replicas of the
British Crown Jewels.*

*Wausau, the largest city in north central Wisconsin, is known
for its annual June Log Jam Festival, with lumberjacks, Civil
War reenactments, arts-and-crafts booths, music, and world-
class kayak racing on a special man-made course along the
Wisconsin River. The city also has an excellent art museum,
the Leigh Yawkey Woodson Art Museum, as well as fine
restaurants, shopping, and nearby Rib Mountain State Park,
with hiking in summer and cross-country and downhill skiing
in winter.*

*Merrill, a former logging town, is the gateway to the great
Wisconsin northwoods, with thousands of lakes and the
attendant resorts and recreational opportunities. Lac du
Flambeau is the center of a Chippewa Indian reservation,
which is home to not only wilderness lakes but—if travelers
want a change of pace—a large gambling casino.*

Places to Go, Sights to See

Baraboo. Circus World Museum (426 Water St., tel. 608/356–0800), the original Ringling Bros. winter home, re-creates the razzle-dazzle era with an outstanding collection of circus wagons and big-top performances featuring today's circus stars. Both Devils Lake State Park (3½ mi south on U.S. 12, tel. 608/356–8301), highlighting Devil's Lake and several prehistoric Native American mounds, and the International Crane Foundation (5 mi north on U.S. 12, ¼ mi east on Shady Lane Rd., tel. 608/356–9462), a preserve for endangered crane species, offer guided and self-guided tours.

Portage. This river town's historic district has a cache of elegant homes worth touring; one of them is the former home of author Zona Gale (804 MacFarlane Rd., tel. 608/742–4959), now a public library. The Old Indian Agency House (Rte. 33E, tel. 608/742–6362) of 1832, the Surgeon's Quarters (Rte. 33E, tel. 608/742–2949) from the 1820s, and the adjoining 1850s Garrison School recall the pioneering era with period furnishings.

Spring Green. Frank Lloyd Wright chose this farming community on the Wisconsin River for his home, Taliesin, and for his architecture school, Hillside Home (3 mi south on Rte. 23, tel. 608/588–7900), both of which can be toured from May through October. The House on the Rock (9 mi south on Rte. 23, tel. 608/935–3639), eccentric builder Robert Jordan's tour de force perched atop a chimneylike rock 450 feet above the Wyoming Valley, is an architectural wonder of a different stripe. The complex, begun in 1940, includes waterfalls, massive fireplaces, and the millionaire's eclectic collections of dolls, paperweights, mechanical banks, armor, and much more. American Players Theater (Rte. C, Spring Green 53588, tel. 608/588–7401) offers four or five classic plays each summer in a natural outdoor amphitheater. Patrons can picnic on the grounds before the show.

Stevens Point. A branch of the University of Wisconsin (tel. 715/346–4242) is here, and campus tours can be arranged. A planetarium and observatory in the Science Building are open year-round, as is the world's largest computer-assisted mosaic mural. The Museum of Natural History (Albertson Learning Resources Center, University of Wisconsin, tel. 715/346–2858) features one of the country's most comprehensive collections of preserved birds and bird eggs. The regionally famous Stevens Point Brewery (2617 Water St., Stevens Point 54481, tel. 715/344–9310) offers tours and samples.

Wausau. The Andrew Warren Historic District (3rd St. and surrounding area) encompasses 10 blocks of historic homes built between 1868 and 1934. You can pick up maps at the Visitors Council (300 3rd St., Suite 200, tel. 800/236–9728) in Washington Square, the center of Wausau's historic Third Street pedestrian mall. The Grand Theater (415 4th St., tel. 715/842–0988) has been restored to its 1926 Greek Revival splendor at a cost of over $2 million; the structure is now home to the performing arts in the area. The Leigh Yawkey Woodson Art Museum (Franklin and 12th Sts., tel. 715/845–7010) is best known for its annual Birds in Art exhibit. It also has a fine permanent collection and a wonderful sculpture garden.

Wisconsin Dells. The scenic dells of the Wisconsin River are one of the state's foremost natural attractions. Created over thousands of years by the force of the river cutting through soft limestone to a depth of 150 feet, the Upper and Lower Wisconsin Dells comprise nearly 15 miles of fantastic soaring rock formations. While the sandstone cliffs, majestic pines, and gently flowing waters are still popular, man-made attractions nearly overshadow the region's natural wonders. Virtually everything in the dells is casual; shorts and T-shirts are allowed nearly everywhere, and swimsuits, tanning lotion, and comfortable shoes should be considered standard equipment. For more information on the dells' attractions, dining, and lodging, contact Wisconsin Dells Convention and Visitors Bureau (701 Superior St., Wisconsin Dells, WI 53965, tel. 800/223–3557).

Restaurants

The **Springs Resort Dining Room** and **Grill on the Green,** both at the Springs Resort (off Rte. C, 2 mi south of Spring Green, tel. 608/588–7000), offer Continental fare in the Dining Room and more casual meals in the Grill; both overlook woods and a golf course. The town's **Round Barn** (⅛ mi west of Rte. 23N and U.S. 14, Spring Green, tel. 608/588–2568), only a little more formal now than when the cows grazed here, segues from sandwiches to giant Wisconsin steaks. The **Silver Coach** (38 Park Ridge Dr., Stevens Point, tel. 715/341–6588), a railroad car that once streaked through Stevens Point, now turns out a fish fry as upscale as its art-deco quarters, with salmon, garlic shrimp, and tuna. **The Cottage** (1502 Post Rd., Plover, tel. 715/341–1600), where dining is in the comfy rooms of an 1860s house, offers a signature beef Wellington. **Wally's House of Embers** (935 Wisconsin Dells Pkwy., Wisconsin Dells, tel. 608/253–6411) is famous for barbecue ribs, veal dishes, prime rib, and salmon—not to mention the Sunday brunch. **Michael's Supper Club** (2901 Rib Mountain Dr., Wausau, tel. 715/842–9856) is a popular dinner spot that serves excellent fish and seafood, pasta, prime rib, and steaks, as well as wonderful desserts. Also in Wausau, the **Back When Cafe** (606 3rd St., tel. 715/848–5668) turns out gourmet breakfasts and lunch daily, plus weekend dinners from a menu that changes with the seasons.

Tourist Information

Green Lake Area Chamber of Commerce (Box 386, Green Lake, WI 54941, tel. 414/294–3231 or 800/253–7354); **Portage Chamber of Commerce** (301 W. Wisconsin Ave., Portage, WI 53901, tel. 608/742–6242); **Spring Green Travellers Guide** (Box 3, Spring Green, WI 53588, tel. 608/588–2042); **Stevens Point Convention & Visitors Bureau** (660 Main St., Stevens Point, WI 55481, tel. 715/344–2556); **Waupaca Area Chamber of Commerce** (221 S. Main St., Waupaca, WI 54981, tel. 800/236–2222); **Wausau Convention & Visitors Council** (Box 6190, Wausau, WI 54402-6190, tel. 800/236–9728); **Wisconsin Dells Visitors & Convention Bureau** (701 Superior St., Wisconsin Dells, WI 53965, tel. 800/223–3557).

Crystal River Inn

With its white clapboard walls and green shutters, Crystal River Inn is one of the first buildings visitors to Rural see as they turn off busy Highway 22. It is in perfect keeping with the history-rich heritage of its town. And it's quite a town: The entire community is listed on the National Register of Historic Places. Settled by New Englanders in the 1850s, the tiny hamlet has the white clapboard–green shutter look often found along the Eastern seaboard. Fortunately, Rural was bypassed by the railroad early on, and it has a preserved-in-amber air to it. The few dozen Rural residents work diligently to maintain the unique character of their town—and two of the hardest working are Lois and Gene Sorenson, owners of this inn.

They have furnished the inn with a tactful eye for its enduring appeal. The oldest part of the inn was built in 1853 by Andrew Potts, one of Rural's first settlers. Additions followed, the most recent being a sunroom and indoor gazebo built by the Sorensons to provide additional space to serve guests. An antique press-back rocker and wood-burning stove anchor the living room, while the sitting room has a picture window looking out on the Crystal River and the shaded backyard with its gazebo. An indoor gazebo is furnished with casual patio tables and chairs—not Victorian perhaps, but comfortable; guests gather here to eat breakfast, as well as play cards and board games. A nearby sunroom holds an antique feed chest Lois found in the barn.

The bedrooms are furnished in an eclectic mixture of country Victorian and contemporary styles. The Canopy Room has a four-poster bed Gene made from boards and pillars of the porch of a house about to be demolished. The Attic Room has a window seat overlooking the woods and an antique brass bed. Andrew's Room has an iron bed, behind which is hung a decorative filigreed gable peak from a 19th-century church. Helen's Summer Room features a tiny porch overlooking the river as well as a gas fireplace.

Many guests come to the inn to enjoy not only the town but the neighboring river, which winds through the community and is crossed by four bridges. The Crystal is popular for canoeing because it is cool, clear, fast, and shallow—if paddlers tip over, they just stand up and climb back into the canoe. Bicyclists also like the area because there's plenty of scenery and—even better—lots of lightly traveled paved roads.

🏠 *E1369 Rural Rd., Waupaca, WI 54981, tel. 715/258–5333 or 800/ 236–5789. 5 double rooms with baths, 2 double rooms share 1 bath. Air-conditioning, TV in common room, ceiling fans, double whirlpools in 2 rooms, fireplaces in 4 rooms. $65–$115; full breakfast, evening refreshments. MC, V. No smoking, no pets.*

Dreams of Yesteryear

Designed in 1901 by architect J. H. Jeffers (who was also the architect of the Wisconsin Pavilion for the 1904 St. Louis World's Fair), Dreams of Yesteryear was singled out from among its Victorian peers by Bonnie and Bill Maher, a couple determined to save the attractive, grand, old Queen Anne from destruction. Bonnie, an antiques collector, recognized the value and aesthetic potential in the oak woodwork, hardwood floors, leaded-glass windows, and footed tubs that remained in the house. She replaced a rotting roof with wooden shingles and restored the Queen Anne lines of "a chimney you could watch the sunset through." Then, with the major overhaul complete, she began "gathering" Victoriana. The voluptuously carved parlor sofa became theirs when a stranger telephoned to say, "Aunt Minerva just died at 93—could you use it?"

Today that sofa, along with a revolving library table discovered at a church bazaar, faces the fancy fireplace with its Victorian cascade decorations and surrounding tools. Sheet music for "Lola" sits on the vintage upright piano, alongside a 1904 phonograph that still has its wooden needles. Bonnie's lavish breakfasts, which feature local cranberry juice and pecan-stuffed French toast, are served on the inn's original dining room set.

Upstairs, it's hard to choose: Gerald's Room, done in French blue with a pineapple-post bed, is next to a tiny balcony; Isabella's Room, with an elaborately carved headboard, has an ivy-filled bay window, and a cozy reading nook; Florence Myrna's Room, with gardenia wall coverings comes with its own deep-green ceramic-tiled bathroom lit by antique wall sconces; and the cozy Maid's Quarters offers telephone access and a desk, making it appealing to business travelers.

The two suites on the third floor each has a bedroom and sitting room. One is furnished with a white wrought-iron bed and has a whirlpool bath, while the other is done in brown wicker and has a black wrought-iron bed.

1100 Brawley St., Stevens Point, WI 54481, tel. 715/341–4525. 2 double rooms with baths, 2 doubles share bath, 2 suites. Air-conditioning, fans in rooms, whirlpool in 1 room, fireplace in common room, TVs in suites and 1 room. $55–$129; full breakfast, afternoon refreshments. AE, D, MC, V. No smoking, no pets.

Historic Bennett House

Historic Bennett House is a pleasant alternative to the many hotels and resorts in the Wisconsin Dells. A handsome 1863 Greek Revival mansion, the inn helps guests recall a gentler era. It was here that Civil War veteran Henry Hamilton Bennett became a pioneer photographer; his stop-action pictures, the first ever taken, are displayed today in the Smithsonian Museum. Gail and Richard Obermeyer, a former stage actress and a university communications professor, are running the inn in their retirement years. "We wanted the change of seasons. We'd visited relatives in the Dells and loved it." The couple knew exactly what they wanted: the intimate atmosphere of a European bed-and-breakfast and a "historic home with warmth and charm," Gail says.

First they found the perfect house, complete with a white picket fence, only a block from downtown and the Wisconsin River. Then they waited for it to come on the market—which it soon did.

Guests from as far away as Germany and South Korea have come to this casually elegant inn. Before dinner, visitors relax with a glass of wine on the floral-patterned sofa or in a pair of wing chairs drawn up to the white, wood-burning fireplace in the living room. Breakfast is served at the communal table in the other half of the long room, which has a walnut-toned china cabinet and buffet and, on cool days, an open fire. Here Gail brings out the house specialty, eggs Bennett, or another favorite, toast Bennett (a variation on stuffed French toast). There's also a small, cozy den with a TV and comfortable sofa.

The ground-floor suite has a bedroom with Eastlake furniture, a parlor furnished with a love seat, antique table and chairs, and a framed antique tapestry; there's also a VCR and video library. Upstairs, the English Room has the original black floors, a walnut canopy bed, and an antique armoire from Britain. It shares a bathroom with the snug Garden Room, fitted with a brass bed and wicker furniture. The bathroom, with its gold fixtures, hand-painted Italian sinks, and claw-foot tub, is so seductive that some guests call it a therapeutic environment.

🏠 *825 Oak St., Wisconsin Dells, WI 53965, tel. 608/254-2500. 2 double rooms share bath, 1 suite. Air-conditioning, TV in suite and common room, fireplaces in common rooms. $70–$99; full breakfast, evening refreshments. No credit cards. No smoking, no pets.*

Rosenberry Inn

This 1908 Prairie schoolhouse built for Judge Rosenberry, in what is now Wausau's Andrew Warren Historic District, was divided into efficiency apartments back in the 1940s. Fortunately, two enthusiastic devotees came along and returned the old home to life as a B&B. By the time Fred and Laurie Schmidt bought the Rosenberry in 1995, it had a well-established reputation. The Schmidts haven't rested on the inn's laurels, however. They turned one of the downstairs rooms into a dining room for guests. They painted and refurnished and generally improved the rooms and the historic feel of the Rosenberry House. They also own the DeVoe House across the street; it's the oldest home in the historic district, dating from 1868.

Today, each guest room in the Rosenberry House contains a tiny kitchen (a remnant of its efficiency apartment days), eating nook, bath, and rustic Victorian furnishings—patchwork quilts, wooden rockers, and braided rugs. The three first-floor bedrooms still have tiled working fireplaces; rooms with western exposure are the sunniest and most spacious.

An imposing staircase with a breathtaking stained-glass window on the landing leads to the second floor. Here, four rooms evoke a comfortable and Victorian setting. The Rosenberry Room, in the corner overlooking the street and gardens, has a bird's-eye maple bed, wicker armchairs, and a tiled fireplace. In one corner is a china cabinet showcasing a collection of antique tea sets. Decorations in other rooms include a calliope horse, a stenciled bed, and a wicker settee. The Schmidts have mixed antiques and contemporary furniture in pleasing combinations.

Across the street, the DeVoe House has been divided into two guest suites; both the downstairs and upstairs accommodations contain whirlpool tubs, fireplaces, and open-to-view kitchen appliances, all in one large room with partitions. Throughout the house are collections of antique hope chests, patchwork quilts, and, in the room under the rafters, a rope-suspended porch swing.

Both establishments on this quiet, almost aristocratic residential street have porches and gardens for relaxation. Fred serves breakfast on the spacious porch of the Rosenberry House in warm weather, and, in cooler days, in the dining room, accented with its antique lace tablecloth. Hustle and bustle aren't too far away: The inn is only a quick walk from downtown.

🏠 *511 Franklin St., Wausau, WI 54401, tel. 715/842–5733. 7 double rooms with baths, cottage has 2 double rooms with baths. Air-conditioning, fireplace in 4 rooms. $65–$125; full breakfast. MC, V. No smoking, no pets.*

Bettinger House

Marie Neider's hilltop brick home, built in 1904, has been in her family since 1913, when her grandfather moved in. Today, it's a walk-in album of family history: Vintage photos line the walls of the house where her grandmother, a midwife, delivered more than 300 of Plain's babies.

Relatives' names are scrolled in brass on the doors of the four guest rooms. Uncle Edmund's Room has a handmade Star of Bethlehem quilt and matching wall hanging, white ruffled curtains, and floral stenciling. The front room, named for Grandma Elizabeth, has a round bed, lace curtains, and white wicker furniture. The large basement room has a king-size bed, but its small windows keep it on the dark side.

The common rooms are more modern and have less personality than the rest of the house. Breakfast is informal; guests gather around the oak kitchen table. Wicker chairs and a swing on the front porch catch the action in this small town, but don't let the relaxed atmosphere fool you: The Bettinger House fills up fast in the summer because it's only 7 miles from Spring Green and its many attractions.

🏠 *855 Wachter Ave., Hwy. 23, Plain, WI 53577, tel. 608/546–2951. 2 double rooms with baths, 3 doubles share 2 baths. Air-conditioning, 2 rooms have ceiling fans. $50–$65; full breakfast. No credit cards. No smoking, no pets, 2-night minimum summer weekends.*

Breese Waye

Portage, Wisconsin's third-oldest city, sits where the Fox River, flowing north toward the waters of Green Bay, comes within a mile of the Wisconsin River. It was here, in 1880, that banker Llewellyn Breese built the Breese Waye—a brick Victorian mansion,

later remodeled to give it a vaguely Greek Revival look.

In the front foyer, a fireplace with sculpted tiles of classic Grecian profiles catches your eye immediately. Innkeeper Diane O'Connor has furnished the rest of the downstairs rooms with admirable good taste. The dining room has a formal table, a crystal chandelier, and a china cabinet. The living room has two sofas and a wing chair grouped around the fireplace. Textured ivory-toned wallpaper gives the room an elegant feel. The rooms retain their original dark woodwork, and large pocket doors separate the living room from the front parlor.

Guest rooms also have a lot to offer. One has the original parquet floor, a bay window, floral wallpaper, and a four-poster bed. Another has an 1850s Victorian bed, matching dresser and table, and the home's original bathroom, slightly modernized. The two rear guest rooms are smaller and not as airy and light. At the rear of the second floor is a large screened porch, with comfortable wicker furniture, where guests can relax, read, or chat.

🏠 *816 MacFarlane Rd., Portage, WI 53901, tel. 608/742–5281. 4 double rooms with baths. Air-conditioning, ceiling fans, TV and VCR in common room, fireplace in living room. $60–$75; full breakfast. No credit cards. No smoking, inquire about pets.*

Candlewick Inn

Built by lumber baron and civic leader Henry Wright in the 1880s, this classic Victorian has been carefully restored to its late-19th-century elegance. The original quarter-sawn oak woodwork includes intricately carved crown molding in the living and dining rooms and library. The living room, furnished with antique and reproduction wing chairs and sofas, has a green glazed-brick fireplace and a large bay window that looks out onto a comfy screened porch. Adjoining the living room is the more casually furnished library, which, besides books, houses a TV and VCR. The dining room has a fireplace rimmed in blue glazed bricks and a built-in buffet with leaded-glass doors; a crystal chandelier hangs from the beamed ceiling. It's here that innkeepers Ken and Jane Oswald serve their wonderful, and filling, breakfasts.

Upstairs, the four guest rooms include the Lane Room, popular with honeymooners because of its pink glazed-brick fireplace, king-size brass bed, and sitting area with wing chairs in the large bay window. The McCord Room features a four-poster queen-size bed, and the Wright Room has an antique oak bed, washstand, table, and chairs.

🏠 *700 W. Main St., Merrill, WI 54452, tel. 715/536–7744 or 800/ 382–4376. 4 double rooms with baths. Air-conditioning, fireplace in 2 rooms and common rooms. $55–$95; full breakfast, afternoon refreshments. MC, V. No smoking, no pets.*

Hill Street

All the woodwork in this Queen Anne house is hand-carved, making Kelly and Jay Phelps's Hill Street one of the nicest bed-and-breakfasts in Spring Green. The grand central staircase has a striking design, and throughout the main floor you'll find contemporary furnishings mixed with Mission- and Shaker-style chairs and tables.

Guest rooms, named after prominent settlers of the town, are each decorated differently. Most attractive is the Harry Gray Room, banded by four windows in a turret alcove, with a brass bed and a ceiling fan. The Marion Kanouse Room has a half-canopy bed with a floral-print quilt, wicker chairs, a love seat, and a Victorian dresser; a quilt made by Kelly's grandmother hangs on the wall. In the basement are

two guest rooms furnished in a contemporary style, as well as the TV lounge.

Before setting out for the day, guests feast on Kelly's large breakfast and often linger on the wraparound porch with its wicker chairs and swing.

🏠 *353 W. Hill St., Spring Green, WI 53588, tel. 608/588–7751. 4 double rooms with baths, 1 triple with bath, 2 doubles share bath. Air-conditioning, ceiling fans. $65–$75; full breakfast, evening refreshments. MC, V. No smoking, no pets, 2-day minimum weekends June–Oct.*

Nash House

The Nash House, in Wisconsin Rapids, recalls some of the state's historic past. Built in the early 1900s, it was home to Guy Nash, father of Philleo Nash, special assistant to President Harry S. Truman and head of the Federal Bureau of Indian Affairs. When Phyllis and Jim Custer bought the house in 1987, their love of historical homes prompted them to draw the Nash family's past into the inn's future by naming the rooms after Philleo and his siblings.

The beds in the three guest rooms are covered with antique quilts; Philleo's Room, decorated in mauve and white, features one crafted by a local Amish woman. Jean's Room displays hand-stenciled furniture, and Tom's Room has an antique brass bed and walnut highboy. Each sunny bedroom has floor-to-ceiling windows and all rooms offer the comfort of a private bath (Jean's and Tom's have claw-foot tubs).

Breakfast is usually served on the screened back porch, giving guests a chance to appreciate the array of daylilies, phlox, and impatiens blooming in the inn's garden.

🏠 *1020 Oak St., Wisconsin Rapids, WI 54494, tel. 715/424–2001 or 800/*

429–6834. 3 double rooms with baths.
Air-conditioning, ceiling fan in rooms,
fireplace in common room, tandem
bike. $45–$65; full breakfast, afternoon
refreshments. AE, MC, V. No smoking,
no pets.

Oakwood Lodge

Guests at Oakwood Lodge are part of a
long tradition. This graceful "cottage"
is the sole survivor of a once-famed
resort built on the shores of Green
Lake in 1866. In what was then the
Wisconsin wilderness, it was the first
full-scale vacation resort west of Niag-
ara Falls, intended to cater to well-to-
do families of Midwest metropolises
such as Chicago and Milwaukee. The
resort eventually went out of business
and all buildings save this one were
eventually razed to make way for modern homes. The shores of Green Lake
are still a playground, though, and the
relaxed ambience remains, lingering
along the lakeshore under the verdant
oaks.

Because Oakwood Lodge itself was
built as a cottage there are no stained-
glass windows, no ornate woodwork or
other elaborate decorations. What
makes up for all that are the lake
views from nearly all the rooms—and
to take advantage of the site, there are
balconies and windowed cupolas
galore, a wraparound porch on three
sides, a shaded lawn sloping down to
the lake, and a private dock.

Guests are warmly greeted by
innkeepers Bob and Mary Schneider,
who maintain the place as a traditional
lake cottage with modern amenities.
The parlor now holds a TV/VCR in
addition to a pair of floral print sofas
and two wing chairs. The dining room
has been converted into an informal
gathering room for guests, with an
antique dresser holding a coffee and
tea service. The porch is chock-full of
wicker rockers, settees, and easy

chairs, while Adirondack-style chairs
are scattered throughout the shaded
yard. Serious sun worshipers head for
the deck.

The guest rooms are similarly informal, with high ceilings, white lace curtains, and white chenille bedspreads.
Furnishings are of the summer-cottage
variety—simple, casual, not always
perfectly matched. Room 3, which is on
first-floor corner, has an entrance from
the front porch, four large windows,
pink floral print wallpaper on two
walls, and a white wicker bed; Room 4
also has a separate porch entrance.
Oakwood remains a favored spot for
families, who particularly cotton to the
accommodating layouts of the double
rooms.

Breakfast is served on the four-season
porch. Mary acts as a "short-order
cook" for breakfasts, offering guests
several breakfast menu options at a
time of their choosing. She gets raves
on her omelets—but don't dare miss
her apple cake.

▦ *365 Lake St., Green Lake, WI*
54941, tel. 414/294–6580. 12 double
rooms with baths, 2 double rooms
share a bath. Ceiling fans, private pier,
TV/VCR in parlor. $62–$108; full
breakfast, coffee and snacks. MC, V.
No smoking, no pets.

Parkview

Tom and Donna Hofmann used 43 rolls
of wallpaper and 35 gallons of exterior
paint to turn this Queen Anne Victorian into a bright, homey place. A few
steps from downtown on a corner in
Reedsburg's historic district, Parkview
is surrounded by other Victorian
homes and churches. But Parkview is
different. Built in 1895 by a local hardware merchant, the house has an abundance of ornate hinges and doorknobs,
not to mention original oak woodwork
throughout. The backyard is just as
fanciful, crowded with a playhouse,

goldfish ponds, stone flower pots, trellises, and a windmill built of pebbles.

The guest rooms upstairs are furnished with antiques bought at local auctions. One room has a high-top bed with carved head- and footboards; another has a dresser with a swinging mirror; another features a brass bed.

🏠 *211 N. Park St., Reedsburg, WI 53959, tel. 608/524–4333. 2 double rooms with baths, 2 doubles share bath. Air-conditioning, ceiling fan in rooms, fireplace in common room, refreshments on arrival. $60–$75; full breakfast. AE, MC, V. No smoking, no pets.*

Pinehaven

Enjoy the ride between the twin allées of spruce trees lining the drive of the 80-acre Pinehaven retreat. Overlooking a private pond on the edge of Baraboo, the house is the dream of Lyle and Marge Getschman, who began its construction in 1971.

In the living room, sliding glass doors frame bucolic vistas, a wall of white luma-stone surrounds a dramatic, modern corner fireplace, and a baby grand piano invites guests to tinkle. There are two levels of guest rooms, all with private baths and three with queen-size beds. Of the four rooms, the Victorian, done in white wicker, has the most dramatic views.

You can sit in the screened porches or outside on shady decks, swim, row, or lounge on rafts. Other activities include strolling to the nearby Baraboo River and petting one of Pinehaven's sturdy Belgian draft horses. The horses team up in the summer for wagon rides and in the winter for sleigh rides.

🏠 *E13083 Rte. 33, Baraboo, WI 53913, tel. 608/356–3489. 4 double rooms with baths, 2-bedroom cottage with kitchen. Air-conditioning, candy in rooms, fire-place in common room; small private lake with paddleboat and rowboat, whirlpool in cottage. $65–$125; full breakfast (no breakfast in cottage). MC, V. No smoking, no pets.*

Sherman House

In 1904, Chicago architect Robert Spencer, a close friend of Frank Lloyd Wright, was hired to design this 14-room house. The stucco-and-sandstone, Prairie-style home, which overlooks the Wisconsin River, was commissioned by wealthy Chicago attorney J. M. Sherman as a summer retreat.

The living and dining rooms, which retain their original woodwork, are divided only by back-to-back tan brick fireplaces, angled to form two sides of a triangle. The point of the triangle directs the eye through wide doors to the large screened porch, which overlooks a shady yard, towering oaks, and the river below. Innkeeper Norma Marz serves breakfast on the porch when weather permits. With the exception of a couple of antique tables, the downstairs is furnished in comfortable, if slightly frayed, sofas and chairs.

Upstairs, the woodwork is painted white, and Norma has painted each room a solid color—deep green, peach, sage green, and mauve—to contrast with the woodwork, creating an uncluttered backdrop for her mixture of antique and contemporary furnishings. Ask for a room with a river view.

🏠 *930 River Rd., Box 397, Wisconsin Dells, WI 53965, tel. 608/253–2721. 3 double rooms with baths, 1 suite. Air-conditioning. $55–$70; Continental breakfast. No credit cards. No pets, closed Nov.–Mar.*

The Swallow's Nest

Although the Swallow's Nest bed-and-breakfast, a modern cedar-shingled lake house, nestles among tall timbers and wildflowers of the forest, you can catch a glimpse of the lake's sparkling water from its windows. This scenery is the inspiration for the photography and paintings of innkeeper Rod Stemo.

The house is built around a sunny, two-story atrium. An open staircase leads to a bridge that overlooks the plant-filled atrium and connects the four guest rooms. In the Tamarack Room, blue-gingham-covered walls and lace curtains offset an antique mirrored dressing table. Paintings and floral plates grace the soft-pink walls of the Wild Rose Room, complementing the room's heirloom English walnut furniture. Twin knotty-pine beds and deep green and rust accents make the Whispering Pine Room quite masculine. The suitably named Sunburst Room is done in pale yellows, with a queen-size brass bed.

After a breakfast served by Mary Ann Stemo, guests can take a woodland walk or rent a boat to explore the lake.

🏠 *141 Sarrington St., Box 418, Lake Delton, WI 53940, tel. 608/254–6900. 4 double rooms with baths. Air-conditioning, fireplaces in common rooms, pool table, TV in common room. $70–$75; full breakfast. MC, V. No smoking, no pets.*

Ty-Bach

Ty-Bach is smack in the middle of thousands of acres of the Lac du Flambeau Chippewa Indian reservation—an almost Edenic area dotted with hundreds of lakes, public forests, and parks. More civilized pleasures also await: There's plenty of shopping, nightlife, and restaurants in the nearby resort communities of Minocqua and Manitowish Waters.

Janet and Kermit Bekkums's contemporary two-story home is built into the hillside so that the second-floor guests enter their quarters at ground level from the rear and walk through the house out onto a deck. Beyond lays a wooded lawn that slopes to a beautiful lake and the Bekkums's private dock. Guests may use the canoe and paddleboat or to take a dip in the cool, clear water of the 50-acre lake. The enormous property also features 85 acres of woods through which the Bekkums have cleared hiking and cross-country ski trails.

Guests are given the run of one floor of the house. Two guest rooms, each with private bath, share the spacious living room and deck. One of the guest rooms is furnished with a brass bed and family antiques. The other has a private deck and a Northwoods ambience. There's also a kitchen, where Janet and Kermit appear every morning to prepare a fine breakfast and even finer conversation.

🏠 *3104 Simpson La., Lac du Flambeau, WI 54538, tel. 715/588–7851. 2 double rooms with baths. No air-conditioning, swimming, boating, private pier, bikes, outdoor hot tub, hiking and cross-country ski trails, kitchen for guests, TV/VCR in common area. $65–$70; full breakfast. No credit cards. No smoking, inquire about pets.*

Victorian Swan on Water

Joan Ouelette's Victorian Swan on Water, appropriately named for its Water Street address, is easy to find—the town's water tower looms behind it. A row of pine trees screens the tower from the 100-year-old blue clapboard house, which is flanked by a beautiful garden of annuals and perennials.

Ivy trails through the home's sunny dining room where the daily three-course breakfast is served. Before retiring to one of the four bedrooms, guests can relax on the large front porch with its old-fashioned wicker chairs or in the Victorian drawing room, which has distinctive black-walnut inlaid floors and elaborate crown moldings.

In the peaches-and-cream Newport Chaney Room, Jean turned an alcove into a sitting area with a skirted table and two antique chairs. The Rothman Travel Suite features antique travel mementos in the bedroom and a handcarved antique dressing table. Its huge bathroom has a whirlpool and fireplace, in front of which are a sheepskin rug and wrought-iron chairs. A wonderful touch: Joan painted one wall with a mural of Rome. The Balcony Room, romantically decorated in rose and lilac chintz, has a canopy-draped wrought-iron bed; a small balcony overlooks the front yard and Water Street.

▦ *1716 Water St., Stevens Point, WI 54481, tel. 715/345–0595. 3 double rooms with baths, 1 suite. Air-conditioning, fireplace in parlor and in suite, whirlpool in suite. $55–$120; full breakfast. AE, D, MC, V. No smoking, no pets.*

Hidden Valleys
Including La Crosse and Prairie du Chien

*The rumpled rural terrain known as Hidden Valleys hugs the
eastern edge of the Mississippi River as it flows southward
from La Crosse to the Iowa border, rolling inland in some
spots for 60 or so picturesque miles. As viewed from a plane,
the land is a pincushion marked by church steeples and grain
silos, towers of strength that neatly summarize what this
somnolent slice of small-town America is all about.*

*Faith first arrived in these parts in the 17th century in the
person of Jesuit priest Jacques Marquette, who busily
converted Native Americans even as he and explorer Louis
Jolliet searched for the Mississippi. Agriculture appeared not
long afterward, as successive waves of immigrants from
several European nations literally and figuratively set down
roots in the rich topsoil.*

*Many of these communities proudly maintain their Old World
character, a task made easier by their relative isolation. The
region has the Midwest's largest concentration of hardwood
forests and is unblemished by an interstate highway system,
allowing the Norwegian heritage to survive in Westby and
helping Hillsboro to keep its distinctive Czech culture. In New
Glarus, founded in 1845 by immigrants from Glarus,
Switzerland, many residents are still bilingual—a pleasant
discovery for visitors to such annual events as the Heidi
Festival in June, the Volksfest in August, and the Wilhelm
Tell Festival on Labor Day weekend. Like the other festivals in
the area, these are genuine ethnic celebrations that have so far
resisted becoming cloying.*

*Another ethnic enclave is Mineral Point, just south of
Dodgeville along U.S. 151. Here Cornish miners in the 1830s
sat out the bitter winters in underground dwellings called
badger holes. The lead and zinc mines contributed to
Wisconsin's admittance to the Union in 1848, and the*

prospectors' dugouts accounted for its nickname as the Badger State. Mineral Point today is a growing artists' colony reflecting a wide variety of influences, but its British roots are still very palpable, from the old stone houses to the formidable meat pies called pasties. Visitors to Mineral Point should not miss Pendarvis, a state-managed historic site with restored limestone and log Cornish cottages dating from the 1840s.

The two largest towns in the region, La Crosse and Prairie du Chien, were settled by French traders eager to exploit their strategic locations on the Mississippi River. The distance between these ports can be leisurely traversed via riverboat or Route 35. The latter, part of the Great River Road, is a 55-mile drive that offers a succession of scenic vistas; it's particularly spectacular in October, when the statewide Colorama autumn festival is in full swing.

Places to Go, Sights to See

Bike Trails. The Elroy-Sparta State Trail (tel. 602/463–7109) was the first abandoned railroad grade to be converted to a recreation trail. It winds through 32 miles of wooded valleys, small towns, and railroad tunnels, with interpretive stops, parking, and picnic facilities along the way. The valley's other biking trails include the Great River State Trail (tel. 608/534–6409), 22½ miles along the Mississippi Valley, and the 23-mile Sugar River State Trail (tel. 608/527–2334), which runs south from New Glarus.

Cassville. Visit Stonefield Village (north on Rte. VV, tel. 608/725–5210), home to the State Agricultural Museum and a replica of an 1890s village, complete with costumed guides. Across the road, Nelson Dewey State Park (tel. 608/725–5374) is a perfect place to catch the drama provided by river-bluff vistas.

La Crosse. The Convention and Visitors Bureau in Riverside Park (tel. 608/782–2366) is also the home of Riverside USA, an exhibition describing early life on the Mississippi. The bureau also provides maps for a Heritage Tour, which details 42 historic buildings throughout the town, beginning at the Hixon House (429 N. 7th St.), now the County Historical Museum, and including the G. Heileman Brewery and Christina Winery. Nearby, *La Crosse Queen* (tel. 608/784–2893 or 608/784–8523) and *Island Girl* (tel. 608/784–0556) offer paddleboat river excursions. Granddad's Bluff towers 530 feet above the city; the summit offers a panoramic view of three states and three rivers.

New Glarus. The town known as "Little Switzerland" honors the Alpine life of its founders in the pastoral Swiss Historical Village (612 7th Ave., tel. 608/

527–2317), where 12 reconstructed buildings depict the homes, trades—including a 19th-century cheese factory—and skills of the Swiss who first settled here. Events such as the Wilhelm Tell and Heidi festivals and the Volkfest, Polkafest, and Winterfest take place throughout the year and include arts-and-crafts fairs, outdoor music, and historical plays.

Norskedalen (Rte. PI, west of Westby, tel. 608/452–3424). "The Norwegian Valley" (in English) has grown from an arboretum to a 400-acre expanse that includes log farmsteads. Trail maps guide hikers past corn and tobacco fields, oak-and-spruce forests, prairies, ponds, and springs. Cross-country skiers use the trails in the winter.

Prairie du Chien. Remains of the American Fur Trading Company's stone warehouses and fort survive on St. Feriole Island. In 1870, fur fortunes built opulent Villa Louis Mansion (531 N. Villa Louis Rd., tel. 608/326–2721), home of Wisconsin's first millionaire; today, tours are offered daily from May through October. Along the river behind the mansion, the St. Feriole Island Railroad's restored railroad cars are filled with shops. Nearby Lawler Park has swimming beaches and marinas.

Restaurants

In Monroe, you have your choice between **Baumgartner's Cheese Store & Tavern** (1023 16th Ave., Monroe, tel. 608/325–6157), in the town's historic square, serving bulky cheese sandwiches and a local brew, or a fancier meal at the century-old **Idle Hour Mansion** (1421 Mansion Dr., Monroe, tel. 608/325–1200), where the Sunday champagne brunch is popular. The **New Glarus Hotel** (100 6th Ave., New Glarus, tel. 608/527–5244) no longer accommodates guests overnight but does serve authentic Alpine dishes such as fondue and raclette. The **Chalet Landhaus** (801 Rte. 69, New Glarus, tel. 608/527–5234), housed in a town landmark, has a similar menu. Mineral Point's **Chesterfield Inn** (20 Commerce St., Mineral Point, tel. 608/987–3682), in a 160-year-old stone building, features seafood, steaks, pasta, and vegetarian items.

Tourist Information

La Crosse Convention & Visitors Bureau (Box 1895, Riverside Park, La Crosse, WI 54901, tel. 608/782–2366); **Mineral Point Chamber of Commerce** (Box 78, Mineral Point, WI 53565, tel. 608/987–3201); **New Glarus Chamber of Commerce** (Box 713, New Glarus, WI 53574, tel. 608/527–2095); **Prairie du Chien Chamber of Commerce** (Box 326, Prairie du Chien, WI 53821, tel. 800/732–1673); **Sparta Chamber of Commerce** (101 S. Water St., Sparta, WI 54656, tel. 608/269–4123).

The Duke House

E ven though it is in the Midwest, this 1870 Federal-style house—one of the oldest in Mineral Point—feels like a New England Victorian. Darlene Duke and her husband, Tom, packed up their antiques collection and left the East Coast fast lane in search of a more pleasant way of life.

One of the reasons Darlene loves the light and airy house is the many windows that enable her to indulge in her needlework, even on a gloomy day. The focus of the creamy white living room is the working fireplace; a plush pastel Chinese rug warms the broad-planked floor. An old brass trunk serves as a coffee table, and there's a Colonial drum table beneath the newel post. These and a few reproduction pieces give the room a lived-in, homey atmosphere, perfect for the early evening social hour the Dukes feel is the best time of the day.

The house is built on the area's highest point of land, so the views from the upstairs bedrooms capture most of the small city, which seems almost untouched by time. The four-poster bed in the Canopy Room is covered with a crocheted string spread and a canopy, and the finials are in the form of pineapples, the symbol of hospitality. With its pierced-tin lamp, its low, wooden Colonial-era rocker, the steamer trunk in the huge walk-in closet, and the copper warming pan hanging on the wall, the room is comfortable without being precious.

Across the hall, in Grandma's Room, more pineapples appear on the four-poster bed, complemented by floral wallpaper, a white rug covering well-polished floorboards, a decorative kerosene lamp, and bookcases filled with tomes of area history and lore. Other pieces find their way here from Duke's Antiques, which is only a short stroll away, close to the artisans' shops that occupy the former miners' dwellings.

🏨 *618 Maiden St., Mineral Point, WI 53565, tel. 608/987–2821. 2 double rooms share bath. Air-conditioning, fireplace in common room. $48–$58; full breakfast, morning coffee, and Cornish appetizers delivered to guest rooms. MC, V. No smoking, no pets, closed Mar.*

The Franklin Victorian

W. G. Williamson, a prominent Sparta banker, personally inspected every piece of wood that went into the interior of this raspberry-red clapboard Victorian. His meticulous standards are evident the minute you cross the white-columned front porch. The floors are of glowing maple complemented by black ash and quarter-cut oak. Pocket doors of curly birch lead to a parlor with russet ceramic tiles, a beveled-glass window, and a double-manteled fireplace with fluted Corinthian columns—elegant reminders of the late 1800s, when Sparta, with its spas and mineral waters, was a hub of social activity.

Cordial innkeepers Jane and Lloyd Larson have integrated their family heirlooms into the house. In the dining room, which has an elaborate parquet floor with a "braided" border, is a built-in buffet with floor-to-ceiling glass doors showcasing china that's been in Jane's family for three generations. In the parlor is the Civil War–era miniature pump organ that belonged to Jane's grandfather. The portable instrument, which he played at funerals, keeps company with a boxy Victorian velvet sofa trimmed in mahogany and its honor guard of stuffed velvet chairs that belonged to Jane's great-grandparents. The intricate sunset-motif stained-glass window faces west, providing a vivid late-afternoon glow to the stairway landing.

Guests love the Wicker Room, with its white wrought-iron bed and wicker furnishings, which contrast with the dark blue floral-design wallpaper. Most requested, however, is the Master Bedroom, which has a grand titled fireplace with decorative columns, an immense oak headboard crafted by Lloyd Larson from the wall of a judge's chamber, and a tall highboy of bird's-eye maple that belonged to Jane's parents. Its bathroom, with tongue-and-groove wainscoting, still boasts the original marble-top sink.

Guests can enjoy a private chat in the upstairs sitting room or sit in rocking chairs and sip lemonade on the side or front porch. They overlook this corner lot in a quiet residential neighborhood, where the trees loom taller than dormers and turrets.

🏠 *220 E. Franklin Pl., Sparta, WI 54656, tel. 608/269–3894. 2 double rooms with baths, 2 doubles share bath. Air-conditioning, fireplace in common room, canoe rental, shuttle service for bikers and canoeists. $70–$92; full breakfast, early morning coffee. MC, V. No smoking, no pets.*

The Inn at Wildcat Mountain

All tall white pillars, with a classic Georgian air, this inn looks like the White House of woodland Wisconsin. A Greek Revival mansion on the edge of the tiny hamlet of Ontario, it was built in 1910 with high hopes as a railroad seemed headed this way: Its builder, who had made a fortune growing ginseng and shipping it to Asian buyers in Chicago, planned to rent rooms in the house to tourists. But the proposed railroad never made it this far, and the interior of the gorgeous house was carved up into apartments.

After undergoing a monumental restoration, the building is the dream come true of innkeepers Pat and Wendall Barnes. With their children grown and gone, turning their home into a bed-and-breakfast seemed natural. "How else could I justify buying a house like this?" Pat laughs. She says she enjoyed restoring the building and likes entertaining people who appreciate the cherry, oak, and bird's-eye maple woodwork she spent years refinishing, according to her calculations.

Pat describes her former life as "collecting things," an understatement once you see the period pieces and vintage clothing hung everywhere on walls, clothes trees, and mannequins. A fan revolves on the parlor's lofty ceiling, and lace-curtained windows rise even higher than the dignified grandfather clock. The focal point of the room is a 1905 oak secretary. In the dining room, connected to the parlor by a columned entry, a silver candelabra casts a warm glow over the Philippine mahogany sideboard.

Of the four upstairs rooms, the most in demand is the Balcony Room, which has a turn-of-the-century brass bed and its own curved balcony. The back room, called Shady Rest, has the house's only closet, as well as a four-poster bed and a bare wooden floor.

The 5-acre woodland setting, in the lap of the forested Wildcat Mountain State Park, makes the inn especially popular with outdoor-sports enthusiasts. Guests can rent horses or canoes at nearby outfitters. Or they can just loll on Pat's wide, inviting front porch or in the spacious backyard and watch the butterflies flit by.

🏠 *U.S. 33 (Box 112), Ontario, WI 54651, tel. 608/337–4352. 4 double rooms (1 sleeps 3 people) share 2 baths. Air-conditioning, ceiling fans. $50–$75; full breakfast, early morning coffee and tea, afternoon refreshments. MC, V. No smoking, pets in outside kennels only.*

The Jones House

This regional showcase looks as grand as it did on the day it was built; oddly enough, it was hardly lived in. William Jones, once commissioner of the Bureau of Indian Affairs for President McKinley, erected the 16-room redbrick mansion in 1906 as a homecoming present to himself after his stint in Washington. He died soon after, and his will forbade its sale until the death of his wife and children. Boarded up intact, a housekeeper faithfully dusted it twice a week until 1986, when June and Art Openshaw purchased it.

A grand, boxy staircase winds around one of the seven unusual fireplaces. The stairs rise from the foyer to a stained-glass skylight that casts patterns on the entry carpet. The mahogany-beamed dining room is graced by forest green woodland scenes painted above the wainscoting. A green-tile fireplace warms guests during breakfast. Twin sideboards topped by graceful arches glint with beveled glass, and padded velvet window seats on either side of the fireplace overlook the broad side lawn. To complete the *après-la-chasse* feel, the hardwood floor is covered with moss green carpet.

The Persian and floral-print rugs, dark patterned wallpapers, and brass lighting fixtures, all of which came with the house, create a decidedly masculine atmosphere. The small Ladies' Parlor overlooking the front walk, however, provides respite for the frill-deprived

with its garlands of roses painted on high, pale walls.

In the Master Suite, a white tile fireplace, original needlepoint chairs, and a floral covering on the daybed in the suite's sitting room also bestow a more feminine air. A screen door leads to a porch-top balcony that overlooks the town. The adjacent front bedroom, with a view of the spreading side yard as well as the avenue, features another white tile fireplace and a Colonial-reproduction four-poster bed with pineapple finials on the posts. The Ivy Suite, which overlooks the hills to the north of town, has a green tile fireplace and a Colonial-reproduction four-poster; the smaller back bedroom, in contrast, has a country-antique look.

There are still traces of William Jones in the house: Outside the Master Suite stand the master's antique golf clubs; his leatherbound books still line the library's shelves; and his umbrella hangs on the door of the vestibule.

▦ *215 Ridge St. (Box 130), Mineral Point, WI 53565, tel. 608/987–2337. 1 double room with bath, 1 suite and 1 double share bath. No air-conditioning, fans in rooms, 7 fireplaces. $58–$88; full breakfast. No credit cards. No smoking, no pets.*

Just-N-Trails

Ask Don and Donna Justin why they added a bed-and-breakfast to their 213-acre working farm, and they just laugh, "We'd been doing it free for 15 years anyway for all the relatives." The accommodations are "all things to all people," claim the friendly, laid-back couple, who delight in welcoming guests. Their 50 head of Holstein cattle occasionally provide visitors with a rare late-night show (no cover charge)—the birth of a calf. An athlete's nirvana, their spread has 10 miles of groomed and mapped hiking and ski trails, six nearby cycling trails (the area calls itself "the bike capital of America"), and five rivers close at hand, where guests can fish or go canoeing. And then, of course, there's always the B&B's own "traditional agrarian fitness center"—decked out with pitchfork and hay bales.

The farm is also a romantic getaway spot, with three private cabins and Laura Ashley–decorated rooms upstairs in the farmhouse. The Granary Cottage has a front deck from which you can watch the sun sinking past the fields and wooded hills. The cabin decor includes a garden-gate queen-size bed, Amish bentwood rockers made by local craftsmen, and its own whirlpool bath. The beds are invitingly comfortable, with an abundance of pillows that make reading a pleasure.

The second log cabin, Little House on the Prairie, has a log bed, country-style furnishings, a fireplace, and a whirlpool bath in the loft under skylights. The Paul Bunyan, the two-bedroom cottage, is made of aspen logs from the farm's woodlots and is furnished with a log bed and other rustic pieces. It also has a double whirlpool bath, and both a rear porch and a rear balcony from which to watch deer coming out of the nearby woods. All three cottages have kitchenettes, and the Paul Bunyan is accessible to wheelchair users.

Guests in the farmstead's bedrooms—such as the Green Room, with a green, pink, and white floral scheme and double bird's-eye maple bed and matching dresser—get the same nine-pillow treatment as those in the cabins. The morning wake-up call is a wren's warble or perhaps a moo, followed by Donna's hearty, farm-style breakfast, served up in the nearby lodge. There's also a microwave guests can use when the hungries hit, as sometimes happens after a ramble on the hills up to the farm pond and down again via the Bambi Trail—so named to reassure novice skiers.

🏠 *Rte. 1 (Box 274), Sparta, WI 54656, tel. 608/269–4522 or 800/ 488–4521. 2 double rooms with baths, 1 suite, 2 1-bedroom cabins, 1 2-bedroom cabin. Air-conditioning, fireplace and whirlpool tub in cabins, hammock, picnic tables, hiking and cross-country ski trails, ski and snowshoe rentals, snow tubes available free. $75–$250; full breakfast. AE, D, MC, V. No smoking, inquire about pets.*

Martindale House

When Anita Philbrook opened the Martindale House in a quiet residential section of La Crosse, she was concerned that bed-and-breakfast establishments would prove to be "a fad, like the vitamin craze." But repeat guests—from as far away as England, Spain, and Scandinavia—have made her fears groundless. "I offer not just a bed, but an experience," Martindale's polished hostess maintains. Luckily, that experience includes a hearty Swedish breakfast served on the fifth-generation family china patterned in wedding-ring gold, which complements antique silver coffee spoons. This repast is served in the white, bright Scandinavian-style dining room, lined with a collection of traditional family portraits.

The imposing green-shuttered house, built in 1859, is a grand architectural mélange of Italianate cupola and Colonial clapboard, with a Victorian-style wraparound porch to boot. Combating years of disrepair, Anita restored moldings and chandeliers discovered in the basement and returned them to their proper places; she also resurrected the iron fence, hidden in the carriage house. Then she replanted the entire garden.

Inside, the parlor is a historian's delight. The room contains a stately grandfather clock, an antique chess table, antique Oriental rugs on the blond-oak floors, floor-to-ceiling windows flanked by their original shutters, and a piano that's been in her husband's family for five generations.

The white staircase in the foyer leads to four bedrooms. The Martindale Room features an 1800 cannonball bed, a warming pan, a 1740 Queen Anne highboy, and quilts from the nearby Amish community. The French Room derives its name from the carved Louis XVI bed that came from a castle in Lyons; its other highlights are a 1640 campaign chest and an antique grandfather clock. The English Room offers a fireplace, a garden view, and a lace-canopied four-poster bed. This room has the advantage of a vast, soothing bathroom, dubbed the "rub-a-dub" by guests. The antique twin beds in the sunny Scandinavian Room came from a convent, and the Lapland dolls on display belonged to Anita's grandmother. Anita also renovated the 1860 carriage house into a two-story, three-room suite. The downstairs sitting room has a microwave, coffeemaker, and small refrigerator. The upstairs bedroom has an iron-and-brass bed and an antique Franklin stove, as well as a heart-shaped double whirlpool bath.

🏨 *237 S. 10th St., La Crosse, WI 54601, tel. 608/782-4224. 4 double rooms with baths, 1 suite. Air-conditioning, use of portable phones, several languages spoken. $80–$145; 4-course breakfast, evening refreshments. MC, V. No smoking, no pets.*

Mascione's Hidden Valley Villas

Phil and Mary Ann Mascione, as Italian as Chicagoans can get, do not at first come across as isolated rancher types. In fact, the fellow with the big grin and hearty handshake was the sports photographer for the *Chicago Tribune* for years. But when their kids grew up and moved away, the couple came here—to a hidden valley reached by a back road that weaves through stands of pine along the bluffs of the Kickapoo River.

All by themselves, the Masciones built an alpine-style guest retreat. Phil scoured the countryside for weathered boards from fallen barns, while Mary Ann collected American crafts. They created a minivillage of chalet-type guest villas, which overlook pastures where young Holstein, relaxing before their milking careers begin, graze peacefully.

The Golden Antler Villa follows a hunting-lodge motif and comes complete with mounted stags' heads, skis, snowshoes, and antlers used as racks for an antique gun collection. The Camelot Villa's decor has a medieval theme. Both villas have two bedrooms and a loft space. The first floors have wagonwheel chandeliers, fireplaces made of local fieldstone that Phil collected, complete kitchens including microwaves, dining areas, and a shared bathroom. They also have decks with umbrella tables and barbecue grills.

Three two-person chalets have been added. The snug living room of each has a fireplace and, in the corner, a minikitchen. Upstairs, under the slanting ceiling, Phil built impressive pine beds that Mary Ann carved and painted in keeping with the theme of each chalet: the Cheyenne, the Aztec, and the Eagle's Nest.

Mary Ann cooks a hearty breakfast of eggs Benedict or soufflé with local bratwurst and serves it in a separate dining cottage, whose entryway houses a gift-and-antiques shop.

Set back in the pines on a hill is an Olympic-size pool surrounded by a deck and umbrella tables. The 80-acre property has two trout ponds, a croquet court, and a baseball field, as well as miles of meticulously tended walking trails.

🏨 *Rte. 2 (Box 74), Hillsboro, WI 54634, tel. 608/489–3443. 2 2-bedroom villas and 3 1-bedroom villas, all villas with private bath. Air-conditioning, coffeemaker, microwave, and fireplace in villas; hiking trails, pool. $90–$190; full breakfast, snacks stocked in rooms. No credit cards. Smoking in designated areas only, no pets, closed early Nov.–Apr.*

Westby House

uess heading for Westby tend to book well in advance at this B&B during the merry month of May, for this is when this very Norwegian town is especially lively, thanks to the Syttendai Mai Festival. Year-round, however, the Old World Norskedalen Village, 6 miles away, attracts visitors. They arrive at a house that is archetypal Midwest American: Topped with an imposing Queen Anne witch's turret, the country manor–style abode was commissioned in the 1890s by a well-to-do Norwegian immigrant. Today, its fine oak woodwork, lighting fixtures, stained-glass accents, and imposing pillared fireplaces are still in place.

Upstairs, in an otherwise undistinguished hallway, the original dining-room buffet stands guard over a pair of spacious front bedrooms. The Tower Room has a small bathroom and a down quilt–covered brass bed set into an alcove of bay windows. The Fireplace Room has a brass bed, tiled fireplace, and a rocking chair; a TV helps to compensate for a lackluster view of storefronts just off the town's main street. The two rooms are connected by double doors and can be rented as a suite. The Anniversary Room is almost a suite, with reproduction wing chairs and a sofa forming a conversation group in its bay window. Its brass bed merits the handmade quilt and white eyelet comforter. The Greenbriar Room's caned chairs, rag rugs, marble-top washstand, and old-fashioned white iron bed, topped with another antique quilt, have the look of Grandma's house—comfortable but not fancy.

200 W. State St., Westby, WI 54667, tel. 608/634–4112. 2 double rooms with baths, 4 doubles share 1½ baths. Air-conditioning, TV in 1 room, fireplace in common rooms. $60–$80; Continental breakfast weekdays, full breakfast weekends, refreshments on arrival. MC, V. Inquire about pets.

Eckhart House

This house, built by local merchant Fred Eckhart, started life in 1897 as a Victorian belle, complete with a large front porch and lots of ornate woodwork and lead-glass windows. By the 1940s new owners had modernized the home, closing in part of the front porch and replacing the clapboard siding with stucco. Fortunately, they left the windows, woodwork, and ornate exterior trim as well as the glazed-brick fireplaces, an imposing entry hall, and the grand staircase to the second floor—all grace notes that remind one of a gentler era.

Today, innkeeper Nancy Rhodes-Seevers welcomes guests on the enclosed porch with coffee, tea, or snacks. The informal gathering then usually moves into the adjacent game room. On the second floor, the bedrooms are eclectically furnished. The Seevers Room has a large bay window, wicker rockers, and a whirlpool bath, while the Dalles Room, formerly the home's master bedroom, has a private balcony. Who can resist going barefoot on the antique carpet in the Eckhart Room? This bedchamber's bathroom has lavender-hued fixtures from Europe and a green-and-white-checked tile floor—a remnant of the 1940s makeover.

Nancy also owns the Viroqua Heritage Inn directly across the street, where she serves breakfast to Eckhart House guests each morning.

🏠 *220 E. Jefferson St., Viroqua, WI 54665, tel. 608/637–3306. 3 double rooms with baths, 2 doubles share 1 bath. Air-conditioning, fireplace in common room, whirlpool bath in 1 room, TV available, refrigerator and microwave. $55–$79; full breakfast, afternoon refreshments. AE, D, MC, V. No smoking, no pets.*

The Geiger House

This sleepy river town is chock full of history. It was the home of several prosperous businessmen in the 1850s and 1860s, just after Wisconsin became a state. This stately 1855 Greek Revival home on a spacious corner lot just two blocks from the Mississippi River was a town showpiece when completed. It still appears as if it just stepped out of the 19th century, with a trim white picket fence, white clapboard siding, and green shutters. Guests can relax on the front porch—a great box seat to take in Cassville's annual Twins Parade—or under the shade trees in the yard or on the second-floor porch. Even better, the backyard affords stunning views of the Mississippi River bluffs that border Cassville on the east.

Many of the inn's rooms showcase owner Kathy Polich's antiques, although she's not shy about adding contemporary pieces and mixing different vintages to create a comfortable setting for guests. One guest room has an antique oak bed with carved legs and an armoire with a beveled-glass mirror in the door; another has a four-poster bed and wicker chairs. The third also is furnished in oak and wicker. In the winter, the dining room's fireplace makes a cozy gathering place for breakfast, which Kathy is proud to serve on her best china.

🏠 *401 Denniston St., Cassville, WI 53806, tel. 608/725–5419. 3 double rooms share 2 baths. Air-conditioning, fireplace in common room, bikes, shuttle to river ferry. $50–$60; full breakfast, morning coffee, afternoon refreshments. AE, MC, V. No smoking, no pets.*

Oak Hill Manor

First a word about breakfast: *Gourmet* magazine has asked for the eggs Benedict recipe. When Glen and Donna Rothe left the fast-paced lifestyle of

Chicago to buy an inn in this rural community, they also inherited many of the wonderful recipes for which the former owners were known—so get set for a wonderful assortment of breakfast treats. But Glen and Donna's main passion is the terraced garden behind their house. The couple lived in England for several years and have created a garden that would fit nicely into the Cotswolds—complete with gazebo and an arbor spanning the entrance. Guests can drink in all this verdant beauty from the porch that spans this 1908 four-square house. The wicker sofas and swing are perfect spots to relax.

The proud farmwife for whom the house was built insisted on being able to survey the comings and goings from both directions, so the inn sits diagonally on its corner. The house showcases some of the lady's upscale tastes: Original ivory-embossed wallpaper hangs in the entry hall; the dining room is appointed with oak pocket doors and a built-in buffet; the living-room fireplace has tall wooden Ionic columns and a shiny brass grate; and rich oak woodwork is visible throughout. Upstairs, off a wide, sunny hall that leads to a cheery sitting room, are the two most popular bedrooms: the Hearth Room, with a white-tile, pillared fireplace, and the Oak Hill, with a private sunporch filled with wicker furniture.

🏨 *401 E. Main St., Albany, WI 53502, tel. 608/862–1400. 4 double rooms with baths. Air-conditioning, TV and VCR in sitting room and parlor, fireplace in 1 room and common rooms, bikes. $60–$70; full breakfast, afternoon refreshments. MC, V. No smoking, no pets.*

The Parson's Inn

The cross on the sign is the clue you've found the Parson's Inn—a 12-room, turn-of-the-century brick rectory that once served the church right across the street. Just off the wraparound porch, which overlooks the wooded river valley and the Mississippi River bluffs beyond town, is the original priest's office. "It's where I signed my marriage papers," says Mary Huser, mother of proprietor Julie Cull and native of this secluded river hamlet.

In decorating the inn, mother and daughter combined eclectic furnishings with family antiques. The living room is comfortably furnished in overstuffed couch and chairs. The bird's-eye maple bed with ruffled half-canopy that belonged to Mary's grandmother sits in Granny's Room, and the dining room set was a wedding present from Mary's mother—it's now where Julie serves a breakfast that includes melt-away pecan rolls and homemade jellies, both from her mother's recipes.

The two-room Bell Suite has a nonworking fireplace in the sitting room and a bedroom with armoires, woodwork, and pretty blue-and–gold-hued bed. From its private deck, the nearby bluffs spread out before your eyes.

🏨 *Rock School Rd., Glen Haven, WI 53810, tel. 608/794–2491. 3 double rooms share bath, 1 suite. Air-conditioning, TV in common room. $50–$70 ($85 for 4 in suite); full breakfast, afternoon refreshments. No credit cards. No smoking, inquire about pets.*

Sugar River Inn

The Sugar River is the source of many pleasures for the Albany community and its visitors. The inn's backyard abuts the river shore, so guests can linger in the gazebo and watch canoes drift by or enjoy the view from the windows of the inn's country-style bedrooms—the River Room even has a small balcony.

Jack and Ruth Lindberg have furnished their 1920s brick home with Colonial-reproduction furniture, but their unique touches are what give the rooms charm. The quilt on the Country Room's four-poster Shaker-style bed depicts the same farm scene you see on the room's wallpaper border. The Rose Room's antique dolls fit perfectly with its pink walls and white lace.

Ruth sends her guests off with a hearty breakfast featuring her "golden treat," a mélange of granola, golden raisins, bananas, vanilla yogurt, and honey, while a full cookie jar awaits guests at the end of every afternoon.

🏠 *304 S. Mills St., Albany, WI 53502, tel. 608/862–1248. 2 double rooms with baths. Air-conditioning, fireplace in parlor, turn-down service. $52–$62; full breakfast, wake-up coffee, afternoon refreshments. MC, V. No smoking, no pets.*

Trillium

These two cottages are nestled amid 85 acres of rolling hills in the heart of Amish farm country. The innkeepers, the Boyett family, live in the nearby frame house, and they still raise cattle, sheep, and chickens on their acreage. Farmwife Rosanne Boyett arrives each morning with a freshly cooked breakfast for guests. Rosanne's husband laboriously hauled sandstone from the banks of the nearby Kickapoo River to build a huge fireplace in each cabin.

Grandma's Cottage—the smaller of the two—has a sitting room whose humble and well-used look comes from over-stuffed armchairs and treadle sewing machines; the sofa bed allows the room to double as a bedroom. Beyond an arched doorway is a cozy inner bedroom with a neatly folded double-wedding-ring quilt made by Rosanne's aunt at the foot of the bed. An old woodstove dominates the kitchen (with a 1950s electric range as backup). The

Hill Cottage has a open living-dining-kitchen area arranged around the stone fireplace. Upstairs are three bedrooms. Both cottages' spacious covered porches are equipped with swings. Paths lead to a brook and waterfall in the woods.

🏠 *Rte. 2 E10596 Salem Ridge Rd., La Farge, WI 54639, tel. 608/625–4492. 1 1-bedroom cottage, 1 3-bedroom cottage, each with bath. No air-conditioning, fireplace and kitchen in cottages, tree house, hiking trails, picnic area with grill. $65–$70 double, $25 for each additional person over 12; full breakfast. No credit cards. No pets.*

Victorian Garden

Trees shade the arched front porches of this 110-year-old Victorian belle on a quiet street in Monroe. But what takes your breath away is the double lot's gardens, crossed by meandering brick pathways. A carved stone fountain from Italy greets guests in the front garden, and another decorates the garden at the rear of the house.

Inside, the light and airy first floor has a sitting room with a baby grand piano and stereo system. The informal parlor has a TV, with the formal parlor reserved for conversation and reading. Innkeepers Pete and Jane Kessenich serve a delicious three-course breakfast in the formal dining room.

Three guest rooms are named after the garden's flowers, seen from the rooms' windows. The White Lace and Roses Room has what is surely the largest bathroom in Monroe. Roses bloom on its black wallpaper and its folding screen. Live plants twine around the claw-foot tub and antique pedestal sink, and French doors overlook the garden.

The spacious Rhapsody in Blue Room features a bay window that affords a particularly lovely garden view. The Tulip Room, a small adjoining single room, can be rented with either the Rhapsody in Blue or the Rosebud Room.

🏨 *1720 16th St., Monroe, WI 53566, tel. 608/328–1720. 3 double rooms with baths, single room can be rented with one of the doubles. Air-conditioning, robes for guests. $70–$80; full breakfast, afternoon or evening refreshments. D, MC, V. No smoking, no pets.*

Viroqua Heritage Inn

Restraint was the last thing the Boyle family had in mind when they built this Victorian extravaganza in 1890, and present owner Nancy Rhodes-Seevers has lovingly restored every last curlicue. This grand house rises in blue-shingled splendor, its porch embossed with a floral garland and its corner tower topped with a conical cap.

More flowers bloom inside on the carved, ornately tiled fireplaces. Polished hardwood floors peep out from under the Oriental rugs in the parlor, nearly outshining the brass-and-crystal chandelier. Lace curtains, a pair of fringed settees upholstered in tapestry print fabric, and a globe gas lamp complete the mood. In the music room is another intricately carved fireplace, as well as a baby grand piano and a working Victrola.

Each guest room is furnished with antiques; the largest has a brass bed and a sitting area in the turret and shares a balcony that overlooks the garden. The inn is the perfect setting for the Murder Mystery Weekends Nancy hosts throughout the winter.

🏨 *220 E. Jefferson St., Viroqua, WI 54665, tel. 608/637–3306. 2 double rooms with baths, 2 doubles share 1½ baths. No air-conditioning, phones and TVs available for rooms, robes, refrigerator, and microwave available to guests. $50–$79; full breakfast. AE, D, MC, V. No smoking indoors, no pets.*

Hiawatha Valley
Including Hudson, River Falls, and Stockholm

Wisconsinites owe their outdoorsy image to the year-round opportunities provided by nature. But you don't have to sport snowshoes or float a kayak to appreciate what the residents of this rugged wedge of water, prairie, forest, and farmland take for granted. Instead, spend a couple of hours on the Great River Road (Route 35), which snakes along the east bank of the Mississippi River and continues along the St. Croix River.

Navigating the rising and falling terrain is like riding the chest of a gently snoring giant, but the eye-popping scenery guarantees you won't fall asleep at the wheel. This primeval nature show hasn't changed since the days of Chief Red Wing and Princess Winona. Limestone bluffs fringed with fir trees rise dramatically around you, while hawks and eagles dip in and out of the shadows. All along the way, old river towns such as Hudson, Prescott, Alma, Maiden Rock, and Stockholm cling to coves and bluffs, each wearing its own unique personality.

Many things in this area look as it they've just bounded off hand-tinted postcards: vintage bandstands centered in shady parks, elegant mansions recalling the glory days of the lumber barons, and red-and-white farmsteads sprinkled over the surrounding hills. Given this heady dose of Americana, it should come as no surprise that the village of Pepin was the inspiration for Laura Ingalls Wilder's first book, Little House in the Big Woods.

The fur trade and the logging industry shaped the area, as newly rich lumber barons filled towns with mansions that seemed to spring up overnight. Today, the area is the playground of Minnesotans seeking an escape from the urban pressures of Minneapolis and St. Paul. And they find it. With state and local parks providing hiking, biking, and cross-country trails; with canoeing and motorboating on the Mississippi and on the St. Croix, designated a National Scenic River; and with plenty of shopping, historic sites, and winding back roads, it's easy to while away a weekend or a week—or longer.

The calendar is filled with antiques shows, arts-and-crafts fairs, and farmers' markets on warm-weather weekends, but autumn is the finest time of year in Hiawatha Valley. Be prepared: The leaves start turning in early September, causing the valley's biggest tourist logjam and making both film and accommodations premium items.

Places to Go, Sights to See

Interstate State Park (Hwy. 35, St. Croix Falls, tel. 715/483–3747) is Wisconsin's oldest state park, and one of its most spectacular. Here, the St. Croix River, designated a National Scenic River, flows through craggy and weathered granite rock formations, called the Dalles of the St. Croix. The park offers miles of hiking and cross-country ski trails with great river views; there is also an interpretive center.

Mabel Tainter Memorial Auditorium (205 Main St., Menomonie, tel. 715/235–9726). This tribute to a lumber baron's daughter was built in 1980—an imposing Romanesque-style fortress harboring a jewel box of a theater done in Victorian Moorish style. Frequent performances range from jazz concerts to children's theater. Tours are also offered.

Nelson Cheese Factory (Rte. 35, Nelson, tel. 715/637–4725). This fifth-generation family-owned shop produces 50 varieties of what the state's cows are best at.

Red Cedar Trail (from Menomonie at Rte. 29, south to Dunnville on Rte. Y). This limestone-surfaced trail follows an abandoned railway right-of-way along the wooded banks of the Red Cedar River to its junction with the Chippewa River 15 miles south. Owls, eagles, deer, otters, and beavers share their habitat with hikers, bikers, and cross-country skiers.

Stockholm. This tiny Mississippi River hamlet shows many signs of its Swedish heritage, from the names in its romantic graveyard to the stores offering food and antiques and art from the Old Country in galleries, shops of traditional wares, and a charming old-time museum in the former post office.

Restaurants

The valley's specialty is its Friday fish fry, found in nearly every small-town bar and grill. The **Harbor View** (1st and Main Sts., tel. 715/442–3893), in Pepin, is one of those corner cafés, with a twist. While it retains its just-folks atmosphere, the place has become a destination for Twin Citians, who are undaunted by the 90-mile drive and no-reservations policy when hungry for Swedish dumplings, coq au vin, or salmon with shiitake mushrooms. The **Creamery** (1 Creamery Rd., tel. 715/664–8354), in Downsville, comes up with equally imaginative food, from lamb curry to fettuccine with morels, in a contemporary setting with a river-valley view. Durand's **Cafe Mozart** (311 W. Main St., tel. 715/672–4103) ladles out *Gemütlichkeit* (that warm, cozy feeling) along with its Wiener schnitzel, while Prescott's **Steamboat Inn** (307 Lake St. N, tel. 800/262–8232) is a classic '50s supper club with the bonus of a riverside deck. The **Little Star Cafe,** in Stockholm (161 Hwy. 35, tel. 715/442–2023), prepares seasonally changing gourmet lunches and dinners from fresh local ingredients. Their Friday and Saturday dinners are a five-course set menu.

Tourist Information

Prescott Chamber of Commerce (Box 244, Prescott, WI 54021, tel. 715/262–3284); **River Falls Chamber of Commerce** (115 E. Elm St., River Falls, WI 54022, tel. 715/425–2533); **Hudson Chamber of Commerce** (421 2nd St., Hudson, WI 54016, tel. 715/386–8411 or 800/657–6775); **St. Croix Falls Chamber of Commerce** (Box 178, St. Croix Falls, WI 54024, tel. 715/483–1851); **Eau Claire Convention and Visitors Bureau** (3625 Gateway Dr., Suite F, Eau Claire, WI 54701, tel. 715/831–2345).

The Knollwood House

The comfortable atmosphere of the two-story Knollwood House and the warm hospitality of owners Jim and Judy Tostrud quickly transform guests into friends. Built in 1886 with red bricks from a local factory, the house, set on 85 acres in the rolling Kinnickinnic River valley, draws people into its rich history. Jim has farmed the land for many years, as his father did before him, and Judy, a horticulturalist, fills the landscape with perennials and hydroponically grown plants. Inside, you'll appreciate the Tostruds' personal touches, displayed in the plants that grace the windowsills and the family heirlooms that furnish the rooms.

Christie Ann's Room is filled with Tostrud family memorabilia. The queen-size bed with carved head- and footboards and matching dresser belonged to Jim's parents. An Amish quilt covers the bed. The suite includes an unusually spacious bathroom with tub and shower. The Country Rose Room is decorated in forest green and mauve and is furnished with an antique oak four-poster bed and an armoire of similar vintage.

The Sherlock Wales Room, a smaller room with wainscoting and an antique brass bed, overlooks a garden and small goldfish pond below the window. The aptly named Garden Room, on the first floor, allows guests access to the plant-filled solarium, which has a hot tub, and to the Daybed Room, which indeed has a daybed—and a small enclosed porch. The Garden and Daybed rooms are usually rented as a suite.

The kitchen contains an antique cast-iron stove, a glazed pottery water-cooler, and a farmhouse pie cabinet with screen doors to tempt the hungry. Judy prepares a down-home breakfast featuring muffins made with the strawberries and raspberries she grows herself. The meal is served either in the solarium or on the arbor-draped deck beside the swimming pool.

There is no lack of activities at Knollwood; just about everything you could want is right outside the door. Badminton, croquet, basketball, softball, shuffleboard, boccie, a swimming pool, an in-ground trampoline, and a 180-yard par-three golf drive are found within the 3½-acre yard. The more ambitious athlete can try the 2 miles of well-maintained hiking and cross-country ski trails on land owned by the Tostruds. Ready to assist hikers are the Tostrud's two llamas, Hustler and Rivera.

🏨 *N. 8257 950th St., Knollwood Dr., River Falls, WI 54022, tel. 715/ 425–1040 or 800/435–0628. 2 double rooms with baths, 1 double and 1 suite share bath. Air-conditioning, fireplace in common room, ceiling fans, robes, ceiling fans and robes, hot tub, sauna, pool, hiking, cross-country ski trails. $80–$150; full breakfast. No credit cards. No smoking, no pets.*

Otter Creek Inn

The original house on this site was built in 1920, then enlarged in the 1960s and again in the 1980s. The additions were well done—it's impossible to tell the old from the new. In 1987, Shelley and Randy Hansen purchased the house and have run it as a B&B ever since. Approaching the inn up the wooded drive, visitors feel they are in the country. The truth is, busy Highway 12 is nearby, and the Eau Claire city limits are only a few yards away.

The house has a Tudor Revival look, with steep gables and half-timbered stucco on the upper story; a brick, stucco, and stone chimney add to the Tudor image. The country-manor feel is enhanced by the beautiful landscaping done by Shelley and Randy; the tidy flower beds on the 1-acre wooded lot are often abloom. At the rear of the house, guests enjoy a deck and a brick terrace. Here awaiting you is a relaxing swimming pool, at one end of which lies a flower-bedecked gazebo—just the place to enjoy an iced tea after a dip in the water.

Inside, the spacious two-story common area has two dark brown leather couches in front of a wood-burning stove, a favorite gathering place on winter evenings. Off in a corner, surrounded by large potted plants, is the cozy breakfast nook, but Shelley likes to serve breakfast poolside in warm weather. However, guests often prefer to have breakfast brought to their rooms; a selection of cheese omelets or waffles can be made the night before.

The six large guest rooms are furnished in country-Victorian style. The Palm Room, actually a two-room suite, features an antique-sleigh bed, a sitting room, and a bathroom that's so big Shelley has furnished it with a wicker chair and étagère. Most guests prefer serious quality time in the double whirlpool bath. The Gardenia Room, decorated in tones of mauve and cream, has white rustic French furniture. The Jasmine Room has an ornately carved antique bed and a sunken whirlpool bath set within a 9-foot-wide bay window. A mahagony canopy bed is the centerpiece of the Violet Room. The Rose Room features an iron-and-brass bed with an Eastlake dresser and matching chair and an antique mission-style rocker. The Magnolia Room is furnished with mission-style furniture and a canopy bed.

🏨 *2536 Hwy. 12, Eau Claire, WI 54701, tel. 715/832–2945. 5 double rooms with baths, 1 suite. Air-conditioning, TVs, whirlpool bath in rooms, swimming pool. $79–$139; full breakfast, afternoon refreshments. AE, D, DC, MC, V. No smoking, no pets.*

The Phipps Inn

This Queen Anne house has remained virtually untouched since its debut in 1884. From the octagonal tower under the witch's-cap roof to the wraparound veranda with scrolled friezes and pedimented gables, the house, which is on the National Register of Historic Places, is the showplace of the river town.

William Phipps, a prominent Hudson banker, politician, and philanthropist, moved here to serve as land commissioner for the railroad and certainly wasn't averse to living well. The interior of his former house is equipped with six fireplaces that are flamboyantly carved, guarded by Ionic columns, and set with Italian tiles. Ornate brass hardware, stained-glass windows, and parquet flooring in intricate geometric designs add to the got-it-flaunt-it look.

Innkeepers John and Cyndi Berglund bought the mansion intact but empty. This gave them the mandate of filling it with antiques from the St. Croix River valley, including an 1890s pump organ and Victorian sofas and chairs in the two parlors. In the music room, they've installed a snazzy 1920 baby grand piano; these days it's set with afternoon snacks. Guests linger over breakfast in the dining room, warmed by sun streaming through the stained-glass windows and by one of the fireplaces.

The Bridal Suite boasts a wicker canopy bed and wicker dresser, table and chairs, and a fireplace with Italian ceramic tile. The Master Suite has a canopied four-poster pine bed, another fireplace, and a large, climb-through window that leads to a private balcony. Victoria's Room, a more intimate hideaway done in a black-and-gold Victorian floral motif, is furnished with a brass bed and antique armoire; the Queen Anne's Room features hand-stenciled walls, a half-tester brass bed, and a gas fireplace that opens on both the bedroom and the adjoining whirlpool room. Guests can sit in the whirlpool bath and look out the windows on one side and enjoy the fireplace on the other.

Above all looms the third floor's grand ballroom. Once the site of the Phipps's elegant gatherings, it has been converted into the Willow Chamber, which is furnished with willow furniture, and the Peacock Chamber, with its antique walnut half-tester bed and redwood paneling. Guests will find Jacuzzis in every bathroom.

🏨 *1005 3rd St., Hudson, WI 54016, tel. 715/386–0800. 6 double rooms with baths. Air-conditioning, fireplace in 5 rooms and in common rooms, whirlpool tub in 6 rooms; bathrobes, picnics available with advance notice and at an extra charge. $89–$179; full breakfast, afternoon refreshments. AE, D, MC, V. No smoking, no pets.*

Arbor Inn

On a bluff overlooking downtown Prescott and the St. Croix River, this inn is fitted out with two porches, both vine-covered and serene, wicker-furnished, and perfect for watching the river below. It turns out Prescott is just upstream from the confluence of the Mississippi and St. Croix rivers and is the start of the Great River Road, which winds south along the Mississippi through Wisconsin, Minnesota, Illinois, Iowa, and Missouri. There's plenty of river traffic, but the porches are also perfect for reading or for quiet conversation—beguiling places that welcome visitors to this B&B.

In 1902 a local banker named Longworth built this Arts and Crafts home. Three owners later, innkeepers Marv and Linda Kangas took over the substantial abode and refurbished it with an eye for comfort. The living room, with exposed wood beams and original woodwork, is furnished with a mix of Linda's antiques and contemporary pieces. An overstuffed plaid sofa and matching ottoman face the large brick fireplace and are a favorite spot for guests in the winter. Linda serves her famous four-course breakfast either in the adjoining dining room, with its Victorian dining set and matching sideboards, on one of two screened porches, or in guest rooms. Linda believes in the dessert-first theory of breakfast, so she starts with her signature strawberry parfait, then moves on to fresh fruit, fresh scones or muffins, an egg dish such as quiche or an omelet, finishing up with waffles or pancakes topped with syrup made from her grandmother's recipe.

The ground-floor Silhouette Room houses Linda's distinctive collection of antique black-on-glass silhouette pictures. Linda's sister made the quilt that covers the king-size bed. An ice-cream-parlor table and chairs provide a quiet spot for breakfast. An arbor-covered private deck holds an outdoor hot tub for the use of guests who rent this room.

Upstairs, Patti's Room, decorated in shades of sage green and rose, features an antique armoire and a handmade star quilt. The huge bathroom also houses a double whirlpool bath. The Longworth Room, the inn's largest, is decorated in hunter green and burgundy, has a private deck overlooking the river and a wood-burning fireplace, and has probably the inn's most intriguing accessory—a handmade trip-around-the-world quilt, which adorns the queen-size bed.

🏨 *434 N. Court St., Prescott, WI 54021, tel. 715/262–4522. 3 double rooms with baths. Air-conditioning, TV/VCR in rooms, fireplace in 1 room and common area, whirlpool bath in 1 room, outdoor hot tub for 1 room, bikes. $105–$145; full breakfast. MC, V. No smoking, no pets.*

Cedar Trails Guesthouse

This was a working farm until 1984. These days, there's a new deck—big enough to hold a hoedown—surrounding this comfy, modernized 80-year-old farmhouse, where city folk can watch cattle amble to the barn and horses enter the paddock. Proprietor Barb Anderson also invites guests to mosey over to her second farm nearby, where she "raises sweaters." Her sheep provide wool for the handmade comforters and mattress pads that warm the guest beds in the six-level house.

The furnishings are an eclectic mix ranging from art-deco squatting-peacock chairs to framed needlework pillow shams. One guest room features an antique rooming-house washstand with drawers, while another has a modern sleeping loft complete with a futon by a window. The overall effect is informal. "It's like visiting relatives, without the relatives," Barb says (she always invites guests to raid the cookie jar). The living room has a welcoming over-stuffed couch and chair and a turn-of-the-century rocker, and the picture window in the parlor offers lovely views of the trees beyond the long driveway.

🏠 *E4761 County Road C, Menomonie, WI 54751, tel. 715/ 664–8828. 2 double rooms with baths, 2 doubles share bath. Air-conditioning. $45–$65; full breakfast, afternoon refreshments. MC, V. No smoking.*

The Creamery

Although this redbrick building began life in 1904 as a cooperative creamery, turning local cream into butter, today, thanks to a tasteful renovation by a family of hands-on proprietors, the building has a clean, contemporary look. The windows of its bright, white dining room frame a garden terrace sloping to the wooded riverbank. The Creamery is known for imaginative American cuisine, and the wine list is excellent. From the lounge, which is lined with old milk bottles, wildlife can frequently be spotted beyond the adjoining open deck.

Upstairs, guest rooms with the same bucolic view are done in cherry wood-work and modern walnut furnishings. Handmade pottery lamps and bath-room tiles—including a mosaic mural in the suite's bathroom—originated in the resident pottery shop. The tiny town of Downsville is a quarter mile down the road, where riders on the 14-mile Red Cedar Bike Trail sail by. A friendly crew of college kids augments the family staff.

🏠 *1 Creamery Rd., Box 22, Downsville, WI 54735, tel. 715/ 664–8354. 3 double rooms with baths, 1 suite. Restaurant, air-conditioning, phone, TV, and whirlpool tub in rooms; fireplaces in common rooms, bar, lounge, restaurant. $100–$130; Conti-nental breakfast (in restaurant or in rooms). MC, V. No smoking in rooms,*

inquire about pets, closed Jan.–Mar., restaurant closed Mon.

The Gallery House

This neat 1861 mercantile brick build-ing has served as a store with a family residence above it ever since its Civil War–era beginnings. The general-mer-chandise and post-office trappings have been replaced by innkeeper and pho-tographer Joe Hopkin's work, including pictures of Europe, Wisconsin, and points between. His wife, Jan, sells spices, teas, and gifts in the shop. Guests share actually are made wel-come in the couple's home on the sec-ond floor, where bedrooms open off a wide, hotel-like hall that's lined with paintings by local artists. The inn fea-tures antique furnishings, including family heirlooms and a cast-iron bed. The Alma Room features a cushioned window seat, a four-poster bed with half canopy, and an antique rocker. The rooms overlook a broad, white-spindled veranda, ideal for viewing barges chug-ging toward the nearby Mississippi River locks. Along the front of the building is a full balcony where guests can watch the river and keep an eye on Main Street comings and goings.

Joe and Jan treat guests to breakfast by candlelight in the dining room, which has a view of the Mississippi River. But who can watch the river when tempted with Jan's fruit soup, stuffed French toast, vegetable pâté, individual soufflés, and other delights?

🏠 *215 N. Main St., Alma, WI 54610, tel. 608/685–4975. 3 double rooms with baths. Air-conditioning, ceiling fans. $70–$85; full breakfast. MC, V. No smoking, no pets.*

The Grapevine Inn

The man who built this house was named Hans Andersen—whether or not he was related to Hans Christian is not exactly known, but he went on to make his family name famous across

America by founding Andersen Windows, now the world's largest window manufacturer. In 1886, the new Danish immigrant had arrived in Hudson to manage the local lumber company. By 1901 he was prosperous enough to build this Queen Anne–Greek Revival home up the hill from downtown Hudson, a few blocks from the mansions of the town's reigning lumber barons. Not surprisingly, he is said to have personally inspected each piece of lumber used in the house.

Avery and Barbara Dahl bought the home in 1990, and after three years of remodeling and decorating—and personally checking *almost* every piece of lumber—they opened the Grapevine Inn in 1993. Guests enter the front parlor, furnished with a bentwood rocker and Victorian sofa and chairs. The library, furnished with a comfy contemporary sofa and wing chair, has a TV and VCR with a video library for guests.

Upstairs, the three guest rooms are furnished in country-Victorian. One has an antique walnut bed with a lavender upholstered settee facing the fireplace. Another has a large bay window with table and chairs, where Barbara will serve a private breakfast. The third has an 1880 bedroom set with a 7-foot-high headboard. Outside, a treat awaits: a lovely swimming pool.

🏠 *702 Vine St., Hudson, WI 54016, tel. 715/386–1989. 3 double rooms with baths. Air-conditioning, fireplace in 1 room, whirlpool bath in 1 room, swimming pool. $89–$139; full breakfast, morning wake-up tray, afternoon refreshments. MC, V. No smoking, no pets.*

Great River Bed & Breakfast

This pioneer stone farmhouse was built in 1869 by the Peterson family, who founded the community of Stockholm in 1854. The home remained in the family until 1980, when Leland and Lydia Krebs purchased it for their home. These days, they live nearby and rent the entire house to guests. In addition to having the building to themselves, guests are welcome to stroll the 45-acre farm or just relax under the century-old trees in the yard.

The downstairs areas, including an enclosed porch, as well as the upstairs guest rooms and bath, are simply furnished in an elegant Scandinavian-influenced combination of antiques and contemporary pieces. The original woodwork and some of the floors are painted in shades of brick red, deep green, and dark gray-blue. Antique tables, chairs, and bedsteads maintain the feel, as does the kitchen, which includes an antique stove on which Leland and Lydia prepare breakfast for guests.

The owners rent the entire house to only one couple or family, allowing complete privacy. Upstairs, the front bedroom has a gray painted floor, ornately carved antique bed and matching dresser, and a 1920s woodstove. The rear bedroom is smaller, with fir flooring and an antique oak bedstead and dresser.

🏠 *Rte. 35, Stockholm, WI 54769, tel. 715/442–5656 or 800/657–4756. 2-bedroom farmhouse. No air-conditioning, woodstove in 1 room and in living room. $95 2 people, $170 4 people; full breakfast. No credit cards. No smoking, no pets, reservations required.*

The Harrisburg Inn

Grandmotherly Carol Crisp calls her place "a view with a room"—not an understatement when used to refer to this century-old, small-town house perched high on a bluff above Lake Pepin in the Mississippi River valley. Actually, there are four rooms lining the upper hallway, all with valley views and homey, turn-of-the-century rustic furniture and a country look accented by colorful quilts. The two end rooms, each with old-fashioned claw-foot tubs, are the most coveted because they sport roomy balconies good for watching towboats and soaring eagles on the river and for listening for the whistle of passing trains.

Just beyond the common rooms, the open porch and large, screened summer room, with its cache of wicker rockers, catch the last of the evening sun. The breakfast room also faces the river, and guests can watch barges and speedier craft while enjoying Carol's homemade breakfast. On cool or rainy days guests like to relax in the living room to listen to the tapes from Carol's classical and jazz library.

▦ *W3334 Rte. 35, Maiden Rock, WI 54750, tel. 715/448-4500. 4 double rooms with baths, 2 rooms can be joined to make a suite. Air-conditioning, ceiling fans. $68-$98; full breakfast, afternoon refreshments. D, MC, V. Smoking on porches only, no pets, closed Jan.-Feb.*

The Jefferson-Day House

The Tyler family's pre–Civil War Italianate house is full of details that give it a gracious air. The inn's bedrooms combine historic flavor with modern luxury. The Captain's Room contains a brass bed and lace curtains; the Harbor Room sports stenciled walls and matching quilt; and the Hudson Suite holds a display of antique dolls. Guests will also find the decidedly modern addition of whirlpool baths for two. The more luxurious three-room St. Croix Suite has soft rose-and-blue accents on ivory walls and a sitting room; the bedroom features a queen-size bed and double Jacuzzi. The Hudson Suite also includes a full private bath and a sunporch on which guests can enjoy a specially delivered four-course breakfast.

The inn is within walking distance of downtown Hudson and the St. Croix River. Favorite recreations include river cruises, visits to local museums, and concerts and plays at the Phipps Center for the Arts.

▦ *1109 3rd St., Hudson, WI 54016, tel. 715/386-7111. 3 double rooms with baths, 1 suite. Air-conditioning, fireplace in 4 rooms, double whirlpool bath in 4 rooms. $99-$169; full breakfast, afternoon refreshments. MC, V. No smoking, inquire about pets.*

Pine Creek Lodge

When Judith Atlee built this stunning contemporary home in 1992, she included two additional bedrooms so guests could share her hilltop home. In the wood-floored living room, a large stone fireplace anchors the 25-foot vaulted pine ceiling. Picture windows offer a view of the surrounding 80 acres of woods and wildflowers, and an outdoor deck overlooks Judith's herb garden. Breakfast, which Judith cooks to order for each guest, is served in the airy dining room or on the deck.

The South Bedroom, painted white and accented by pine ceiling beams and woodwork, is furnished with a contemporary-rustic pine bed and matching dresser. The bath includes a two-person steam room. The North Bedroom, also white with pine trim, has a contemporary mission-style bed and dresser accented by a stained-glass lamp; a double whirlpool tub is in the bathroom. The Treetop Suite, which is half the second floor, has a private deck, a queen-size bed next to the window, a sofa and antique rocker in the sitting area, and a large bathroom.

▦ *N447 244th St., Stockholm, WI 54769, tel. 715/448-3203. 3 double rooms with baths. Climate-controlled guest rooms, whirlpool bath in 1 room, steam room in 1 room; TV, VCR, and CD player in common room; kitchen access, masseuse on call, hiking, cross-country skiing. $85-$120; full breakfast. MC, V. No smoking indoors, inquire about pets.*

Pleasant Lake Inn

This has been Richard Berg's family homestead since 1894. While he and his wife, Charlene, wished to retire from farming, they wanted to keep the property, so in 1990 they built this secluded rural retreat on 32 wooded acres of Berg land overlooking 40-acre Pleasant Lake, taking maximum advantage of the lake view. The airy and open living/dining/kitchen area on the first floor has picture windows looking out on the lake and a door opening onto a deck. And guests don't have to just gaze longingly at the lake; a canoe and paddleboat await on the shore for anyone who wants to explore.

The guest rooms are just as open and inviting. Downstairs, Julia's Room, which features a brass bed, fireplace, and whirlpool bath, has a private deck with steps that lead to a lake path. The three upstairs rooms each have a sitting area or deck with lake views. All the rooms are furnished with an eclectic and comfortable combination of family antiques and contemporary pieces.

Every morning, Charlene greets guests with coffee, herbal teas, and fresh baked muffins to start the breakfast. They're followed by such favorites as honey-baked French toast. She also makes coffee cake and even her own bread with custom-ground flour.

🏠 *2238 60th Ave., Osceola, WI 54020, tel. 715/294–2545 or 800/294–2545. 3 double rooms with baths, 1 suite. Air-conditioning, fireplace in 1 room, whirlpool bath in 3 rooms, lake access, canoe and paddleboat, evening bonfires, TV/VCR in common room. $55–$125; full breakfast. MC, V. No smoking, no pets.*

The Rosewood

In 1912, local banker A. W. Hofer ordered this large Arts and Crafts home from a catalog company in Davenport, Iowa—the kit cost $1,634. Debra and Steve Knutson bought the home in 1990, spent a good deal more money remodeling and refurbishing, and opened the Rosewood in 1993.

The living and dining rooms retain their original woodwork, including columned room dividers, built-in bookcases, and a china cabinet. The living room's central attraction is the green glazed-brick fireplace surrounded by heavy oak framing and an oak mantel surmounted by a large mirror. On the other side of the large entrance hall, the informal parlor is furnished with modern pieces, including a big-screen TV and a VCR.

Upstairs, the three guest rooms share a small sitting room that opens onto a front balcony. The Blue Room has the original teardrop-crystal-and-brass ceiling fixture. The Master Bedroom has a fireplace that's a smaller version of the one in the living room, as well as a four-poster bed, an antique dresser, and lace curtains. The Brass Room, smallest of the three, has a private bath and a large brass bed.

🏠 *203 S. Main St., Cochrane, WI 54622-7228, tel. 608/248–2940. 1 double room with bath, 2 doubles share bath. Air-conditioning, fireplace in common room and in 1 bedroom, TV/VCR in common room. $58–$78; Continental breakfast. No credit cards. No smoking, no pets.*

The Ryan House

In 1890, Patrick Ryan, an accomplished carpenter, built this stately home for his bride, Emma, on his Bear Creek Valley farm, 4 miles from town. With a yellow exterior capped by an elegant mansard roof, the farmhouse was like no other in the area and became the talk of the county.

The living room's strong points are its original oak woodwork, pocket doors, and stained-glass windows. The dining room features an elegantly carved fireplace that was found in the attic; it has been restored to its rightful place of honor, warming guests as they breakfast on homemade cinnamon rolls.

A grand oak stairway leads upstairs to the guest rooms. The Hat Room is where the Ryans traditionally boarded teachers. In fact, innkeeper Lorena Weiss can recall visiting her teacher here when she was a girl. The Garden Room holds Lorena's old dressing table and the four-poster bed her husband built. There's a nice window view of the flower garden below.

🏠 *W4375 U.S. Hwy. 10, Durand, WI 54737, tel. 715/672–8563. 1 double room with bath, 2 doubles share bath. No air-conditioning, fireplace and TV in common room. $40–$60; full breakfast, afternoon refreshments. MC, V. No smoking, no pets, closed Jan.–Mar.*

St. Croix River Inn

Local pharmacist C. W. Staples built this solid stone Dutch Colonial home overlooking the St. Croix River sometime after the turn of the century. Developer Robert Marshall bought it from the Staples family in 1984 and spent more than a half million dollars reconfiguring the interior and creating a luxury inn. It was money well spent. The home's original porch, along the side of the house, is now the inn's lobby area, where guests are greeted by innkeeper Bev Johnson. There's plenty of space to relax in the lobby and enjoy the eye-gratifying view of the river 100 feet below; to encourage you, Bev puts out cheese and crackers, coffee, and other drinks. Just outside the lobby is an open deck with a wooden swing— here, guests love to read or nibble on snacks as they watch the world go by.

Each of the seven guest rooms is named for a steamboat built in Osceola, and all are furnished with antique reproductions. The three lower-level rooms each open onto a private brick terrace that faces the river. These rooms have striking whitewashed stone walls—the original foundation supports of the house. The Minnie Will and Nellie Kent rooms each feature a breakfast nook that overlooks the river. In the Nellie Kent, guests can enjoy the whirlpool bath and river views simultaneously.

Upstairs, the Linn J. Room includes a bathroom with a skylight above the whirlpool bath, as well as a four-poster canopy bed and a blue velvet–upholstered chaise longue. Unfortunately, the huge arched picture window looks out on a parking lot. The G. B. Knapp Room also has a canopy bed, plus a pair of wing chairs near the fireplace. Guests in this room also have a large river-view sitting room furnished in casual wicker and a large upholstered sofa. The Jenny Hays Room, with a private balcony, is furnished with a four-poster bed from which guests, looking out the large cathedral window, can see the river.

Every morning at about 8 Bev or an assistant delivers hot coffee and a newspaper to each room. A half hour or so later a delicious breakfast of banana French toast, an omelet, or other goodies is delivered. Everything is freshly made and piping hot—even the maple syrup is warmed. Every room has a small breakfast table next to a window; no need to dress for breakfast here.

🏠 *305 River St., Osceola, WI 54020, tel. 715/294–4248 or 800/645–8820. 2 double rooms with baths, 5 suites. Air-conditioning, TV in 1 room, TV/VCR in 2 rooms, fireplace in 2 rooms, stereo/cassette player and whirlpool bath in rooms, robes for guests, grill and picnic table for guest use. $85–$200; full breakfast, afternoon refreshments. AE, MC, V. Smoking in lobby and game room only, no pets.*

Door County

Jutting into Lake Michigan like the thumb on a mitten, Door County is a 70-mile-long, 13-mile-wide peninsula that is often called the Cape Cod of the Midwest. And not without reason: Quaint coastal villages dot 250 miles of shoreline, with the waters of Green Bay on the west and Lake Michigan on the east. Lighthouses, wide sand beaches, apple and cherry orchards, quiet back roads, commercial fishing boats, and offshore islands complete the picture. Fishing, sailing, bicycling, and cross-country skiing are popular Door County sports, and most visitors at some point sample the region's famous fish boil—a 100-year-old traditional way of cooking whitefish steaks in a cauldron over a wood fire (boiled red potatoes, coleslaw, and cherry pie are the de rigueur side dishes). Nearly 2 million people flock here each summer, many of them repeat visitors. Substantial crowds also come to view the brilliant leaf colors in autumn.

Door County was named after Portes des Morts (Doors of Death), a strait of water separating the peninsula from Washington Island, at the tip of the mitten's thumb. The name, coined by 17th-century French explorers, derives not (as some have suggested) from the treacherous currents there, but from a bloody encounter between war parties of the Potawatomi and Winnebago tribes—an encounter from which virtually no one emerged alive. Since 1891, northern Door County has also been separated from the Wisconsin mainland by a ship canal at Sturgeon Bay, one of the busiest shipbuilding centers in the nation. The largest private motor yacht built in the United States in more than 50 years was recently completed by Sturgeon Bay's Palmer Johnson Boatyard.

First-time visitors often make a circle tour via Routes 57 and 42. The Lake Michigan side of the peninsula is somewhat less settled and the landscape more rugged. It is not uncommon for the Lake Michigan side to be foggy and stormy with choppy waters, while just a few miles across the peninsula, the bay is calm and the skies blue and sunny. The Green Bay side offers other advantages: warmer water for swimming and breathtaking views of the sunset from its many limestone bluffs.

Sturgeon Bay is more or less the gateway to the peninsula; Routes 42 and 57, the main roads leading to and around Door County, converge in Sturgeon Bay. Heading up the Green Bay side of the peninsula on Route 42, you'll pass first through Egg Harbor and then Fish Creek, which today is full of gingerbread Victorian homes housing several bed-and-breakfasts and boutiques. Just north of Fish Creek lies Peninsula State Park, where you can marvel at the views from atop Eagle Bluff.

Two miles north of Fish Creek is the picturesque town of Ephraim, known as the White Village because its tiered hills rising from the bay are heavily covered with white wooden houses and churches. Founded in 1853 by a group of Moravians of Norwegian heritage, the town remains dry to this day. A short distance up Route 42 from Ephraim is Sister Bay, whose early settlers were mostly Scandinavian and German immigrants. Farther north is Ellison Bay, founded in 1870; the quiet back roads around here make for particularly good biking and hiking (nearby Newport State Park is a good camping spot). The fishing village of Gill's Rock is the next town north; the passenger ferry to Washington Island leaves from here, while the car ferry leaves from Northport, at the very tip of the peninsula.

Washington Island has nearly 100 miles of roads and is a popular cycling spot. Its population of 600 inhabits the oldest Icelandic settlement in the United States. Ferries from Washington Island take visitors on to remote Rock Island, once the private estate of millionaire inventor Chester Thordarson and now a state park permitting only backpacking and primitive camping.

Back on the mainland, retrace your route along Route 42/57 until Route 57 branches east to follow the Lake Michigan shore. *Bailey's Harbor, the largest village on the lake side of the peninsula, was named for Captain Justice Bailey, who found refuge there from a storm in 1844. He and his men spent several days ashore, feasting on wild berries, and their glowing reports soon lured settlers to the area. A few miles south lies the quiet village of Jacksonport, according to legend the site where most of the lumber was cut to rebuild Chicago after the its famous 1871 fire. Nearby Cave Point, where the hammering Lake Michigan surf has carved elaborate grottoes into the stern limestone, is one of the most photographed sites in Wisconsin. In many respects, Cave Point symbolizes the enduring appeal of the Door: It remains a place only lightly touched by human hands.*

Places to Go, Sights to See

Al Johnson's Swedish Restaurant and Butik (702–712 Bay Shore Dr., Sister Bay, tel. 414/854–2626). Tourists wait in line for hours to feast on Swedish pancakes, meatballs, and all manner of other Swedish delights. To keep them occupied while they wait, diners are invited to go outside and watch the goats grazing on the sod roof.

Bjorklunden Chapel (7603 Chapel La., Baileys Harbor, tel. 414/839–2216). A replica of an ancient Norwegian church, this beautifully decorated chapel was constructed over a period of many years by the late Winifred Boynton and her husband, Donald. This labor of love is chronicled in their book, *Faith Builds a Chapel.*

Cana Island Lighthouse (Rte. Q, northeast of Baileys Harbor). Connected to the mainland by a low stone causeway often covered with water, this 1851 lighthouse is still in use.

Cherryland Brewery (341 N. 3rd Ave., Sturgeon Bay, tel. 414/743–1945). In the former train station, this lively microbrewery is open for tours throughout the year.

The Clearing (just off Rte. 42, Ellison Bay, tel. 414/854–4088). This 128-acre oasis is the home of a summer residential school patterned after Danish folk tradition. Designed in 1935 by landscape architect Jens Jensen, the retreat is open to the public on weekends for self-guided tours through the rustic buildings built to fit the peaceful bluff-top site.

Door Community Auditorium (Rte. 42, just north of Fish Creek at Gibraltar School, tel. 414/868–2728). Nationally known musicians, dance companies, and theater troupes perform here throughout the year. It's also the home of the

Peninsula Music Festival (tel. 414/854–4060), a three-week-long celebration of the finest in classical music.

Door County Historical Museum (18 N. 4th Ave., Sturgeon Bay, tel. 414/743–5809). Native American relics, pioneer items, and an early firehouse are displayed here daily from May through October.

Door County Maritime Museum. There are two branches of this museum, one in Sturgeon Bay (101 Florida St., tel. 414/743–8139) and the other in Gills Rock (12724 Wisconsin Bay Rd., tel. 414/854–1844). The Sturgeon Bay location, right next to the city's extensive modern-day shipyards, exhibits a refurbished ship's pilothouse, antique engines, turn-of-the-century sailboats, and artifacts from sunken ships; in Gills Rock you'll view nautical paintings and items illustrating the history of commercial fishing. The museum is open from Memorial Day through mid-October.

Door Peninsula Winery (5806 Rte. 42, Sturgeon Bay, tel. 414/743–7431). Wine tastings and guided tours are offered here.

Edgewood Orchard Galleries (4140 Peninsula Players Rd., Fish Creek, tel. 414/868–3579). Housed in a beautifully restored fruit barn made of stone, this is one of the premier art galleries in the Midwest. All media are represented, but special emphasis is placed on works in glass.

Fishing Charters and Guides. The waters surrounding Door County offer some of the finest and most diverse fishing in North America. Tackle-busting salmon, brown trout, and steelhead roam Lake Michigan's cold, clear depths, while trophy walleye, smallmouth bass, and northern pike lurk in the shallower bays. A number of guides and charter captains operate out of Door County's harbors; two of the best are Fritz Peterson (1229 Georgia St., Sturgeon Bay, tel. 414/743–7877) and Tim Dawidiuk (848 S. 16th St., Sturgeon Bay, tel. 414/746–9916). For general information about fishing in Door County, contact Mac's Sport Shop (43 S. Madison Ave., Sturgeon Bay, tel. 414/743–3350).

Hardy Gallery (Anderson Dock, just off Rte. 42, Ephraim, tel. 414/854–5535). A fixture on the Door County arts scene for over three decades, this gallery, in a funky, graffiti-covered wooden warehouse, specializes in work that draws inspiration from the peninsula's enduring beauty.

Maple Grove Gallery (Rte. F between Fish Creek and Baileys Harbor, tel. 414/839–2693). It's worth a drive to visit this crafts store, featuring traditional Door County pottery and handwoven clothing, throws, pillows, and wall hangings.

Miller Art Center (107 S. 4th Ave., Sturgeon Bay, tel. 414/746–0707). Painting and graphics by Door County artists and others from the Midwest are featured in this gallery, in the Door County Public Library.

Peninsula Players (W4351 Peninsula Players Rd., Fish Creek, tel. 414/868–3287). The oldest professional summer-theater company in the nation performs hit musicals, comedies, and dramas from late June through mid-October.

Peninsula State Park (Rte. 42, just north of Fish Creek, tel. 414/868–3258). The state's busiest park, Peninsula offers miles of bike trails, beaches, an 18-hole golf course (tel. 414/854–5791), and the American Folklore Theater (tel. 414/839–2329), which presents original musicals on an outdoor stage from late June through late August.

The Ridges Sanctuary (Rte. Q, ½ mi north of Baileys Harbor, tel. 414/839–2802). Hiking trails wind through this beautiful 1,000-acre nature and wildlife preserve.

Sailing Cruises. Try Bella Sailing Cruises (South Shore Pier, Ephraim, tel. 414/854–2628) or Classic Yachts of Door County (42 Kentucky St., Sturgeon Bay, tel. 414/743–2478).

Uncle Tom and Aunt Marge's Candy Shop (Europe Bay Rd. and Timberline Rd., Ellison Bay, tel. 414/854–4538). Uncle Tom has passed away, but Aunt Marge still welcomes visitors eager for her sublime fudge or peanut brittle.

Washington Island Tram Tours. Two operators—Washington Island Cherry Train (tel. 414/847–2039) and Viking Tour Train (tel. 414/854–2972)—run narrated tram tours of Washington Island from Memorial Day to mid-October, which leave from the ferry dock (purchase ticket with your ferry ticket at Northport or Gills Rock).

Whitefish Dunes State Park (3701 Clark Lake Rd., Sturgeon Bay, tel. 414/823–2400). This park boasts the highest sand dunes on the western shore of Lake Michigan and what one recent poll ranked as the best swimming beach in Wisconsin.

Restaurants

Time was when dining in Door County meant fish boils, supper clubs, and ice-cream parlors—period. Good, hearty fare, to be sure, but somewhat lacking in imagination. Happily, while there are more fish boils and ice-cream parlors than ever, the level of creativity and sophistication displayed by Door County's restaurants has increased markedly in the past few years. Two of the trendsetters in this regard are the **White Gull Inn** (4225 Main St., Fish Creek, tel. 414/868–3517) and the **Inn at Cedar Crossing** (3rd and Louisiana Sts., Sturgeon Bay, tel. 414/743–4249). Critics consistently rank both among the top restaurants in Wisconsin. Fresh, regionally produced ingredients (whitefish, duckling, veal) are emphasized, and the sumptuous breakfasts are a match for the romantic candlelight dinners. The White Gull also serves what is arguably the best fish boil on the Door, presided over by master-boiler-cum-raconteur Russ Ostrand.

Currently, Door County's most exciting restaurant is the **Black Locust** (Rte. 42, at the entrance to Peninsula Park, Fish Creek, tel. 414/868–2999), where chef Christopher Kuhnz changes the menu nightly to take advantage of the current season's harvest. The decor is a bit stark, perhaps, but the food is positively voluptuous. Other innovative kitchens that stand out from the crowd include **Hotel du Nord** (Bay Shore Dr., at the north end of Sister Bay, tel. 414/854–4221), the **Common House** (8041 Rte. 57, Baileys Harbor, tel. 414/839–2708), and **Trio** (at the corner of Rte. 42 and Rte. E, Egg Harbor, tel. 414/868–2090).

For marvelous pies, pecan rolls, cookies, and other delights, check out the **Town Hall Bakery and Daily Special Cafe** (6225 U.S. 57, Jacksonport, tel. 414/823–2116) or **Grandma's Swedish Bakery,** in Ellison Bay (1041 Rte. ZZ, at the Wagon Trail Resort, tel. 414/854–2385). Last but hardly least, the quintessential Door County ice-cream cone is scooped at **Wilson's Restaurant and Ice Cream Parlor** (9990 Water St., Ephraim, tel. 414/854–2041).

Tourist Information

Baileys Harbor Business Association (Box 31, Baileys Harbor, WI 54202, tel. 414/839–2366); **Door County Chamber of Commerce** (U.S. 42/57, just south of Sturgeon Bay; Box 406, Sturgeon Bay, WI 54235, tel. 414/743–4456); **Door County Fishing Hotline** (tel. 414/743–7046); **Egg Harbor Business Association** (Box 33, Egg Harbor, WI 54209, tel. 414/868–3717); **Ephraim Information Center** (Box 203, Ephraim, WI 54211, tel. 414/854–4989); **Fish Creek Civic Association** (Box 74, Fish Creek, WI 54212, tel. 414/868–2316); **Sister Bay Advancement Association** (Box 351, Sister Bay, WI 54234, tel. 414/854–2812); **Sturgeon Bay Area Advancement Group** (Box 212-C-1, Sturgeon Bay, WI 54235, tel. 414/743–3924); **Top-of-the-Thumb Association** (Box 10, Ellison Bay, WI 54210, tel. 414/854–5448; **Washington Island Chamber of Commerce** (RR1, Box 222 Washington Island, WI 54246, tel. 414/847–2179).

The Ephraim Inn

In the picture of his son that inn owner Tim Christofferson carries in his wallet, another man is included—the Wal-Mart photographer who took the picture (yup, the camera timer allowed him to join the son in the photo). Tim just wanted to make sure he remembered the guy. That's the kind of good humor Tim exudes, and inn guests feel it from the time they walk in the door. A former McDonald's marketing executive, Tim had always wanted his own business; he and his wife, Nancy, moved to Door County in 1979 when they bought Wilson's Ice Cream Parlor, overlooking the harbor in Ephraim's charming historic district. Then, in 1985, the big white house next door, where the town doctor, Dr. Sneeberger, had lived and practiced for 40 years, went up for sale. Tim and Nancy bought it and built a large addition that turned it into a sprawling horseshoe-shaped inn with a center cupola. Much to the dismay of their sons, Tim and Nancy sold Wilson's in 1987 (it's still in operation) to concentrate on the inn.

The Christoffersons live in most of the old main house; all of the 17 guest bedrooms are in the new addition, where such modern essentials as soundproofing, air-conditioning, and private baths were easy to install. Each room has its own motif, often Shaker-inspired, it shows up on the room's wooden key tags, the painted symbol on its door, and the hand-stenciled border on its ceiling. Shaker-style peg rails around the walls hold such decorative touches as dried flowers, grapevine wreaths, straw hats, and even chairs. The furniture is a mix of reproductions and antiques revealing the couple's preference for the simple, clean lines of country furniture.

The large common room with its harbor view brings guests together around a large fireplace or in a well-stocked library nook. Full breakfasts, served in three small dining areas, may include homemade granola, fresh-baked pastries, and an Ephraim Inn omelet, a quichelike dish of baked eggs, cheese, and spices.

The shorefront location, a decided asset, gives the inn wonderful water views and puts guests within walking distance not only of Ephraim's historic sights but also of an unspoiled beach just around a curve of the road. Not much farther up the road are Peninsula State Park and its fine 18-hole golf course.

🏨 *Rte. 42 (Box 247), Ephraim, WI 54211, tel. 414/854–4515 or 800/622–2193. 17 double rooms with baths. Air-conditioning, TV in rooms, beach across street. $79–$145; full breakfast. MC, V. No smoking, no pets, 2-night minimum.*

The Griffin Inn

Converted from a private house to a summer hotel in 1921, the Griffin Inn is a classic country retreat, on 5 acres of rolling lawn shaded by maple trees. Long verandas with porch swings and a gazebo give guests plenty of places to sit and enjoy the breeze. Besides the main building, a Dutch Colonial–style house built in 1910, there are two cottages on the property, each with two guest units.

For innkeepers Paul Ennis and family, who recently purchased the Griffin from Jim and Laurie Roberts (who now own the Whistling Swan in Fish Creek; *see below*), it's a case of having come full circle. A brother and sister-in-law had managed the property in the mid-'70s. When Ennis decided to return to his northeastern Wisconsin roots from Maryland where he'd been living, his search for a business to run ended when he learned the familiar old inn was available.

Though the bedrooms are fairly small, they have been comfortably furnished with a collection of pieces reflecting the tastes of the inn's various owners throughout the years.

Common rooms include the dining room, a downstairs living room with a large fieldstone fireplace where guests gather for popcorn every night, and a small library where guests can curl up on a love seat with a good book.

The cottages, which are open from May through October, are a bit more rustic, with open-beam ceilings, rough cedar walls, and ceiling fans. Cottage guests can either pick up a breakfast basket each morning or make arrangements to join the main-house guests for the dazzling gourmet breakfast always prepared from scratch. Fresh fruit and baked goods (scones, muffins, and breads) are always on the menu, along with a changing selection of temptations such as baby Dutch pancakes topped with lemon butter and cherry sauce, stuffed blueberry French toast, and made-to-order omelets.

Only two blocks from downtown Ellison Bay, the inn is within walking distance of the waterfront. It sits on a well-traveled bike route, and the Peninsula Cross-Country Ski Trail literally runs through the backyard. Guests often play badminton or croquet on the inn grounds, a sight that conjures up images of the inn's venerable role as a summer retreat.

🏨 *11976 Mink River Rd., Ellison Bay, WI 54210, tel. 414/854–4306. 8 double rooms and 2 triples share 2½ baths; 4 cottages each sleep 4 people. Air-conditioning in inn, TV in cottages. $79–$86; full breakfast for inn guests; Continental breakfast with full-breakfast option for cottage guests. No credit cards. No smoking, no pets, 2-night minimum weekends, 3-night minimum holidays.*

The Whistling Swan

A fixture on Fish Creek's Main Street since 1907, what is now the Whistling Swan was originally built in 1887 in Marinette—22 miles due west, more or less, across the waters of Green Bay. Dr. Herman Welcker, a legendary figure in the history of tourism in Door County, had the white-frame Victorian towed across the ice to its present location, where it became part of a resort complex that also included the current White Gull Inn (*see below*).

Now meticulously restored, the inn features such touches as floral prints, brass fixtures, and claw-foot tubs, recalling the romance of that bygone era. Guests will find fresh flowers on their nightstands, too, along with complimentary bottles of spring water. An expanded Continental breakfast is served on the sunny, glass-enclosed porch during clement seasons; come winter, full breakfast becomes the rule. Afternoon tea is served year-round.

While owners Jim and Laurie Roberts are newcomers to the Whistling Swan—they purchased the property in 1996—they're no strangers to innkeeping, after owning and operating the nearby Griffin Inn for the previous 10 years. In addition to elegant accommodations, they offer sophisticated women's fashions in their boutique on the building's main level. It's one of the many upscale specialty shops that make the neighborhood one of the peninsula's toniest.

⊞ 4192 Main St. (Box 193), Fish Creek, WI 54212, tel. 414/868–3442. 4 double rooms with baths, 1 deluxe queen room with bath, 2 suites. Air-conditioning, cable TV in rooms, telephones in selected rooms. $98–$134; expanded Continental breakfast (full breakfast in winter). AE, D, MC, V. No smoking, no pets, 2-night minimum weekends, 3-night minimum holidays.

The White Gull Inn

One of the oldest lodging establishments in Door County, the White Gull Inn was founded in 1896 by a Dr. Welcker as a lodging for wealthy German immigrants who came to Fish Creek by steamer. Its current owner and manager, Andy Coulson, is a former journalist. He was traveling in Australia when a friend contacted him about joining a group of investors seeking to buy the White Gull. Andy said yes—on the condition he could run the place. The other partners happily agreed. One of Andy's first managerial decisions was to hire a new housekeeper, Jan; five years later, wedding bells happily rang.

The Coulsons have worked hard to maintain the original feel of the white-frame inn, with its inviting front porches (upstairs and down), gleaming hardwood floors covered with braided rugs, and country-style antiques. The main entry is the focus of activity; it's here that guests watch television or gather around the large fieldstone fireplace. Besides overnight guests, crowds of people visit the inn's restaurant, famous throughout Door County for its traditional fish boils, on Wednesday, Friday, Saturday, and Sunday nights in summer (Wednesday and Saturday in winter). The restaurant serves three meals a day; breakfast may include eggs Benedict, hash browns, or buttermilk pancakes.

The inn is perfectly situated: To the left is Sunset Beach Park; to the right, the charming shops of Fish Creek and then Peninsula State Park. Accommodations are spread around a number of buildings. The main house has several guest rooms, each with a comfortable wrought-iron or carved-wood bed, and each decorated with antiques, some of them once owned by Dr. Welcker himself. Behind the inn is the Cliffhouse, whose two suites have fireplaces and lush furnishings; the inn also owns three nearby cottages, which make wonderful little family vacation homes.

🏨 *4225 Main St. (Box 160), Fish Creek, WI 54212, tel. 414/868–3517. 6 double rooms with baths, 3 suites, 5 cottages each sleep 2–8 people. Restaurant, air-conditioning, cable TV, complimentary coffee, and newspaper each morning in rooms. $96–$185, cottages $157–$251; breakfast extra. AE, D, DC, MC, V. No pets, 2-night minimum weekends, 3-night minimum holidays.*

The Barbican Guest House

If your aim is a romantic getaway, this is the place. All accommodations are two-room suites decorated with thick carpets, floral-print wallpapers, and English country house–style antiques. Each suite has a queen-size bed, a double whirlpool bath, its own fireplace, cable TV, a stereo, a refrigerator, and room-service breakfasts, so if guests don't want to, they never have to leave the room. The Barbican is one block from the waterfront in the heart of Sturgeon Bay's historic district.

🏨 *132 N. 2nd Ave., Sturgeon Bay, WI 54235, tel. 414/743–4854. 18 suites. Air-conditioning, cable TV and VCR, fireplace, whirlpool bath, stereo, and refrigerator in suites. $110–$175; Continental breakfast. MC, V. No pets, 2-night minimum weekends, 3-night minimum holidays.*

The Eagle Harbor Inn

In addition to the Cape Cod–style inn there are a dozen cottages scattered among pines, cedars, and birches. These include six grand guest houses, each unique, but each reflecting the indigenous Ephraim farmhouse–style of architecture: white clapboards; dormer windows; and a minimum of gingerbread. Inside, however, they're positively luxurious, offering one- and two-bedroom suites with fireplaces, whirlpool baths, four-poster beds, full kitchens, and private decks. All of Ephraim lies within easy walking distance.

🏨 *9914 Water St. (Box 558), Ephraim, WI 54211, tel. 414/854–2121 or 800/324–5427. 9 double rooms with bath, 16 1-bedroom suites, 16 2-bedrooms suites. Air-conditioning, cable TV, whirlpool bath in 1 room and all suites, sauna, lap pool, fitness center. $79–$156; full breakfast for inn guests; breakfast available at additional charge for suite guests. MC, V. No smoking, no pets, 2-night minimum weekends, 3-night minimum holidays.*

The French Country Inn of Ephraim

Architect Walt Fisher and his wife, Joan Fitzpatrick, were immediately drawn to this square, white-frame house in the Door County village of Ephraim. Built in 1912, it was a classic summer beach house, with large casement windows to catch breezes off Green Bay, just down the road. One room has a bed from an old French hotel; in another, a whole wall is covered with hats that Joan, a former teacher, once kept in her classroom to amuse students. Walt says that guests love to watch Joan mow the lawn—using, of course, an old-fashioned push mower.

🏨 *3052 Spruce La. (Box 129), Ephraim, WI 54211, tel. 414/854–4001. 2 double rooms with baths, 5 doubles share 2 baths; 1 2-bedroom cottage. No air-conditioning. $55–$89; cottage $485–$580 per week; Continental breakfast, evening refreshments. No credit cards. No smoking, no pets, 2-night minimum weekends, 3-night minimum holidays.*

The Gray Goose Bed and Breakfast

If husband and wife innkeepers John Bruzenas and Sandra Hoff seem to have a knack for anticipating their guests' every need, it could be because they came to Door County for much the same reasons their clientele does: to escape the stress of high-pressure jobs and fast-paced urban life of Chicago. Built in 1862, their frame house, now painted a warm, autumnal red, features an airy front porch with wicker furniture and on the second floor, huge dormer windows that face the sunset. In each bedroom, look for that special touch—old cookie cutters hung as a ceiling border in one room, dried-flower bouquets draped across the rafter in another. Comforters and quilts accompany country-style antique furniture. It all adds up to a casual atmosphere, in keeping with the inn's quiet, wooded setting.

🏠 *4258 Bay Shore Dr., Sturgeon Bay, WI 54235, tel. 414/743–9100. 4 double rooms share 2 baths. No air-conditioning, TV in guest lounge. $70–$80; full breakfast. AE, MC, V. Smoking on porch only, no pets, 2-night minimum holidays.*

The Harbor House Inn

Else Weborg laughingly tells visitors she never really wanted to be an innkeeper—still doesn't, as a matter of fact. But it's hard to believe this charming Danish woman since she runs Harbor House Inn with such vigor. Guest rooms in the lovely Victorian-gingerbread main house have turn-of-the-century furnishings. Ground-floor bedrooms have bay windows, while those upstairs have private balconies. A new wing of four one-bedroom suites features floral-print fabrics and blond-wood furniture. The charming Troll Cottage preserves the stove-wood construction used by the region's early Scandinavian settlers.

🏠 *12666 Rte. 42, Gills Rock, WI 54210, tel. 414/854–5196. 12 double rooms with baths, 2 cottages each sleep 4. Air-conditioning, TVs, sauna, hot tub; private beach, bicycle rentals. $49–$109; Continental breakfast. AE, MC, V. No smoking.*

The Inn at Cedar Crossing

Pressed-tin ceilings, stenciled walls, secluded balconies, and a TV room just like Mom used to have are features that make the Inn at Cedar Crossing charming. The setting is convenient, if not secluded—right in Sturgeon Bay's downtown historic district, at the junction that used to be Cedar and Cottage streets (hence the inn's name). Downstairs is a restaurant; upstairs are nine guest rooms. Each room has its own look: golden oak in one, hand-carved mahogany in another, Victorian walnut in another.

🏠 *336 Louisiana St., Sturgeon Bay, WI 54235, tel. 414/743–4200. 9 double rooms with baths. Restaurant, air-conditioning, whirlpool bath in 5 rooms. $85–$145; Continental breakfast. D, MC, V. No smoking, no pets, 2-night minimum weekends, 3-night minimum holidays.*

The Inn on Maple

Guests at the Inn on Maple may feel like they've checked into an old country grocery, with its pink awnings and expansive storefront windows. The inn, which is listed on the National Register of Historic Places as one of the finest surviving examples of the stove-wood construction style, was a combination private home and meat market in the early 1900s. It's been a B&B now for several years, taking advantage of a pleasant location on a quiet side street off Route 42, within easy walking distance of Sister Bay. The present owners, Bill and Louise Robbins, took over in 1995 and gave the inn its present name (it had been the White Apron). This is very much a traditional bed-and-breakfast: small, simple, and intimate. The cozy guest rooms are furnished with sturdy vintage beds, cheery linens, and a few carefully chosen accessories.

🏠 *414 Maple Dr., Sister Bay, WI 54234, tel. 414/854–5107. 5 double rooms with baths, 2 single rooms with baths. Ceiling fans. $55–$75; full breakfast. MC, V. No smoking, no pets, 2-night minimum, 3-night minimum holidays.*

The Scofield House

Fran and Bill Cecil believe in letting life take them where it will. In 1987, it took them down a street in Sturgeon Bay, where they saw a gabled Victorian frame house built in 1902 by Herbert Scofield, Sturgeon Bay's mayor. They promptly bought the house, then superlatively renovated it. Special touches in the guest rooms include stained-glass windows, hand-crocheted lace curtains, marble-top dressers, and roomy antique armoires. The most impressive (and most expensive) room is the third-story suite, which has skylights, Oriental rugs, a double whirlpool bath, golden oak wainscoting, and a pressed-tin ceiling.

🏨 *908 Michigan St. (Box 761), Sturgeon Bay, WI 54235, tel. 414/743–7727 or 888/463–0204. 6 double rooms with baths. Air-conditioning, cable TV and VCR in 5 rooms, whirlpool bath in 5 rooms. $89–$190; full breakfast. No credit cards. No smoking, no pets, 2-night minimum, 3-night minimum holidays.*

Directory 1
Alphabetical

Directory 2
Geographical

Michigan

Ahmeek
Sand Hills Lighthouse Inn *43*
Alden
Torch Lake Bed & Breakfast *80*
Au Train
Pinewood Lodge *43*
Battle Creek
Greencrest Manor *30*
Bay City
William Clements Inn *14*
Bay View
The Gingerbread House *79*
Beulah
Brookside Inn *65*
Big Bay
Big Bay Point Lighthouse *42*
Thunder Bay Inn *44*
Blaney Park
Celibeth House *42*
Brooklyn
Chicago Street Inn *16*
Charlevoix
Belvedere Inn *74*
The Bridge Street Inn *79*
Coldwater
Chicago Pike Inn *23*
Detroit
Blanche House Inn *15*
The Castle *15*
Corktown Inn B&B *16*
Dundee
Dundee Guest House *16*
Ellsworth
House on the Hill *76*
Farmington Hills
Botsford Inn *15*
Fennville
Crane House *24*
Kingsley House *25*

Harbor Springs
Kimberly Country Estate *77*
Veranda at Harbor Springs *80*
Holland
Parsonage 1908 *32*
Kalamazoo
Stuart Avenue Inn *33*
Lake Leelanau
Centennial Inn *61*
Lakeside
Pebble House *27*
Laurium
Laurium Manor Inn *41*
Leland
Aspen House *64*
Snowbird Inn *69*
Mackinac Island
Bay View at Mackinac *50*
Bogan Lane Inn *54*
Cloghaun Bed & Breakfast *54*
Haan's 1830 Inn *51*
The Inn on Mackinac *52*
Metivier Inn *53*
Murray Hotel *54*
1900 Market Street Inn *55*
Maple City
Leelanau Country Inn *66*
Marshall
McCarthy's Bear Creek Inn *31*
National House Inn *26*
Mendon
Mendon Country Inn *32*
Northport
North Shore Inn *63*
Old Mill Pond Inn *67*
Omena
Omena Shores Bed and Breakfast *67*

Petoskey
Bear River Valley *79*
The Benson House *75*
Stafford's Bay View Inn *78*
Port Huron
Victorian Inn *13*
Port Sanilac
Raymond House Inn *11*
Saginaw
Montague Inn *10*
St. Joseph
South Cliff Inn *28*
Saugatuck
Fairchild House *30*
Maplewood Hotel *31*
Twin Oaks Inn *34*
Wickwood Country Inn *29*
Sault Ste. Marie
Water Street Inn *45*
South Haven
Yelton Manor *35*
Suttons Bay
Lee Point Inn *66*
Open Windows Bed & Breakfast *68*
Tecumseh
The Stacy Mansion *12*
Traverse City
Bowers Harbor Bed & Breakfast *64*
Chateau Chantal *65*
Cherry Knoll Farm *65*
Linden Lea *62*
Neahtawanta Inn *67*
The Victoriana 1898 *70*
Union City
Victorian Villa Inn *34*
Union Pier
The Inn at Union Pier *31*
Pine Garth Inn *33*
Walloon Lake Village
Walloon Lake Inn *81*

Minnesota

Afton
The Afton House Inn *98*
Alexandria
Carrington House *143*
Blue Earth
Fering's Guest House *153*
Cannon Falls
Quill & Quilt *116*
Chaska
Bluff Creek Inn *98*
Crookston
Elm St. Inn *136*
Crosby
Hallett House *137*
Deerwood
Walden Woods *145*
Duluth
The Ellery House *123*
Fitger's Inn *129*
The Mansion Bed & Breakfast Inn *125*
Mathew S. Burrows 1890 Inn *130*
The Olcott House *126*
Dundas
Martin Oaks *116*
Embarrass
Finnish Heritage Homestead *124*
Falcon Heights
The Rose Bed and Breakfast *103*
Fergus Falls
Nims' Bakketop Hus *144*
Glenwood
Peters' Sunset Beach *141*
Grand Marais
Bearskin Lodge *122*
Naniboujou Lodge *130*

Pincushion Mountain Bed & Breakfast *127*
The Superior Overlook B&B *131*
Hastings
Thorwood Historic Inns *111*
Lake City
Red Gables Inn *117*
The Victorian Bed & Breakfast *112*
Lanesboro
Carrolton Country Inn *115*
Historic Scanlan House *115*
Mrs. B's Historic Lanesboro Inn *109*
Little Marais
The Stone Hearth Inn Bed & Breakfast *128*
Marine on St. Croix
Asa Parker House *92*
Minneapolis
Elmwood House *99*
Evelo's Bed & Breakfast *100*
Le Blanc House *95*
Nicollet Island Inn *102*
1900 Dupont *103*
Nevis
Park Street Inn *140*
New Prague
Schumacher's New Prague Hotel *104*
New York Mills
Whistle Stop Inn *146*
Northfield
The Archer House *113*
Park Rapids
Heartland Trail Inn *143*
Pelican Rapids
Prairie View Estate *145*

Pequot Lakes
Stonehouse Bed and Breakfast *145*
Preston
JailHouse Inn *108*
Princeton
Oakhurst Inn *139*
Red Wing
The Candle Light Inn *114*
Pratt-Taber Inn *110*
St. James Hotel *117*
Round Lake
Prairie House on Round Lake *153*
St. Paul
Chatsworth B&B *99*
Covington Inn *93*
The Garden Gate Bed and Breakfast *100*
St. Peter
Park Row Bed and Breakfast *151*
Sanborn
Sod House on the Prairie *152*
Silver Bay
The Inn at Palisade Bed & Breakfast *129*
Spicer
Spicer Castle *142*
Stillwater
The Ann Bean House *91*
Elephant Walk *94*
Harvest Restaurant and Inn *100*
James A. Mulvey Residence Inn *100*
Laurel Street Inn *101*
Lumber Baron's Hotel *102*
The Rivertown Inn *96*
The William Sauntry Mansion *97*